WITHDRAWN

Gramley Library
Salem College
Winston-Salem, NC 27108

Ben Jonson's
1616 Folio

Reproduced with the generous permission of the Huntington Library, San Marino, California.

PR
2643
.B46
1991

Ben Jonson's 1616 Folio

Edited by
Jennifer Brady and W. H. Herendeen

DELAWARE

Newark: University of Delaware Press
London and Toronto: Associated University Presses

Gramley Library
Salem College
Winston-Salem, NC 27108

© 1991 by Jennifer Brady and W. H. Herendeen.

All rights reserved. Authorization to photocopy items for internal or personal use, or the internal or personal use of specific clients, is granted by the copyright owner, provided that a base fee of $10.00, plus eight cents per page, per copy is paid directly to the Copyright Clearance Center, 27 Congress Street, Salem, Massachusetts 01970. [0-87413-384-X/91 $10.00 + 8¢ pp, pc.]

Associated University Presses
440 Forsgate Drive
Cranbury, NJ 08512

Associated University Presses
25 Sicilian Avenue
London WC1A 2QH, England

Associated University Presses
P.O. Box 488, Port Credit
Mississauga, Ontario
Canada L5G 4M2

The paper used in this publication meets the requirements
of the American National Standard for Permanence of Paper
for Printed Library Materials Z39.48-1984.

Library of Congress Cataloging-in-Publication Data

Ben Jonson's 1616 Folio / edited by Jennifer Brady and W. H. Herendeen.
    p.   cm.
    Includes bibliographical references.
    ISBN 0-87413-384-X (alk. paper)
    1. Jonson, Ben, 1573?-1637—Criticism, Textual. 2. Jonson, Ben, 1573?-1637—Bibliography—Folios. 1616. I. Brady, Jennifer, 1952–
. II. Herendeen, Wyman H., 1948– .
PR2643.B46 1991   89-40448
                                                   CIP

PRINTED IN THE UNITED STATES OF AMERICA

The Catalogue.

Euery Man in his Humor,	To Mr. CAMBDEN.
Euery Man out of his Humor,	To the INNES of COVRT.
Cynthias Reuells,	To the COVRT.
Poëtaster,	To Mr. RICH. MARTIN.
Seianus,	To ESME Lo. Aubigny.
The Foxe,	To the VNIVERSITIES.
The filent Woman,	To Sir FRAN. STVART.
The Alchemift,	To the Lady WROTH.
Catiline,	To the Earle of PEMBROK.
Epigrammes,	To the fame.

The Forreft,
Entertaynments,
Panegyre,
Mafques,
Barriers.

¶ 3

Reproduced with the generous permission of the Huntington Library, San Marino, California.

Contents

Acknowledgments

Beyond thanking the contributors to this volume who accepted our invitation to write essays addressing key aspects of the 1616 Folio's achievement, we have incurred other debts, both personal and institutional. At various stages this project has benefited from the counsel of Earl Miner, Jeanie Watson, William Stoneman, Charles Fantazzi, and Cynthia Marshall. I would like to express particular gratitude to Gerald Duff; my own essay is an offspring of the early leave I received upon his recommendation. Rhodes College and the University of Windsor have both supported this undertaking with grants and, in the case of Windsor, with the resources of their word processing center. Special thanks are due to Lucia Brown and her staff and to Kofi Asare for their assistance in preparing the volume for press.

I want further to take this opportunity to thank the Rhodes community, as also my family, for the kind practical help I was given after an accident in February 1988. My recuperation was eased by friends and colleagues I cherish: Adelaida Lopez, Susan Kus, Carolyn Jaslow, Kate Mehuron, Lisa Rone, Carol Devens, Sunil SenGupta, Dan and Margaret Handwerker, Beth McCullough, Charles Wilkinson, and Dorothy Worsham, among many.

Our final acknowledgment is of another order. We dedicate this volume to the memory of Richard C. Newton, in gratitude for work that has enabled our own.

JENNIFER BRADY

Introduction: On Reading the 1616 Folio

W. H. Herendeen

> So a Lion is a perfect creature in himselfe,
> though it bee lesse, then . . . that of a *Buffalo*,
> or a *Rhinocerote*. They differ; but *in specie:*
> either in the kinde is absolute. Both have their
> parts, and either the whole.
>
> (Discoveries, 2711–15)

There are many ways to skin a rhinoceros. The principle behind
this is fundamental to pluralism; Jonson himself was, and this
volume of essays is, essentially pluralistic. It is about *THE
WORKES OF Benjamin Jonson*, printed in London by William
Stansby in 1616. That is to say, it is about a large folio having
a unique place in the history of printing; about a single volume
having its own aesthetic design; about a collection of plays,
poems, and entertainments of interest in themselves; and about
an imaginative work by a man with a significant literary and
public career both before and after the Folio's appearance.

Physically, historically, and artistically, the Folio is an object
of considerable magnitude. To try to describe it, to locate it
historically, or to analyze it, is to raise basic questions about
our ability to perform any one of these three tasks, much less
all of them. As a printed work, the Folio is more than a milestone
in the history of printing: the physical, economic, social, and
literary issues associated with its production alone might occupy a few monographs, or a career. Physically imposing, the
volume is a good deal more impressive than its thinner but
better connected contemporary, *The Workes of James, King of
Great Britaine, France, and Ireland*. Within its 22.5×33 cm and
1,015 folio pages are nine plays, each with its own dedication
and its unique performance and publication history. There are
133 numbered epigrams, here published together as a collection
for the first time, as are the fifteen verses in different genres
gathered under the title "The Forrest." These are followed by

Gramley Library
Salem College
Winston-Salem, NC 27108

a collection of entertainments, "panegyres," masques, and barriers, works whose textual status is even more problematic than that of the plays. Falling into three broad categories of drama, verse, and entertainment, the literary contents of the volume range from comedy, to satire, to tragedy, from lapidary epigram to the lithe lyric, from the reminiscence of an entertainment to the operatic masque. Added to these major literary works are various kinds of apparatus that enrich the artistic design and enlarge the thematic and historical implications of the whole: these include an engraved title page and prefatory poems for the Folio; separate title pages for the plays, epigrams, royal masques, and some of the entertainments; dedications to the plays and epigrams; marginal gloss for some of the masques. A mine of material—with some work more gemlike than others—Jonson's Folio offers a variety of generic, formal, textual, and other critical problems sufficient to intimidate the solitary literary prospector. As historical object and event, it is unique as the first collected works by an English dramatist. As social historians will recognize, the significance of this is compounded by Jonson's closeness to James's court, despite his low birth, and by his avoidance of contractual ties with the acting companies, despite his literary profession. Such anomalies raise extraliterary questions about the politics and economics of the creative life in a world both medieval and modern.

In raising such questions, the Folio resists any single critical or methodological approach. That there are many 1616 Folio *WORKES OF Benjamin Jonson* the postmodern reader will probably grant unflinchingly. Today, it is perhaps more controversial to say that there is also only one such text: the questions posed by the Folio are defined by their association with Jonson. The Folio's problems are his problems—as the work of a man marginally of the court, as a friend, a playwright, a sometime Catholic, as a man of a certain social class humanistically educated beyond reasonable expectation, as a man of flesh and blood, but distinctly Jonsonian flesh and blood. Some of these concerns are universal while others are particular to the time and the individual; the mingling of the two dimensions is what makes Jonson and his Folio artistically and intellectually rewarding, while their unique, historically specific place in the seventeenth century gives them their distinctive Jonsonian importance. Jonson, after all, thought of himself and his art in historical terms.

Granting the multiple dimensions in which the Folio exists, and a range of problems exceeding the scope of one volume, we can, nevertheless, take an approximate measure of the importance of the work. We do so in this collection, in part, by following Jonson's own suggestions in *Discoveries*. What he argues about rhinoceroses, buffaloes, epics, tragedies, and other prodigies can be argued of his *opera*: it has mass, density, a shape of its own, and component parts appropriate to its function as a whole. As readers of Jonson's epigrams will understand, one needs to approach his work as an experience, as a process where meaning emerges through relationships. This is so fundamental to Jonson's art and his theory that we have let his own ideas direct us in our approach to the Folio. As Jonson has stressed, one perceives and apprehends a work through a sequence of experiences involving the different faculties. So too the Folio exists physically as a whole, serially, as a fable with an action that unfolds as one reads, and critically, or morally, as one looks back over the work, assesses it and understands it. Judgment draws on the senses, memory, understanding:

> Therefore, as in every body; so in every Action, which is the subject of a just worke, there is requir'd a certaine proportionable greatnesse . . . . For that which happens to the Eyes, when wee behold a body, the same happens to the Memorie, when wee contemplate an action. . . . So in a *Fable*, if the Action be too great, wee can never comprehend the whole together in our Imagination. . . . The same happens in Action, which is the object of Memory, as the body is of sight. (2716–2732)

In finding new approaches to his work, critics have recognized the need to be led by him. These remarks from *Discoveries* emphasize the interdependence of the components of a work of art, an economy of meaning in which a two-way transfer of sense between the part and the whole occurs. As in life, so in art—in each there is an inevitable contingency of being where the individual parts of a work are isolated, pretend to completeness, but finally acquire life and meaning only through their participation in the whole, in the body politic, as it were.

This metaphor of the body in the *Discoveries* is more than a trope. Central as it is to his aesthetic theory, it is also a dominant theme in his verse and drama, as it was for his major classical sources. Jonson uses it particularly as an image that carries with it a cluster of associated ideas about growth, creativity, and productivity that implicate simultaneously biological, artistic, economic, and political systems. As can be seen in many of the essays that follow, the body provided an image of art and reality that haunted Jonson's imagination and pervades the Folio as well as his theory with its suggestions of ways of being and understanding. Questions about what a "body of work" (like the Folio) is and how to approach it knowingly are not academic for the reader of Jonson. The images that he used to deal with such aesthetic matters are, as we see from his *Discoveries*, ones that pose the essential Jonsonian questions—how to read and how to live—and they enter as major preoccupations of the Folio.

Contingency, marginality, interdependence: Jonsonians will recognize these important ideas for Jonson's art and his view of life. They have been central in recent discussions of the epigrams, where clusters of poems and organizing sequences have been found. No longer understood as a collection of isolated poems, they have become, in fewer than twenty years, a sequence of works commenting on one another. The same problems of contingency pertain to the Folio as a whole, where one progresses from drama through verse to the masques with an increasing sense of meaningful direction and purpose. At the outset, in *Every Man In His Humour*, we encounter art imitating life, and with the final masque, *The Golden Age Restored*, life (the performing courtiers) imitates art. For the reader coming to the Folio without preconceptions and willing to let the Folio take its own shape, much happens in the intervening 1,015 pages.

In organizing this volume, then, we have carried to its next logical step some of the critical approaches that have recently been used fruitfully for the epigrams and plays. As we move from play to poem to performance we are forced to adapt to different kinds of problems—not only timeless literary problems, but ones raised by the poet about himself and his relation to his friends, his monarch, and other aspects of his cultural environment that encroach upon him and his art. Jonson repeatedly undermines the status of his text, breaking the barriers that tend to segregate art from life. His readers cannot confine themselves to the disinterested contemplation of gem-like works as if they were the *Emeaux et Camées* of the seventeenth century. We say this recognizing that this has not been the accepted critical view, and that Jonson's classicism, his formalism, the lapidary nature of the epigram, all invite the more static, abstracted view of individual works that critics have generally held.

The critical view of the present volume, however, sees a strategic tension, first of all between the art and its environment, and relatedly between form and fluidity, definition and meaninglessness, being and nonbeing—tensions that are evident within individual works and among different works, and that exist between the Folio's status as work of art, and as a historical, archaeological object. As a result, one of the achievements of this volume is the radical redefinition of the major critical tenets traditionally associated with Jonson's art. For example, as Kevin Donovan and Jennifer Brady show, from very different perspectives, the monumentality of Jonson's Folio and the art he bestowed on it should not lead us to presume stability of text on the one hand or too congenial an identification between text and author. Similarly, writers who have done much to illuminate the classicism that is inseparable from Jonson's name here submit it to radical redefinition. William Blissett, Katharine Maus, and Stella Revard show how classicism enters the Folio as an ethic severely hedged in by reality, a form potentially as destructive as any form is for Jonson, and as an aesthetic perhaps more modern than ancient in nature.

In this collection we try to represent a range of problems, fully aware that the kinds of issues raised are too varied and complex for one person or one volume to deal with comprehensively. The critical challenge has been enhanced by the strikingly good critics Jonson has and has had in the past, many of whose names recur throughout these essays. Much of the most interesting new work in Renaissance studies has been generated by Jonsonians. This is not just because much has been happening in the period, but also because of the uniqueness of Jonson and his work. Jonson's marginality—literary, social, professional (playwright and not a playwright), and economic—is as much a function of his place in history as it is of his personality. This is what makes him a pivotal historical figure for the postmodern reader whose views of the period tend to be eccentric.

Given the kinds of questions currently being asked about the relationship between printed and other media in an early modern economy such as London's, and given the current interest in conflating historical context and literary text, one cannot set about a book on the 1616 Folio in the way that one might have twenty years ago. In the following pages, many of these questioners bring their larger intellectual concerns directly to bear on the Folio and its content. In the framework of the Folio, critical categories and questions become less discrete; issues overlap in ways that they seemed not to before. To be a classicist is not what it once was; bibliographical studies do not lead where once they seemed to; as a number of the essays show, plays and poems reach beyond the borders of their form to implicate economies and ideologies. One cannot simply define the copy-text; study of one or more plays is impossible in isolation—they are inseparable from the context implied by their dedications, and their importance is qualified by their place in the volume.

The Folio's importance exceeds itself in other ways as well. It has a place in Jonson's career—in mid-career, in fact, and in this way too it has a marginal status, looking as it does both forward and backward in the author's development. The Folio gains in meaning from what follows it, as well as from what it is and where it came from. Here also, Jonson's sense of form raises questions: a folio collected-works implies some manner of terminus, closure of one sort or another. Jonson (aged 43 in 1616) certainly viewed his Folio as a turning point marking both an end and a beginning. That he retired from the theater for a decade after its publication is one of a number of details reinforcing such a view of Jonson's intentions. But as Jennifer Brady's essay shows, Jonson's view of the Folio's symbolic significance was not the same as his contemporaries', a disparity in perspective that is reflected in his later work.

In content and design the present volume responds to some of these multidimensional problems raised by the Folio. The essays have been invited for the volume from scholars having different critical and personal approaches to Jonson; the result is that each knows a different poet. Men and women at different stages in their careers, each author has a markedly different voice, and this should remind us of the basic Jonsonian theme of the inseparability of art and life. The polyphony of the collection will, we hope, contribute to the richness and complexity of current Renaissance studies.

In trying to see the Folio from different angles, in the round so to speak, we have tried to let it give shape and definition to our volume and the questions we ask. Existing first as a physical object in space and time, but as Kevin Donovan points out hardly fixed stably in those dimensions, the Folio is a book with an identity and history whose description poses an initial challenge to the bibliographer. The direction followed by the subsequent essays is that of the Folio itself; as gloss to the

text, they parallel a reading of its contents. Thus, as preface
to the plays themselves, in Wyman Herendeen's paper on the
dedications, we encounter Jonson's relations to friends, institutions, and even genres, and hear in extraliterary contexts the
themes that recur in the plays, verse, and masques. Their influence is felt as one moves into the world of Jonson's art, into
the claustrophobic center of his plays. We are repeatedly forced
to cross the borders between created world and the world of
the creator. In contrast with the destructive illusion of self-
sufficiency and security dreamt by Sejanus, Volpone, and Subtle,
and their eventual confrontation with a world outside their own,
in the Folio, Jonson keeps a healthy traffic between art, or
the imagination, and reality and controls the overlap between
spheres of experience. The tensions that William Blissett and
Katharine Maus identify within the plays are also those of the
Folio as a whole, and—as Sara van den Berg and Jennifer Brady
show—of Jonson's growing preoccupation with himself and his
role as poet. Each section of the Folio is contingent upon the
other. As Blissett argues, Jonson's Roman plays lack the classical
temper present in the verse. Maus describes a drama where
tensions exist between ideal and real economies that are firmly
based in psychological and social realities of the seventeenth
century.

The studies of the dedications and the plays acknowledge
Jonson's classicism, but go far to qualify what has traditionally
been viewed as the Roman Ben Jonson. Both Blissett and Maus
demonstrate, in different ways, the city limits of Rome in Renaissance England, particularly as the classical ideal jars with the
moral, economic, and political realities of the world in which
the Folio must survive. The first four essays show how classicism, like all Jonsonian artifacts, is contingent upon people,
patronage, politics, economics, and other values that challenge
the presumed stability of the Roman ideal for the humanist.

In the next three papers, Jonson's interest, as reflected in the
shape of the Folio, is shown shifting from the world of drama
to the drama of the world. From Stella Revard's essay it can
be seen that the process is also one that displaces classicism
with a neoclassical ideal, where Latin models are redefined according to Neo-Latin rhetoric. The epigrams also present the
emergence of authorial identity in a way unsuited to drama.
As Sara van den Berg illustrates, the Renaissance individual
steps forward in Jonson's works to claim authority for his art.
The audacity behind Jonson's publication of his Folio becomes

an implicit concern as the author asserts his personal, no less than his social and economic, independence. Joseph Loewenstein's study of the masques brings a number of these related themes together in his discussion of Jonson's awareness of the anomaly of the printed masque, an anomaly that pits a modern medium against a medieval and hierarchic patronage system. In doing so, Jonson pushes the social and historical role of his literary art to its fullest potential and succeeds in an iconoclastic act that allows him to address the king and court in ways that his contemporaries, such as Daniel and Shakespeare, could not.

Much of the drama of the Folio is, as Maus, van den Berg and Loewenstein argue, the creation of the ideal of authorship, embodied in Jonson himself, and figuring an act of creation and authority that has personal, psychological, and socioeconomic dimensions. Moving beyond the historical terminus of the 1616 Folio, Jennifer Brady's essay evaluates the hazards of Jonson's success. She looks back on the vulnerability of the voluntarily disenfranchised author and examines the limits of the "modern" author's control of his medium when he aspires to making life coextensive with his art. Jonson and his Folio stand here as an exemplum for the artist as a solitary figure who achieves his moment of fame and lives to watch its demise. The instability of the Folio text that Donovan describes is an extension of the psychological estrangement and corruptibility of Jonson the man analyzed by Brady. It is also, as Jonson realized and as this volume suggests, the logical and historical evolution of the role of the artist in a political economy differing from that of the sixteenth century. Looking back on Jonson, we see him as the embodiment and victim of the fame he earned through an unusual ability to see the uniqueness of his age and to use its media to capitalize—artistically and socially—on its social instability. As a result, his Folio, creating worlds of its own while responding to its age, comments with striking perspicacity on what we can identify as characteristics inherent in early modern society.

We have, then, followed the design of Jonson's Folio throughout: our divisions are those of the volume set forth in the Catalogue. Several assumptions lie behind such a seemingly logical approach. First of all, we assume that there is an artful pattern to the Folio and the sequence of its contents, that the movement from drama to masque is a progression in which the volume's dominant themes are redefined, and where ideas of individual works are shown to be contingent upon a significant whole. Our ordering also makes assumptions about the Renaissance and about the uniqueness of the Folio's (and Jonson's) place in it. As Jonson studies have demonstrated in recent years, his career and work exemplify some key changes that occurred implicitly in the early seventeenth century and that culminate in the death of Charles I. As Huizinga suggested long ago, the end of the Middle Ages is also the end of the Renaissance. This cultural transition finds its emblem in the Folio—an individual, historical, social, and economic feat more symbolic in some ways than the publication of the Shakespeare First Folio, itself a son of Ben. No invidious comparisons should be made: the men and their works are monumental enough to stand on their own. But while Jonson might say Shakespeare was for all ages, we hope to show here that Jonson was a man of his age.

Ben Jonson's
1616 Folio

Jonson's Texts in the First Folio

Kevin J. Donovan

The essays collected in this volume testify to the growing awareness among literary scholars of the 1616 Folio's significance
not only in Jonson's career but in the larger history of English
Renaissance literary and dramatic culture. This renewed interest
in the Folio underscores the need for greater understanding of
the material production of the book and for a reevaluation of
Folio readings where they differ from other authoritative texts,
such as the quarto editions of the plays and the manuscript
copies of the poems and masques. Ironically, however, while
recent scholarship enhances our sense of the Folio's historical,
literary, and cultural significance, reevaluation of Jonson's texts
in the Folio tends to diminish the preeminent authority accorded
to the Folio in the received text of Jonson as established in
the monumental Oxford edition.[1]

Given the amount of attention paid to other Elizabethan and
Jacobean dramatic texts by analytical bibliography and textual
criticism in the twentieth century, the neglect of the Jonson
Folio by bibliographers is remarkable.[2] The singular importance
of the book in the literary culture of the English Renaissance
is widely recognized, and several studies have called attention
to the material structure and arrangement of the book itself
as significant media for Jonson's artistic expression;[3] however,
compared to the Shakespeare Folio of 1623 or the Beaumont
and Fletcher Folio of 1647, little is known about the printing
of Jonson's 1616 *Workes*. Perhaps as a result of the unfortunate
rift in modern scholarship between literary interpretation and
textual criticism, scholars have apparently been content to rely
on the account of the Folio's printing found in the Oxford edition, though the textual scholarship behind that edition is now
outdated.[4]

Both textually and historically, the 1616 *WORKES OF Benjamin Jonson* is an extraordinary book. Certainly as far as dramatic

23

texts are concerned nothing comparable can be found in the Elizabethan and Jacobean periods. The publication of plays from the professional theater in an impressive folio volume whose title recalled the *Opera* of the Latin classics was a bold claim for the literary status of the often denigrated professional drama and set an important precedent for the publishers of the Shakespeare First Folio.[5] By 1616 Jonson was already remarkable for the pains he took to publish his plays in authoritative texts for readers, his practice in this respect, as in so many others, contrasting strikingly with that of Shakespeare.[6] The publication of the Folio was the culmination of Jonson's use of the printing press to "interpret himself to his age as a writer whose individual works formed a unified corpus animated by his conception of the poet's function."[7]

Thanks in large part to Herford and the Simpsons, the Folio has continued to exert a powerful influence on the received text of Jonson in our own day:

> Percy and Evelyn Simpson correctly identified the extant witnesses to the text of Jonson's dramatic works and, in disentangling the bibliographical complexities of the Folios . . . with their numerous variant and reset formes, performed a magnificent labor of scholarship to which following generations of scholars must always be indebted. *Herford and Simpson* is the first point of consultation for information about all matters of Jonsonian interest.[8]

However, many advances in the practice and theory of bibliographical and textual scholarship have been made since the publication of this great edition. It is a consequence of the Oxford edition's monumentality, as well as its limitations, that any discussion of the present state of Jonson's text must continually refer to, while occasionally contradicting, the findings of Herford and Simpson.

The Oxford editors believed that the Folio provided the most authoritative text for virtually all of the work it contains, and it contains most of the work which we consider Jonson's best. In many cases the supreme authority of the Folio is undeniable: it is the sole authority for *Epicoene*, the revised version of *Every Man In His Humour*, most of the *Epigrammes*, *The Forrest*, and eleven of the eighteen entertainments and masques that it prints, as well as for several lengthy passages in *Cynthia's Revels* and *Poetaster* that are not found in the Quartos.[9] Jonson himself selected and arranged for publication in the volume those works that best represented his own idea of his artistic achievement. In addition, he thoroughly rewrote *Every Man In His Humour*, and corrected and revised the earlier versions of many of the works, especially the early plays.

Jonson apparently marked up the Quartos, which served as copy for the Folio printers when they set up the eight previously published plays, introducing a host of minor revisions, especially in the plays before *Sejanus*.[10] In addition Jonson was responsible for a number of press corrections in the Folio, mainly in the texts of the "comicall satyres" (*Every Man Out Of His Humour*, *Cynthia's Revels*, and *Poetaster*) and *Sejanus*. Many of the press corrections are further departures from the Quartos, and thus constitute another stage of revision. Thus, there are two general classes of revision: changes already made in the copy given to the printers, and press corrections. Both classes of revision include many changes in punctuation, spelling, capitalization, and italicization, as well as a number of added stage directions and many changes of word or phrase.

There is no reason to doubt that the verbal changes and many of the changes in accidentals are authorial; they are so extensive and, in many cases, so inconsequential that no one but the author would have taken the trouble to make them. This is especially true of the revisions made as press corrections; certainly no efficient printer would interrupt a press run to make such changes on his own. Henry DeVocht, who in a series of books published between 1934 and 1958 vehemently maintained that almost none of the Folio's departures from the Quartos is authoritative, was forced to postulate a meddling Folio editor possessed by a "mania for changing indiscriminately."[11] DeVocht's theories have been universally rejected. However, while DeVocht was obviously wrong invariably to prefer the Quartos over the Folio, Herford and Simpson sometimes err in the other direction, too readily ceding authority to the Folio over the Quartos where variants occur in accidentals as well as in substantive readings. They take virtually no account of the possible effect of compositors on the spelling and punctuation of Folio variants. Similarly, they too readily accept as authoritative most variants resulting from press correction, even though some of these are also clearly compositorial.

Having recognized that Jonson revised to some extent most of the earlier works and oversaw press correction in the early stages of the Folio's production, Herford and Simpson invariably chose the Folio over the Quartos as copytext for the works, and, except in cases of obvious error, adopted all of the readings found on press-corrected pages. Textual critics schooled in the theory of W. W. Greg's "Rationale of Copy-Text" will readily recognize two problems resulting from the consistency with which the Oxford editors adhered to these choices.[12] First, the choice of copytext sometimes is mistaken; for some of the plays and masques a modern editor would choose an earlier Quarto text over the Folio. Second, in the matter of press correction, the editors succumb to "the tyranny of the copy-text,"[13] by taking all the readings from a press-corrected page, even though some are clearly compositorial. Generally speaking, a modern editor would be more eclectic in the handling of variants than Herford and Simpson were. However, it is only fair to note that the theory of textual editing that justifies such eclecticism was not available to Herford and Simpson. Greg's "Rationale" appeared when the edition was almost complete, when, in fact, all of the actual works of Jonson (as opposed to the commentaries found in the last three volumes) were already edited and published. Indeed Greg seems to have reached his theoretical conclusions in the course of evaluating some of the more problematic decisions reached by the Oxford editors.[14]

The Oxford editors' frequently mistaken choice of copytext is perhaps the most serious shortcoming of the edition. Fredson Bowers goes so far as to say that "the Herford-Simpson Jonson was ostensibly an edition of the works which by a mistaken choice of copy-text for many parts turned itself into an edition of the Folio."[15] The editors chose the Folio as copytext for almost all the work it contains on the basis of the revisions Jonson made in the Quartos used as printers' copy and because of their belief, based on the authorial press corrections, that Jonson closely supervised the printing. However, they chose the Folio as copytext for all but one of the previously printed masques, even though they recognized that revision in the masques was minimal and that Jonson did not supervise the printing of the section of the Folio containing the masques.[16] Clearly these masques are mere reprints, inferior in authority to the Quartos, upon which a modern critical edition should be based. However even in plays that Jonson clearly revised, the Quarto may be preferable as copytext. Where multiple authorities exist for a text, a modern editor of the critical edition will choose his copytext on the basis of the authority of its accidentals, freely introducing authoritative substantive revisions from other texts. As

Bowers points out, the almost unique case of *Every Man In His Humour* is exceptional:

> because of the very thorough substantive rewriting, the accidentals that accompany the altered wording must of course be accepted, and these are so numerous as to make it almost impossible to attempt with any consistency to preserve the Quarto accidentals when revision of the substantives would not necessarily have effected their variation.[17]

For the remaining revised plays the crucial point in determining the choice of copytext is whether "Jonson's marking of his copy was sufficiently detailed to change the texture of the Folio accidentals from derived to 'substantive' status":

> Especially when it is considered that . . . in general . . . Jonson did nothing in the press-corrections about the Folio departures from his ordinary spellings (and these were fairly numerous) a problem does indeed arise whether the supervision [Jonson] gave the play both in the preparation of the marked Quarto copy and in the Folio press-correction is sufficient to elevate the Folio to copy-text status for plays (unlike *Every Man In His Humour*) where the amount of substantive revision was markedly less and so had little or no effect on the separate problem of the accidentals that were independent of revision.[18]

The surviving Jonsonian autograph manuscripts provide a good deal of information about Jonson's spelling and punctuation habits. A comparison of these with the Folio's departures from the spelling and punctuation of the Quartos suggests that while many—perhaps most—of the Folio's changes in punctuation tend to move closer to the "elaborate . . . overloaded . . . and ultralogical" (Herford and Simpson, 2.432) practice of the autographs, spelling changes tend to move further away from Jonson's habits and seem principally determined by compositorial preference. This was Bowers's "theoretical opinion after a cursory run-through of the Simpson apparatus [to *Sejanus*] and the Jonsonian manuscripts."[19] My own study of the orthography of Jonson's autographs and of the variants between the Quarto and Folio texts of *Every Man Out Of His Humour* and *The Alchemist* supports this conclusion. In the earlier play, although some of the Folio's changes in punctuation are inadvertent, the majority testify to Jonson's careful revision of the

Quarto. The autographs provide support for the authority of the Folio's frequent addition of hyphens, dashes, apostrophes, parentheses, and especially the host of commas added to set off interjections, vocatives, appositives, prepositional phrases, relative clauses, and indirect statements. Of particular interest is the addition in *Every Man Out Of His Humour* of over 200 Jonsonian "coordinating commas," used after the first of two words or phrases joined by a coordinating conjunction. While many of the changes in punctuation in the Folio text of *The Alchemist* are also supported by the evidence of the autographs, a number of deletions of punctuation marks seem due to compositorial oversight. The few and obvious press corrections in the Folio text of *The Alchemist* show that Jonson probably did not supervise the printing of this play, certainly not with the scrupulous attention he paid to the printing of *Every Man Out Of His Humour*, the most heavily press-corrected work in the Folio.

In contrast to the punctuation changes, with a few exceptions—notably the addition of the digraph œ in "tragœdy" and "comœdy"—the Folio's changes in the spelling of the Quartos are due mainly to compositorial preference. Many Jonsonian spellings retained in the Quartos are regularly changed in the Folio. For instance, where Jonson's autographs show a marked preference for internal *ay* over *ai*, the Folio usually prints *ai*, often changing *ay* spellings in the Quarto; such changes are especially frequent in *The Alchemist*. Similarly, where Jonson's autographs invariably spell the words *near, clear,* and *year* with *ea*, the Folio usually spells these words with *ee*, often departing from the Quartos to do so.[20] While compositorial preference is certainly a factor in the spelling of the Quartos,[21] the Quarto versions seem as a rule to retain more Jonsonian spellings than the Folio. This is notably true of *The Alchemist*: where the Quarto contained fifteen examples of Jonson's "classicizing" spelling of such words as "æquall," with the digraph æ instead of *e*, the Folio changed all but three to *e*.

With the spelling losing authority and the punctuation gaining authority in the Folio texts of these plays in comparison with the Quartos, the choice of copytext is complicated, demanding an unusually high degree of eclecticism in accidentals as well as substantives. An editor must decide whether to choose the spelling or the punctuation as the primary determinant of the authority of the copytext's accidental texture. Bowers describes the alternatives as follows:

If spelling is chosen as the main determinant (as is customary in Elizabethan editing) and if . . . the normalized spelling forms are on the whole compositorial save for the recognizable idiosyncrasies which present no difficulty, then it would be practicable for an editor to take the Quarto as copy-text in order to preserve its generally superior texture of ordinary spelling forms and to treat the idiosyncratic accidentals of the Folio like the substantives by incorporating such as the editor believes were authentic Jonsonian alterations plus those that he knows are Jonson's by reason of Folio press-correction . . . . If F were chosen as copy-text instead, the list of emendations would comprise a return to such Q spellings as the editor believed, on sufficient evidence, had been unauthoritatively altered by the compositors, plus punctuation in the same category, plus the numerous idiosyncratic accidentals in Q normalized or corrupted in F.[22]

An editor's choices would vary from one play to the next. For instance, an editor would probably decide that the Folio revision of *Every Man Out Of His Humour* is so extensive and minute in matters of punctuation, so much more authoritative than the Quarto in this respect, that its texture of accidentals is quantitatively superior to the Quarto's. By basing a text on the Folio and importing from the Quarto demonstrably authorial spelling and punctuation, an editor would probably retain a certain amount of compositorial normalization in the accidentals while losing fewer authorial traits than if the Quarto were chosen and only such Folio spellings and punctuation as could be convincingly defended were imported. However, the same editor might well choose the Quarto as the copytext for *The Alchemist*. The reduced amount of revision discernible in the punctuation of the play and the Folio's demonstrably compositorial spellings make a Quarto copytext that imports only those changed Folio accidentals that can be ascribed to Jonson, and is more likely to retain the characteristics of his orthography than a text based on the Folio.

Press corrections constitute another area where the Oxford editors tend to be too faithful to the Folio. Herford and Simpson were convinced that "most of the [Folio's press] corrections are the author's, made at the printing-office where he would present himself for this purpose every morning."[23] However, it now seems clear that the Oxford editors gave too much authority to the press variants. This assumption leads to two kinds of confusion. First, they sometimes confuse careless resettings with uncorrected original settings, seeing press corrections where there are none. For instance, Johan Gerritsen has shown that a supposed press correction in the text of *Catiline* on 3R4v is actually "a compositorial variant introduced when outer 3R3,4 was reset."[24] A more striking example occurs in the text of *Mercury Vindicated from the Alchemists*, where one of two variant states of 4P5v prints nonsense. Although Herford and Simpson assumed that the correct state was caused by some fairly obvious press correction by the compositor, in fact the correct state is the earlier, the garbled state appearing in pages which were reimpressed, though not reset.[25]

Another problem appears when Herford and Simpson adopt every reading from a press-corrected page, even though some changes made in the course of press correction are clearly compositorial. For instance, when a press correction adds a word, the compositor may replace *and* with *&* or change the spelling of a previously set word to make the new matter fit. Herford and Simpson invariably adopt these later compositorial spellings and abbreviations merely because they occur in corrected pages. As Gerritsen points out,

> where the Folio exists in two or more states it is incorrect to assume that the succession of states invariably progresses towards the most authoritative reading. This assumption, however, the editors seem to have made on several occasions, due to their having failed to estimate at its proper value the compositor's influence on the text he was producing. So far as substantive variants are concerned the assumption will indeed generally hold good, but where it fails is when we consider the accidentals, especially those of spelling. Too often, in these cases, the editors, by neglecting to distinguish between the author's correction in proof and the compositor's expedients when translating into type, have preferred Stansby to Jonson.[26]

It would be unjust, however, to end this discussion of the Herford and Simpson edition on a note of criticism, especially in a volume dedicated to appreciation of the 1616 Folio, for the Oxford edition everywhere displays signs of the editors' respect and even love for the Folio. One of the pleasures of using the edition, in fact, is encountering the editors' attempts to convey to their readers an approximation of the experience of reading the works in their first collected edition. Thus they reproduce a number of the Folio's typographical features—for instance, in the dedications that precede the Folio plays and the lists of the principal actors in the first performances; in the style of the headlines (italic running titles between horizontal rules); and in the typography of act and scene divisions and speech headings. The most striking example of the editors' fidelity to the Folio—and one which shows their sense of humor—is their printing of the running title *"Cynthias Reuells"* instead of *Poetaster* in the headline over the first verso page containing the text of the play *Poetaster,* a bit of whimsy clearly aimed at readers intimately familiar with the Folio.

Finally, the Oxford editors' seemingly extreme fidelity to the Folio can be better understood in relation to its historical context. Their work preceded the development of Greg's editorial theory, which would have allowed them a greater degree of eclecticism than they felt free to employ. In addition, their work on Jonson's texts was conducted at a time when the primary obstacle to a proper appreciation of Jonson's texts seemed to lie not with overvaluing the Folio but with undervaluing it in favor of the Quartos. During most of the twenty-seven-year period when the Oxford edition was being published, Henry DeVocht was publishing a series of articles that collectively constitute "a wholesale attack on the authority of the [F]olio, an attack distinguished by wrong-headedness and ignorance as much as vehemence."[27] DeVocht was unwilling to concede the slightest degree of authority to the Folio's deliberate departures from the Quartos. So serious did the threat of DeVocht's theories seem to the Oxford editors that they devoted ten pages of their "Account of the Text" in volume 9 to refuting DeVocht. If this refutation reminds modern readers of "the amusing style of an eighteenth-century scholars' feud,"[28] it also indicates the seriousness with which the Oxford editors regarded their defense of "a great classic text."[29]

Since the completion of the Oxford edition, little new textual work has been published on the 1616 Folio. In the late 1950s, Gerritsen published two important but brief articles that corrected Herford and Simpson on a number of facts concerning the printing of the Folio, including the correct order of the variant settings in the first quire of *Epicoene,* and that also revealed such notable facts as the printing of *Every Man In His Humour* out of order and the reimposition of a number of unreset formes at the end of the volume.[30] Gerritsen called the second of these articles "A Preliminary Account" and promised a larger work that would give in detail the evidence for his conclusions, but unfortunately this longer study has not yet appeared. The principal source of Gerritsen's findings is the evidence of changes in the headlines; my own examination

of these confirms the essential soundness of Gerritsen's conclusions. Otherwise the only published bibliographical works on
the Folio since Herford and Simpson are R. B. Parker's excellent
1983 edition of *Volpone* for the Revels Plays, which gives a
much fuller account of the press correction in the section of
the *Workes* containing *Volpone* than that found in Herford and
Simpson; James A. Riddell's 1986 note in *The Library* establishing conclusively the order of the variant states of the Folio's
title page; and my 1987 article in *Studies in Bibliography* demon-
strating the correct order of some variant pages in the final
quires of the Folio, showing that Stansby printed the final quires
concurrently with another work and establishing a more precise
and later date for the conclusion of the Folio than had yet been
proposed.[31] Perhaps these signal a return to a long-neglected
topic. Riddell currently is involved in a new study of Folio
watermarks. These were previously studied by Gerritsen, who
claimed that they help to demonstrate that work on the Folio
began in 1615 "and had reached mid-way by the spring of
1616"[32] but he never published an account of them. The watermarks may provide fuller information on the order in which
different sections of the Folio were printed and the relation
of the Folio to other works from Stansby's shop. Meanwhile,
more work needs to be done on other aspects of the Folio.

Some methods of investigation are more promising than others
in assessing the effect of the printer Stansby's staff on Jonson's
texts in the Folio. The Folio is particularly resistant to the kind
of investigation of identifiable types that has yielded great results in the texts of Shakespeare, Beaumont and Fletcher, and
others. One reason is the relatively good condition of the types
used to print the Folio. In contrast to the battered types from
Jaggard's stock used in the Shakespeare First Folio, Stansby's
English Roman types bear far fewer distinctive marks of damage.
Another factor limiting the effectiveness of type analysis when
applied to the Jonson Folio is the large amount of type that
Stansby had at his disposal. When printing began on the Folio,
Stansby regularly had five to seven formes of type standing
at a time; during the extensive resetting and reimposition that
occurred in the last section of the book Stansby had as many
as "37 folio pages" standing in type.[33] Not only did Stansby
have plenty of type, he also used relatively few per page in
the Jonson Folio. In contrast to the Shakespeare Folio of 1623
and the Beaumont and Fletcher Folio of 1647, both of which
were mainly printed in double columns of pica type, the Jonson

Folio is mostly printed in single columns of English type, which is larger than italic. Consequently an average page of the Shake-speare Folio contains nearly twice as many types as an average page of the Jonson Folio. The combination of Stansby's larger supply of type and the appearance of fewer types per page means that types recur far less frequently in the Jonson Folio than in the Shakespeare and Beaumont and Fletcher Folios, since Stansby was not obliged to distribute the types from printed pages nearly as often as, say, Jaggard did. This low rate of frequency in the recurrence of types means that the evidence derived from type analysis in the Folio is often too sparse to be of much use.

Further hampering the use of types as a method of investiga-tion is the likelihood that the Folio was not printed as a self-contained operation but that printing on the Folio occurred concurrently with the printing of other books. It has recently been discovered that the latter part of the *Workes* was being printed concurrently with another Stansby folio, *The Surveyor* by Aaron Rathborne. If concurrent printing was the norm in Stansby's shop, then types could not recur within a given work without frequent disruption in the pattern of type recurrence. In fact a study of type recurrence in *Every Man Out Of His Humour*, where printing in the Folio began, foundered on just such disruption of the pattern of recurrence in the later quires of the play. If indeed concurrent printing was the norm in Stans-by's shop while the Folio was in progress, then a full account of types in the *Workes* would necessitate investigating the ap-pearance of distinctive types in every work printed by Stansby from 1615 to 1617—a herculean task unlikely to be worth the effort given the low density of recurring types per page.

On the other hand, compositor study promises to be a more fruitful area of research on the Folio. Abundant evidence exists of compositorial spelling preferences in the Folio. In quires M–P and reset pages G5–G6V of *Every Man Out Of His Humour* the pattern of type recurrence supports a division of pages be-tween one compositor who prefers final *y* and another who prefers final *ie*. Compositor identification in the Folio has barely begun, but its usefulness promises to be augmented by the fact that the surviving Jonson holographs enable us to identify a number of Jonson's own habits in spelling and punctuation and so to gauge the authority of the changes in punctuation and spelling effected in the Folio texts of the plays.

Particularly desirable is a study of the many press corrections and resettings in the Folio. Except for A. C. Judson in his single edition of *Cynthia's Revels* in 1912, Herford and Simpson were the first editors to collate different copies of the Folio in order to identify press variants. By modern standards, the Oxford editors collated an insufficient number of copies—eight, with occasional reference to one or two others—though they nonetheless found a large number of variant formes. Gerritsen collated formes known to be variant in forty copies of the Folio, "well above what the law of averages could have made them expect."[34] A fuller collation is bound to uncover more variants than have yet been discovered and give a fuller record of press activity during the volume's printing. Further studies need to distinguish more precisely the areas where Jonson is responsible for the corrections from those due to the compositors alone.

It is now known that Herford and Simpson overestimated the authority of the Folio in comparison with some of the quarto editions of plays and masques that preceded it and made greater claims than are warranted for Jonson's involvement at the press. In this sense the Oxford edition represents the apex of the Folio's textual authority and reputation. However, a growing current of thought among some textual critics would retain a focus on the singularity of individual books, emphasizing their social role and context as well as the nonverbal elements that contribute to the reading experience.[35] The Jonson Folio in particular invites such approaches. The book itself is replete with meaning that goes beyond the individual works it contains. The prestigious folio format and the volume's typographical conventions associated with classical literature are bearers of meaning that profoundly affect the experience of reading the works. Textual critics can and should significantly increase our understanding of such features of the *Workes*.

Notes

1. C. H. Herford and Percy and Evelyn Simpson, eds., *Ben Jonson*, ll vols. (Oxford: Clarendon, 1925–52).

2. See, among others, G. Thomas Tanselle, *Textual Criticism Since Greg: A Chronicle, 1950—1985* (Charlottesville: University Press of Virginia, 1988); and Fredson Bowers, "A Search for Authority: The Investigation of Shakespeare's Printed Texts," in *Print and Culture in the Renaissance: Essays on the Advent of Printing in Europe*, ed. Gerald P. Tyson and Sylvia S. Wagonheim (Newark: University of Delaware Press; London and Toronto: Associated University Presses, 1986), pp. 17–44.

3. See W. David Kay, "The Shaping of Ben Jonson's Career: A Study of Facts and Problems," *Modern Philology* 67 (1970): 224–37; Richard C. Newton,

"Jonson and the (Re-)Invention of the Book," in *Classic and Cavalier: Essays on Jonson and the Sons of Ben*, ed. Claude J. Summers and Ted-Larry Pebworth (Pittsburgh: University of Pittsburgh Press, 1982), pp. 31–55; also Richard C. Newton, "Making Books from Leaves: Poets Become Editors," in *Print and Culture*, pp. 246–64; Edward B. Partridge, "Jonson's *Epigrammes*: the Named and the Nameless," *Studies in the Literary Imagination* 6 (1973): 153–98; and D. F. McKenzie, "Typography and Meaning: The Case of William Congreve," in *Buch und Buchhandel in Europa im achtzehnten Jahrhundert: (The Book and the Book Trade in Eighteenth-Century Europe): Proceedings of the Fünftes' Wolfenbütteler Symposium, Nov. 1–3, 1977*, ed. Giles Barber and Bernhard Fabian (Hamburg: Hauswedell, 1977): 83–123.

4. The limitations of Herford and Simpson's edition were pointed out as early as 1942, in Sir Walter Greg's review of volume 7, "Jonson's Masques—Points of Editorial Principle and Practice," *Review of English Studies* 18 (1942): 144–66. In the late 1950s Johan Gerritsen published two short articles that corrected Herford and Simpson on a number of points: a review of vols. 9–11, *English Studies* 38 (1957): 120–6; and "Stansby and Jonson Produce a Folio: A Preliminary Account," *English Studies* 40 (1959): 52–55. See also Fredson Bowers, "Greg's 'Rationale of Copy-Text' Revisited," *Studies in Bibliography* 31 (1978): 109–18. What is ultimately wanted is a new edition of Jonson; such an edition could serve as a satisfactory basis for a concordance of the poet's works. Such a massive undertaking, however, would require a major commitment of resources and is certainly a long way off. See T. H. Howard-Hill, "Towards a Jonson Concordance," *Research Opportunities in Renaissance Drama* 15–16 (1972–3): 17–32: "Scholars can remedy some of the deficiencies of *Herford and Simpson* in the quiet of the study, with the aid of supplementary studies, but an editor of a concordance could not justifiably, in my opinion, base his concordance on that edition. . . . Nor do I think that *Herford and Simpson* comes so close to a 'definitive' edition and is so well established as a text that a concordance editor could disregard its textual inadequacies. . . . If the standing of the *Herford and Simpson* text is as poor as it has been described, then, regardless of whether or not a concordance to Jonson's plays is desirable, the text of his dramatic works should be edited anew" (pp. 27, 29).

5. See Herford and Simpson, *Ben Jonson*, 9.13.

6. See "Publication," chap. 10, in Gerald Eades Bentley, *The Profession of Dramatist in Shakespeare's Time, 1590–1642* (Princeton: Princeton University Press, 1971), pp. 264–92.

7. Kay, "Facts and Problems," p. 236.

8. Howard-Hill, "Jonson Concordance," pp. 22–23.

9. See the separate textual introductions to the plays in Herford and Simpson, *Ben Jonson*, vols. 3–5.

10. The case of *Every Man In His Humour*, wholly rewritten for the Folio, is, of course, exceptional. Herford and Simpson note that the Folio text of *Every Man In His Humour* reproduces a few of the Quarto's errors of punctuation and lineation, and conclude that the printers' copy was a corrected and interlined Quarto; however, J. W. Lever, in his Parallel-Text Edition of the play for the Regents Renaissance Drama Series (Lincoln: University of Nebraska Press, 1971), holds that

The inference is somewhat far-fetched. So detailed a revision, with its countless deletions, insertions, and transpositions, would have made the corrected text virtually unreadable. . . . It is more plausible to suppose that Jonson had the Quarto before him while preparing his manuscript revision and inadvertently repeated some slightly defective punctuation. (xxvii–xxviii)

The evidence that Quartos of the other previously printed plays were used as a copy by the Folio printers can be found in the textual introductions to these plays in Herford and Simpson. See also the following publications by Henry DeVocht: *Comments on the Text of Ben Jonson's "Every Man out of his Humour"* (Louvain, Belgium: Uystpruyst, 1937), pp. 3–9; *Comments on the Text of Ben Jonson's "Cynthia's Revels"* (Louvain, Belgium: Uystpruyst, 1950), pp. 39–46; *Ben Jonson's "The Alchemist," Edited from the Quarto of 1612, with Comments* (Louvain, Belgium: Uystpruyst, 1950), pp. 203–7; and *Ben Jonson's "Poetaster" . . . with Comments on the Text* (Louvain, Belgium: Uystpruyst, 1934), pp. 104–7. For *The Alchemist* see also Herbert Davis, "Note on a Cancel in *The Alchemist*, 1612," 5 *Library* 13 (1958): 278–80; and for *Volpone*, see Parker ed., p. 5.

11. Henry DeVocht, *Ben Jonson's "Volpone," Edited from the Quarto of 1607, with Comments on the Text, Materials for the Study of the Old English Drama,* no. 12 (Louvain, Belgium: Uystrpruyst, 1937), p. 96. The frequently indifferent nature of many Folio revisions seemed sufficient proof to DeVocht that Jonson was not responsible for them: he cites as the basis for his antipathy to the Folio "the indubitable principle . . . that, if a Ben Jonson brings about a change in the texts of his works, that change *must necessarily testify to his intellectual and literary ability*, it must be worthy of him,—and not merely consist of an interchanging of equivalent terms, or the insertion of a few superfluous commas or marks of exclamation" (p. 3). Of course there is no reason an author's revision of his own work could not sometimes be trifling; in *The Stability of Shakespeare's Text* (London: Arnold, 1965), E. A. J. Honigmann cites numerous examples of authors making quite trifling revisions of their work. DeVocht's "Attack on the Folio" is refuted in an appendix to the Oxford edition (9. 74–85).

12. W. W. Greg, "The Rationale of Copy-Text," *Studies in Bibliography* 3 (1950–51): 19–36.

13. Greg, "Rationale of Copy-Text," p. 25.

14. Howard-Hill, "Jonson Concordance," p. 23, notes that "Greg's work for [his review of Herford and Simpson 7] led him to attempt a reconstruction of Jonson's *Masque of Gypsies*, from which study he developed the first statement of the theory of copy-text."

15. Bowers, "Rationale of Copy-Text Revisited," p. 114.

16. "The [Folio] text of the entertainments and masques is often carelessly printed, and the Latin and Greek quotations in the notes are especially bad. Jonson cannot have read the proofs" (9.72). The exception is the *Masque of Queenes*, printed from the holograph in the British Library.

17. Bowers, "Rationale of Copy-Text Revisited," p. 110.

18. Ibid.

19. Ibid., p. 115.

20. In *The English Grammar* Jonson recognized ẽa as an acceptable "diphthong" (it is actually a digraph), but rejected ẽe (I.v.28–30).

21. For instance, two compositors can be distinguished in the first Quarto of *Every Man Out Of His Humour*: one favors the spellings *Humor, blood, houre, togither, master, Mitre, monsieur, spite,* and *sute;* the other favors *Humour, bloud, hower, together, maister, Miter, mounsieur, spight,* and *suit.*

22. Bowers, "Rationale of Copy-Text Revisited," p. 115.

23. Herford and Simpson, *Ben Jonson*, 9.72.

24. Gerritsen, *English Studies* (1957), p. 123.

25. The Oxford editors' optimism regarding the authority of the press correction in the Folio extends to their discussion of press variants in the Quartos. In editing *Volpone*, Parker found that "there are more states of correction [in the Quarto] than Herford and Simpson supposed; that some of the states they considered compositorial errors seem more likely to be the later results of damage; and that there are several cases of miscorrection: their assumption that nearly all variants are a result of Jonson's own careful correction is, thus, much too optimistic" (p. 4).

A similar situation occurred with the Quarto of *Cynthia's Revels*, where Simpson argued at length that certain variants were the result of Jonson's proofreading, whereas in fact the correct states are the earlier ones, the faulty states resulting from careless resetting. (See Herford and Simpson 4.5–17 and 9.10; also Greg's review of Herford and Simpson 5 in *Review of English Studies* 14 (1938): 218.) Although Simpson acknowledged the error in the "Historical Survey of the Text" found in volume 9, it has been perpetuated in his study of early proofreading, where it appears as one of three examples of Jonson's activity as a press corrector. See Percy Simpson, *Proof-Reading in the Sixteenth, Seventeenth and Eighteenth Centuries* (1935; Oxford: Oxford University Press, 1970), pp. 11–12. The passage is not mentioned among other errata listed in the "Forward to the Reprint."

26. 1937, p. 122.

27. Gerritsen, *English Studies* (1957), p. 125.

28. Ibid.

29. Herford and Simpson, *Ben Jonson*, 9.84.

30. See above, n2.

31. James A. Riddell, "Variant Title-Pages of the 1616 Jonson Folio," 6 *Library* 8 (June 1986): 152–6; Kevin J. Donovan, "The Final Quires of the Jonson 1616 *Workes*: Headline Evidence," *Studies in Bibliography* 40 (1987): 106–20.

32. Gerritsen, "A Preliminary Account," p. 55.

33. Ibid.

34. Gerritsen, *English Studies*, p. 124. Some variants unknown to Herford and Simpson are recorded by Gerritsen (*English Studies*, p. 124; and "A Preliminary Account," p. 55), Parker, and Sidney Musgrove in his edition of *The Alchemist* (Berkeley: University of California Press, 1968). The Lowell copy of the Folio at the Houghton contains a resetting of sheet 2S2.5, an unrecorded variant that the headlines show to be one of the "mysterious resettings" made late in the printing of the volume, "apparently in order to make up incomplete sets" (Herford and Simpson 9.40); for these see also Gerritsen, *English Studies*, p. 55.

35. See McKenzie, "Typography and Meaning"; and Jerome McGann, "The Monks and the Giants: Textual and Bibliographical Studies and the Interpretation of Literary Works," in *Textual Criticism and Literary Interpretation* (Chicago: University of Chicago Press, 1985), pp. 180–99. See also James K. Bracken, "Books from William Stansby's Printing House, and Jonson's Folio of 1616," 6 *Library* 10 (1988): 18–29.

A New Way to Pay Old Debts: Pretexts to the 1616 Folio

W. H. Herendeen

TO THE HIGH AND MIGHTIE HENRY, *Prince of Wales.*
This first part of my intended Poeme I consecrate
to your Highnes.

This, part of Drayton's opening address to Prince Henry, is un-
mistakably a dedication. Its very conventionality makes it a
useful model for some preliminary remarks about the political
economy of prefatory material in the Renaissance. In its expression of fealty to Prince Henry one can readily see an affirmation
of a stable order confirmed by unquestioning acceptance of—or
unwillingness to examine—Henry's deservingness. In its rhetoric, and as a social and political gesture, it is wholly public;
as such it avoids any inward searching, either of Henry or the
poet. It stands in marked contrast with the decorum informing
Francis Bacon's dedication of his translations of the Psalms to
George Herbert. Striving for the greatest possible spiritual or
psychological affinity between book and dedicatee, his dedication does not express a social order, but rather witnesses publicly
a spiritual or moral correspondence: "My manner for dedications [is] to choose those that I hold most fit for the argument"
of the book.[1] Compared with Drayton's, his dedication strives
to express feeling, not form, and works from inner knowledge,
not outward acceptance. Because it implicitly denies social order
in favor of a subjective inner one, it speaks from and about
a world socially less stable and hierarchic than Drayton's.

Naturally, both dedications are public addresses, but the rules
of decorum are used very differently by each. They represent
two extremes in the treatment of prefatory and dedicatory material; each dedication "foregrounds" a different aspect of human
experience. In the process, each writer defines himself and his

work in terms of very different social and psychological struc-
tures.

Prefatory material thus provides readers with their first clues
about the political and spiritual economy of a work, among
other things, and about the social order that must sustain it.[2]
In examining the apparatus accompanying Jonson's folio, we
will find that the poet moves skillfully between the two extremes
marked by Drayton and Bacon. Consider, for a moment, the
dedication (if that is the word) of *Every Man Out Of His Humour*
to the "NOBLEST NOURCERIES OF HUMANITY, AND LIBERTY
. . . The Innes of Court"—"*I Understand you, Gentlemen, not
your houses.*" In its bold public voice, it calls attention to its
social context and values (as Drayton's does), but also speaks
(as Bacon's does) from the assumption that a significant public
gesture must somehow be an expression of inner understanding
or harmony, which the poet admits is rather tentative in this
case. Jonson's distinction between the Inns of Court and the
men themselves is also the distinction between public and private voice, values, and identities; significantly, the address is
first of all to a public audience—to the Inns—although the poet
concedes that he is baffled by them. Reading this against the
two previous models, one can see that unlike Drayton, Jonson
does not posit a stable relationship between himself, the text,
and the dedicatee, and he does not take for granted the deservingness of the dedicatee. Bringing Baconian inner concerns to
bear on the social values that are implicit in a dedication to
the "NOURCERIES OF HUMANITY, AND LIBERTY," Jonson
hopes that the individuals of the Inns will make the institution
worthy of his trust. Jonson creates a similar instability between
himself and his addressee in his prefatory remarks to *Cynthia's
Revels.* Addressing the court as the "FOUNTAINE OF MAN-
NERS" and the kingdom's "glasse," Jonson proceeds to under-
mine the Draytonian sense of order and stability through an
image of Narcissus, and the warning, "*Beware, then, thou render
mens figures truly.*"

Obviously, then, the Jonsonian dedication is not a nostalgic
affirmation of feudal hierarchy based on tenets of *noblesse
oblige.* It hardly offers rank and respect in return for patronage;
it speaks from within a social and economic system but refuses
to abandon the critical independence by which one asserts separateness. The prefatory material generally does not come from
a fixed spiritual and political economy in which fealty is perpetuated as willingly and as "naturally" as it appears to be in

the moral ecology of Penshurst, where self-sacrificing fish offer themselves up for their lord's consumption. Rather, Jonson uses it to suggest a contract of a more modern sort, like the covenant set forth in the Induction of *Bartholomew Fair* that enumerates the material and moral fees, rights, and obligations of all parties. Here, with the one significant exception of the voyeur-king, everyone is servant to someone or something, but no one is slave to anyone, unless it be to his own passions.

The contract spelled out fully in that play, and operating also in the epigrams, is pretty much that which emerges from the *meum* and *tuum* of the prefatory material, and that Jonson bluntly states when he subscribes himself after his address to the court (*Cynthia's Revels*): "Thy servant, but not slave." As we will see in more detail as we study the role of this material, Jonson's relationship to this audience is one which, in destabilizing the social order, is essentially dynamic—even dramatic— and thus provides a significant link with the different sections of the Folio. Indeed, the individual dedications of the Folio not only share stylistic and thematic features with the rest of Jonson's art, but they also introduce additional dramatic elements into the volume as a whole.

Formally, the prefatory apparatus has much in common with Jonson's poetic art, although it ostensibly stands outside its range, in the social, commercial, and political world of authorship.[3] Because Jonson is so concerned with the politics of relationships and with the theoretical and the actual place of art in society, the dedications and other prefatory material in the Folio naturally take on considerable interest: taken together, it promises to be the testing place for the ideas about art and society that are treated in his dramatic and epigrammatic work. Just how Jonson wants to make the dedications serve himself and his art becomes crucial for the Folio and also for a reconciliation of Jonson the theorist with Jonson the opportunist making his way nearer the salt at the king's table.

Even this cursory preliminary discussion of the subject divulges some of the originality of this material and begins to explain Wheatley's elliptical statement in 1887 that "Ben Jonson's series of dedications is of the greatest of interest."[4] Because the Folio itself is wholly original as a volume of collected works by an English playwright, it follows that this apparatus will share, to some extent, that originality. More specifically, we can already see that they are part of Jonson's artistry—part of the selection and editorial process that shaped the volume, and part of the definition of himself and his craft that emerges from the Folio. In them we have another instance of Jonson's redefinition of the nature and use of genre.

1

It is difficult to say what Jacobean readers expected in the way of prefatory material for a folio. Putting aside for the moment individual characteristics of tone and content, we can again take *Poly Olbion* as fairly representative of the form at its fullest. It has all the apparatus that one might encounter: title page, an engraved frontispiece followed by explanatory verses, the dedication to Prince Henry, an engraved portrait of the dedicatee, a table of contents, an address to "The General Reader," an address to "My Friends the Cambro-Britons," and, finally, Selden's remarks about the Illustrations. The elements themselves are fairly typical of folio publication, although tailored to the specific needs of Drayton's poem. While the Shakespeare First Folio was inspired by Jonson's example, in many particulars it resembles Drayton's more closely, notably in its emphasis on the visual image and its use of various voices to address different readers—in this case, the dual dedicatees, the Earl of Pembroke and the Earl of Montgomery, and the address to the General Reader.[5]

Whether in its no-frills form (title page, dedication, text) or in more intricate combinations like that seen in *Poly Olbion*, prefatory material begins the interpretive definition of the text. The process is further refined by the tone of the material, be it sincere and humble, such as in the Drayton example, ironic, as in Marston's dedication of the *Scourge of Villainy* "To his most esteemed and beloved Selfe," or embittered and hurt, as in the desolate tone of Part II of *Poly Olbion*, where Drayton addresses himself "To any that will read this."[6] Conventionally, prefatory material also begins the process of defining the form and interest of the work, implicitly by identifying its readers and their relationship to the text and explicitly, as the author states the form and intention of the work and suggests its level of seriousness. Turning to the Folio, we find Jonson's theory of satire in the dedication to *Volpone,* and his definition of the epigram in the dedication of the *Epigrammes.* This critical use of prefatory material is hardly unique to Jonson and has classical and medieval precedents.[7]

Thus, although it is customary to speak of such prefatory material in the context of the patronage system and the nuances of the rhetoric of power,[8] it is well to remember that these pre-texts also serve as a critical introduction to the work. The impor-tance of this material, then, is by no means confined to the new historicist; although it is certainly part of the author's asser-tion of authority over text, its focus is as much generic and textual as it is social and political. This aspect of the genre gives it a literary and a political status that is usually ignored—it looks simultaneously inward to the literary qualities of the work and outward to the relation of text and author to society and audience. In its infinitely varied rhetorical postures, a dedica-tion, for example, defines the form and ideas of the work while also performing the related function of defining its intentions and status with respect to society outside of the text. In her discussion of censorship, Annabel Patterson has argued power-fully for the need to heed political forces working within genre.[9] Similarly, in looking at prefatory material both aspects of its importance must be recognized: not only its obvious implica-tions for the political life of a work, but also the way in which it defines its generic and artistic identity. In the case of Jonson, in particular, these two roles serve one another. There are many ways to engage a patron, win the favor of an audience, and protect a work, but the way this is accomplished also affects the way the work itself is viewed.

2

This begins to sound perverse when we recognize that Jonson's Folio has no dedication. Although there is a good deal of prefa-tory material, including dedicatory addresses to seven plays and the *Epigrammes*, among all those who are addressed there is nothing remotely resembling Drayton's address to Prince Henry. Still more important, there is no single patron such as might be expected for a folio of this monumentality by a poet who prided himself on his closeness to the king. If Jonson is a self-crowned laureate,[10] which of course in some way he is, one can hardly help feeling that he neglects one of his self-assumed responsibilities when he refrains from dedicating his work, or (if one prefers), when he reverts to the use of multiple dedications.

The explanation lies not in the missing dedication, but in

the relation of the prefatory material to Jonson's strategic composition of the Folio as a whole. This rather full arsenal of material begins with the engraved frontispiece, and also includes nine gratulatory poems from Jonson's friends and colleagues, and a catalogue, or contents.[11] All of this precedes any word from the poet himself: Jonson's voice is heard first in the dedication of *Every Man In His Humour* to William Camden. Only then, upon reading this revised version of the play—set now in contemporary London—does the reader enter the world of Jonson's art. The frontispiece, the verses by playwrights, poets, lawyers, and even gentlemen, and Jonson's dedication of the first play to his teacher-mentor, all influence our response to Jonson's art—when one gets to it—by identifying his themes and artistic concerns. This carefully selected material is part of Jonson's strategy. He has us read seven pages of verse praising his art and defending him against his detractors and censors. We then hear Jonson's own respectful, even filial praise of Camden, a Justice Clement figure, for his judgment and encouragement, before we get to *Every Man In*.

Every Man In is, of course, a light play about a youthful poet-son challenging paternal authority. It opens with mildly satiric portraits of characters who reject poetry (Knowell Senior) and subvert authority (Knowell Junior and Wellbred), a parody of the familiar epistle, and goes on to offer harsher portraits of abusers of poetry and authority and of themselves (notably Matthew and Kitely). Thus, the themes of authority, rebellion, ingratitude, and of sound and unsound judgment in social and literary matters, are reiterated throughout the prefatory apparatus and become the core themes of the opening play. The transition from preface to play is obviously carefully modulated; we move almost indiscernibly from the one into the other (an effect that would have been impossible with the original version of *Every Man In*). Jonson establishes a relationship wherein one element clearly mirrors the other.

Jonson's art is more than a hall of mirrors, however, and his use of the prefatory material is not only reflexive, but critical and interpretive as well. Jonson made strategic use of dedications and other kinds of apparatus appended to his texts; in his quarto texts he regularly explains his reasons for publication. Occasionally, for example, he prepared presentation editions of works to which he appended unique dedications; he also decided to change the dedication to Camden from *Cynthia's Revels* to *Every Man In*.[12] Jonson's attention to such details is well documented. In the Folio particularly, his allocation of prefatory material—notably the absence of a dedication to the work as a whole, and location of the first dedication as far into the text as possible, where it camouflages the passage from pretext to text—all invite questioning of his intentions.

Jonson has been careful to ensure that we approach his work without authority—without the authority of a patron. If we go leaderless into the Folio, we do not go unprepared, for our approach is directed precisely by this material, which defines Jonson's themes and forms and develops a critical independence in more specific ways than have yet been suggested.

In fact, the entry to THE WORKES OF Benjamin Jonson is through the portals of the triumphal facade of the title page, which establishes the critical and generic range of the volume. In so far as it expresses Jonson's literary concerns, it promises the reader comedy, tragedy, satire, pastoral, and tragicomedy. Iconographically, tragicomedy, personified at the top of the facade and embodying aspects of the other figures, would be, if not the highest form aspired to in the Folio, then the dominant one, lording it over both comedy and tragedy. For those whose teaching of Renaissance drama is largely shaped by the Shakespearean mold and whose view of tragicomedy is mainly English and probably defined by Beaumont's introduction to The Faithful Shepherdess, this positioning of tragicomedy will seem implausible since Jonson wrote nothing that resembles the genre as practised by those authors.[13] But this is not so surprising if we remember that Jonson was a neoclassicist, that Plautus, the first to use the word, was also a city dramatist, and that Jonson the theoretician and author of Discoveries, developed his ideas of dramatic form from the Italian formalists. In practice and in theory, then, Jonson is in many respects closer to the critical opinions of Guarini—who had the most to say about tragicomedy—than to those of Sidney, who maligned tragicomedy. Jonson was always an advocate of the proximity and intermixture of forms. Though he almost never uses the term tragicomedy, he was especially interested in the generic overlap between tragedy and comedy. As he states in his dedication of Volpone to the universities, he is aware that his satires often subvert the decorum appropriate for comedy and move through a no-man's land toward a middle, or tragicomic ground:

And though my catastrophe may, in the strict rigour of comick law, meet with censure . . . I desire the learned, and charitable critick

to have so much faith in me, to thinke it was done off industrie. . . .
But my speciall ayme being to put the snaffle in their mouths,
that crie out, we never punish vice in our enterludes, &c. I tooke
the more liberty; though not without some lines of example, drawn
even in the ancients themselves, the goings of whose comœdies
are not alwaies joyfull . . . and fitly, it being the office of a comick-
Poet *to imitate iustice, and instruct to life.*[14]

Moreover, it is certain that Jonson strove to realize in his art
the same ambitious social and artistic goals that Guarini sees
as distinctly those that make tragicomedy superior to tragedy
and comedy:

> . . . what exactly is such a mixture as tragicomedy? I answer that
> it is the mingling of tragic and comic pleasure, which does not
> allow hearers to fall into excessive tragic melancholy or comic relax-
> ation. From this results a poem of the most excellent form and
> composition, not merely fully corresponding to the mixture of the
> human body, which consists entirely in the tempering of the four
> humors, but much more noble than simple tragedy or simple com-
> edy, as that which does not inflict on us atrocious events and horri-
> ble and inhumane sights . . . and which . . . does not cause us
> to be so relaxed in laughter that we sin against the modesty and
> decorum of a well-bred man. . . . It can delight all dispositions,
> all ages, and all tastes—something that is not true of . . . tragedy
> and comedy, which are at fault because they go to excess.[15]

The social and moral considerations, and the unusual kind of
realism that Guarini describes for tragicomedy are very much
in the spirit and idiom of Jonson's art and theory. It is a form
involving real people in recognizable situations, conveying an
atmosphere of verisimilitude rather than the excesses of comedy
and tragedy; it is also very un-Shakespearean.

Jonson's usual eclectic approach to genre, the dramatic and
nondramatic art of the Folio, and the emblematic figure on the
frontispiece, together suggest that Jonson saw his volume as
illustrating the ideal moderation of tragic and comic extremes
in tragicomedy. The signal placement of the figure of tragicomedy suggests that Jonson wants her to be viewed as the presiding
genius of the Folio as a whole rather than as a generic label
for individual works. With this sibylline presence informing
our approach to the Folio, the heterogeneous genres and diverse
elements of the Jonsonian urban world begin to make better
sense and the work seems a "poem of the most excellent form

and composition . . . corresponding to the mixture of the human body"—in short, it resembles a tragicomic view of the world.[16]

Thus the eloquent emblematic title page begins to mold the critical faculty that Jonson expects of his reader and that he challenges in each of the dedications. Tragicomedy, at least as understood by his Italian sources, is a genre that emphasizes the inconclusive and ambiguous elements of human drama. This is certainly the kind of mixed fare met with in the Folio: in the social, political, literary, and moral conflicts of its plays; in the dramatic accounts Jonson gives us of their performance and reception, and of his own successes and precarious encounters; in the congestion of the *Epigrammes*; and in the sophisticated court comedy that lies behind the masques. The Folio is not just a collection of works. It conveys a powerful sense, not so much of dramatic literature, but of the drama of literature—of people, ideas, and values at odds in a real world. These are the characteristics of Jonsonian tragicomedy; they are qualities which emphasize literature's engagement with the poet's world and the legitimacy of their concerns is further heightened by the dedications.

3

Jonson was committed to the principle of the inseparability of art and life. Through the preliminary material he succeeded in making the lives of his contemporaries and himself part of his art and, conversely, in making art comment on his world. This is straightforwardly seen in the drama sketched in the gratulatory poems that precede the works themselves. The verses contributed by Selden, Bolton, Beaumont, and Donne recall the controversies surrounding *Poetaster*, *Sejanus*, and *Catiline* and Jonson's run-ins with audiences and official censors, as well as generally reminding us of the drama of his career.

> Heare you bad writers, and though you not see,
> I will informe you where you happy bee:
> Provide the most malicious thoughts you can,
> And bend them all against some private man,
> To bring him, not his vices, on the stage,
> Your envie shall be clad in so poore rage,
> And your expressing of him shall be such,

That he himselfe shall think he hath no touch.
("Upon *The Silent Woman*," Francis Beaumont)

This strategy is even more evident in the dedications themselves. Attesting to it, for example, is the range of Jonson's addresses: to his mentor, William Camden; to his lawyer-friend Richard Martin; to men of rank and power at court, Lord Aubigny and the Earl of Pembroke; and to people of wit and judgment, such as Lady Mary Wroth. He also has dedications to institutions and groups—the court, the Inns of Court, and the universities. The gratulatory poems and the dedications give us men, and a woman, in the context of a larger society or group, and they present the poet himself in turbulent and occasionally in harmonious relationships with individuals, the public, and institutions. The dramas suggested in the dedications are close to the sorts of dramatic relationships that Jonson brings into his plays and epigrams.[17]

In other ways as well, the prefatory material shares elements of Jonsonian dramatic and epigrammatic art. Like a play, it gives us an imitation of an action that has already taken place. A marked quality of this material is its emphasis on the past. In this it deviates significantly from the usual focus of such epideictic writing, which usually celebrates the present and looks forward, implicitly or explicitly, to favors in the future. Naturally, it is not unusual for a dedication to acknowledge past favors, but its first concern is for continued patronage. Certainly the desire for further support is implicit in some of the dedications, but far more obtrusive is the reiterated and strongly felt claim that the dedications are made in payment for services rendered, a published receipt:

> I send you this peece of what may live of mine; for whose innocence, as for the Authors, you were once a noble and timely undertaker, to the greatest Justice of this kingdome. Enjoy now the delight of your goodnesse. . . . (*Poetaster*, "To . . . Richard Martin")

They sketch out the dynamics of Jonson's previous relations to individuals and institutions, emphasizing the protector's disinterested help through some past crisis, and the poet's free and unexpected acknowledgment of and repayment of the debt. In some cases the historical nature of these obligations is strengthened by the reissuing of dedications that originally appeared in the quarto publications (as in the case of *Catiline*).

The accretions of prefatory and other apparatus to the texts—
epigraphs, dedications, identification of actors and acting companies, the date and place of the first performance, for example—
give the volume a veneer of authority and seniority that the
poet is careful to keep polished. In the case of *Every Man Out*,
for example, he emphasizes that the text is of a play that is
at least a generation old.

This retrospective quality is important for the Folio as a whole.
In thus offering a cumulative record of the past, the volume
and the dedications paradoxically turn the reader's thoughts
to the future. In Jonson there is so little explicit or implicit
solicitation and so much recollection of events past that the
dedications give the impression that the Folio was crafted and
compiled as an artistic account of its own generation. As his
Kunstlerroman, the work reveals Jonson freeing himself from
his vulnerable past. It is in this light that the dedication of
Poetaster to Richard Martin, the lawyer who helped Jonson
through the scrapes arising from that play and *Eastward Ho!*,
can be seen. Jonson stresses that *his* debt is moral rather than
economic: "Sir, A thankfull man owes a courtesie ever: the
unthankefull, but when he needs it." To express his gratitude,
Jonson sends him "what may live of mine." The art and friendship exist in an ongoing present; against it stands the historical
event and mean-spirited human affairs of the past, when "ignorance, and malice of the times, then conspir'd to have [it]
supprest." In the dedication of *Sejanus* to Lord Aubigny, Jonson
creates the same opposition between the durability of art and
gratitude and the ephemerality of ignorance and the accidents
of the history that gave rise to friendship. Jonson recalls the
events surrounding the play's creation and reception: "It is a
poeme, that (if I well remember) in your Lo. sight, suffer'd no
lesse violence from our people here, then the subject of it did
from the rage of the people of Rome." The historical analogy
throws the intimate events in the theater ("if I well remember") further into the past. But outliving this now lifeless
history is the art—"If ever any ruine were so great, as to survive; I thinke this be one I send you"—and it in turn engenders
love and immortality: "For this hath out-liv'd their malice,
and begot it selfe a greater favour then he lost, the love of good
men."

In repaying his debt, Jonson looks back on the accidental,
historical, and political dross of the measurable past; out of

it his art and friendships emerged into a realm free of policy and patronage. Thus, although the dedications to individuals all ring with genuine gratitude, there is an overriding sense that a debt to the past and the world of policy is paid. The often uncomfortable division between past and present, past favor and present friendship, leaves one with the feeling that now only friendship need survive; the necessity for or likelihood of any further service from those addressed is slight. They rose to meet the need occasioned by Jonson's art, but that need is past and the debt paid. With slight variations, this is Jonson's strategy in most of the dedications. Camden was Jonson's mentor, teacher, and lifetime friend. But the 1616 dedication is very emphatically the payment of a debt located far in the past: "It is a fraile memorie, that remembers but present things." Among Jonson's opening remarks in the Folio, these words reach back dramatically to the beginnings of Jonson's career. The specific thanks due to Stuart, Aubigny, and to a lesser extent to Mary Wroth are also located specifically in the past. The effect is not to mark the end of the friendship, but to make Jonson seem all the more alone and free; it is a public accounting from the poet of the Folio, and a record of the rocky path of his road to success. In thus separating occasion and policy from his art, Jonson is throwing the husks of art behind him.

This economy of dedication is also part of the larger aesthetic effect sought by Jonson. In deliberately gathering his early work—all that preceded the experimental *Bartholomew Fair*—Jonson pays off his debt to the past in another way. Thus, professionally and personally Jonson delimits the relationships articulated in the dedications. While he is artistically indebted to many, he remains the author of his own work and slave to no one: the sum of his achievement is greater than any one debt. His goal in this is political as well as platonic and aesthetic. The absence of any single dedicatee, then, becomes important for the artistic economy of self-definition in Jonson. As Leggatt and others have shown in their discussions of the epigrams, Jonson's concern for moral and artistic integrity is expressed in terms of mercantile and commercial economic systems.[18] Through his dedications he acknowledges his many debts while retaining his integrity. The absence of a single dedicatee to the Folio is one way by which Jonson more or less humbly accepts his limitations, but is able to localize them and thus not lose "credit" for the work as a whole.

4

If we think of Spenser's *The Faerie Queene*, with its emblematic
dedication to Elizabeth and reverential verses addressed to a
carefully selected group of courtiers, Jonson's isolated, leaderless dedicatees appear all the more unusual. More varied in
tone than Spenser's, Jonson's addresses hardly seem like dedications at all. They range from humility and self-effacement (in
Every Man In His Humour) to the businesslike voice of a social
and intellectual equal *(Poetaster)*. In the dedication to *Volpone*,
Jonson assumes a carefully modulated literary voice, and in
that to *Cynthia's Revels*, he takes the infinitely subtle voice
of a satirist. In writing to Lady Wroth Jonson's tone is sober,
even reverential, and in his second address to Pembroke his
manner and his frank admission of the hazards of writing epigrams come closest in tone to the language conventionally used
for a patron.

This variety is governed by the kind of decorum described
by Bacon. The concern for protocol shown by Spenser, as he
carefully places the dedicatees in their proper places in a microcosmic image of Elizabeth's court, is treated with characteristic
insouciance in the Folio. Jonson mingles high and low, formal
and familiar, individual and institution. What at first appears
to be a fairly random collection proves to have a controlled
rhetorical and moral order that deviates greatly from the normal
descending order that would be expected. Thus the dedication
to Camden, socially the humblest of the addressees, begins the
volume, and the two dedications to Lord Herbert, Earl of Pembroke, the most powerful and highest born, end it.[19]

But Jonson is not just inverting the usual order prescribed
by protocol. Here and in Epigram 14, Camden is given the warm-
est and fullest expression of respect and praise; Jonson sees
him as his own principal intellectual and moral benefactor, and
speaks of him without irony, and with candor and feeling. If,
however, Camden is the humblest of dedicatees, as educator,
historian, and Clarenceux King-of-Arms, he also is the arbiter
of genuine nobility, learning, and merit. The terms of Camden's
praise are the ideas that give meaning to Jonson's own world
and that of his art. His placement at the opening of the Folio, expressly violating the convention that places birth before
worth, establishes the emphasis on spiritual qualities rather than
outward appearances that pervades Jonson's work. The Folio,
then, begins with an address to the man whose public office

and inner ability together qualify him to judge the relation between title and virtue; its final dedication is to the "great Example of Honor and Virtue"—the man whose "merit" and "title"
are perfectly matched.

The contrast between idea and exemplum, or judge and model,
recurs in other pairs of dedications, and becomes one of the
major organizing motifs of the Folio by which art and social
reality come in contact. The dedication of *Every Man Out Of
His Humour* to the "NOBLEST NOURCERIES OF HUMANITY,
AND LIBERTY . . . The Innes of Court" insists on the distinction
between individual and institution. Arguing that some of his
best friends have been lawyers, Jonson says that in the previous
generation the members of the Inns were wise and judicious
enough to admire the play when it was first performed. In
dedicating the play to their successors, "the inheritors of the
first favour borne it," he juxtaposes past and present. Perhaps
with a slight note of skepticism, he confers on them the charge
to be no less humane and judicious than their predecessors
and then presents them with a play that satirizes their profession. Against this challenging address stands the dedication of
Poetaster—a play about true and false judgment of poets, stupid-
ity and corruption in high places, and the need to defend the
place of the true poet in society—to the lawyer, friend, and
protector, Richard Martin.

The very admonitory dedication of *Cynthia's Revels* "TO THE
SPECIALL FOUNTAINE OF MANNERS: The Court" contrasts
in similar ways with dedications to the men and woman of
the court who, from Jonson's experience, have stood as specific
examples to the anonymous institution. His words to the court
consist of a good deal of moral finger-shaking disguised as advice. In urging them to be as virtuous as they are comely, Jonson
reiterates one of his most serious and persistent themes. As
Leggatt reminds us, the critique implicit in the Folio dedication
was explicit in the original quarto title, where the "fountain
of manners" was called instead the "fountain of self-love."[20]
Jonson describes the court much as he (and others) describe
poetry: it is a mirror of and model to society and so its beauty
should reflect its goodness.

Jonson's injunction to the court articulates a moral and aesthetic principle that is everywhere evident in his ameliorative art.
Its significance is that much greater when one recognizes that
his art in the Folio and throughout his career looks more and
more to the court and its head, the king, as its proper audience.

As so many of the dedications do, this one looks forward to, and prepares the critical reader for what should be for Jonson the ideal art form, the court masques that conclude the Folio. In this first section of the Folio, however, the warning to eschew materialism, to attain spiritual and intellectual beauty, and to be self-critical, prefaces a play which depicts a court which is obtuse, insensitive, and corrupt.[21] Using language and imagery that resonate with the poet's zealous piety, he insists that true beauty deserves to be approached with reverence and veneration; the court, however, must first learn—and earn—such beauty.

Jonson incorporates the same language, imagery, and intensity of feeling in his praise of one of the ladies of the court, Lady Mary Wroth:

> In the age of sacrifices, the truth of religion was not in the greatnesse & fat of the offrings, but in the devotion, and zeale of the sacrificers.

Turning to himself with characteristic self-mockery, Jonson points out that his zeal exceeds the "greatnesse & fat" of his self-sacrifice, "else, what could a handful of gummes have done in the sight of a hecatomb? Or, how might I appear at this altar?" Jonson himself assumes the role of one approaching intellectual and spiritual beauty with the veneration and humility that, the dedication to *Cynthia's Revels* suggests, should be due to the court. Lady Wroth has earned what could also be accorded the court, and Jonson's response to her is a paradigm for the ideal relation between the court and country. But her position in courtly society is rather like the poet's (in *Poetaster* or *Cynthia's Revels*, for example). As a lady of the court, her judgment shines and is safe, though it is "forbidden to speake more; lest it talke, or looke like one of the ambitious Faces of the Time" and thus seem infected with self-love. Exemplary as she is, Lady Wroth—and Jonson's dedication to her—stand in implicit judgment of the court; while Jonson tells the court what it could be, Lady Wroth exposes it for what it is.

Frequently, then, the dedications echo one another and contrast individuals and institutions, and ideal and real forms in order to bring the themes of his art into the political milieu of his life. In this way, the dedications add significantly to what the Folio has to say to its readers. With the help of this apparatus the plays and verses address very pointedly the need for men and women, and even institutions, not only to have judgment, but also to act upon it. Thus Aubigny and Pembroke, socially and politically the highest and most powerful of the dedicatees, are praised for their protection of Jonson and his art. Just as they are the men closest to the sources of power, the plays dedicated to them deal explicitly with political rather than artistic themes. Although the plays stress the need for moral commitment and active involvement in the world of politics and show the unpromising prospects for goodness in a corrupt courtly world, the dedications deal with the steadfastness of Jonson's supporters and acknowledge their judgment and courage in spite of the "violence" and "malice" of the public.[22] In their esteem for Jonson's plays, these people exhibit the combination of critical judgment and conviction that the poet expects of his public, and that he dramatizes in his comedies and in the tragedies dealing with politics and power. The relationship between Jonson, dedicatee, and play or poem, then, embodies Jonson's highly polemical view of the social importance of art.

5

Not just a disembodied aspect of Jonson's neoplatonic aesthetic, the paradigm provided by the dedications has specific relevance for the social, moral, and economic milieu of the poet himself. In particular, it reaches beyond the insulated world of art and touches upon some of the peculiarities of Jonson's career, specifically his aloofness from the acting companies and the maverick independence that he boldly asserts through the publication of the Folio. The Folio is the clearest announcement of the determined independence that can also be seen in his relationship to the acting companies. In specifying at the end of each play which companies originally performed it, and even in identifying the original actors, Jonson proclaims his independence from any single company and presents himself as an employer of actors rather than as an employee.[23] More than most, Jonson insisted on being his own agent, using this freedom to select his companies and his audiences and to publish his works how and when he chose. The Folio itself, of course, is the culmination of an independence that other playwrights, having various kinds of contractual ties to their companies, did not have.[24]

With a readiness that would appal any company manager, Jonson flaunts his unwillingness to be a crowd-pleaser and his determination to choose the audience that he prefers, however small and aristocratic it may be. It is a theme that enters his epigrams and the plays themselves. It is reiterated regularly in the epigraphs of the plays, but significantly, it stands at the head of the Folio itself: "neque, me ut miretur turba, laboro: / Contentus paucis lectoribus."[25] In repeating this idea, Jonson places himself in an open, competitive literary market unlike that enjoyed by the in-house writers in Henslowe's and other companies. In these and other ways the Folio shows us Jonson contending with the *meum* and *tuum* of literary free enterprise. Thus, his preoccupation in the dedications with paying off past debts is also part of the commercial reality that Jonson sees as one of the realities of the poet's life. If his dedications are not exactly requests for patronage—and they are not—they do recognize the reality of the artist's precarious status.

The *negotium* in Jonson's dedications and in his art generally shows his desire to deal in a literary marketplace characterized not by a medieval patronage system like that which tied Daniel for a time to the Herberts, but by a value system in which the parties involved are equals, each benefiting from the relationship. Lord Herbert, Earl of Pembroke, was patron to both Daniel and Jonson, but the relationships were as different as the medieval paternalism of "patron" is from the modern, commercial idea of "patronage." Daniel was a member of the Herbert household, enjoying the protection and support granted other liveried servants, including the members of the Lord Chamberlain's company. Professionally and domestically Jonson refused to wear livery.[26] His "neoconservatism" was not an attempt to secure the kind of support that Daniel had from the Herberts, where the poet is invariably incorporated within the embrace of the patron. Unlike Jonson, Daniel did not enjoy the rivalry that came with the reins of power. Jonson insisted on remaining on the margin of such confining arrangements; he sought independence and influence, not security. His commercialism automatically elevated his status as an artist: disenfranchized, he was able to speak for himself, negotiate for himself, and more important for Jonson, to accept responsibility for the integrity of his artistic and moral vision. Jonson objectifies his relationships to his patrons; as the dedications make clear, Jonson was very specific about the help he received. When Pembroke supported Jonson's plays he was a judicious critic recognizing the importance of the playwright's art; as Daniel's patron, he was midwife to Daniel's art.

To a large extent, Jonson's frequent clashes with authority arise from the vulnerability of being unaffiliated. In a very Jonsonian sense, being unaffiliated paradoxically puts one's identity on the line and necessitates an aggressive approach to artistic and moral self-definition. Jonson's independent status often forced him to define himself: in terms of the Established Church, in his political affiliations surrounding the Gunpowder Plot, and in his conflicts with fellow playwrights and the acting companies.

But if he tended to find himself in hot water, he also had greater influence than any other playwright; one consequence of greater power is a more precarious existence. As a result, we regularly get a sense of Jonson's own sensitivity about the power structure of publication and performance. In spite of his frequent clashes with one authority or another, he regularly boasts in print that his work was performed and published with authority of the Master of Revels. Although he was interrogated about suspect passages in *Sejanus* and *Catiline,* he wrote the former play with the benefit of Lord Aubigny's hospitality. A long-time favorite of the king's and quite at home in his dissolute court, Aubigny was especially well qualified to see the applicability of Jonson's tragedy of political and personal corruption.

Thus, while critics comment on Jonson's brush with authority, it is usually overlooked that the play was written under the roof of one of James's oldest and most intimate friends and acted with the authority of the Master of Revels.[27] Jonson was not exactly defenseless. It was at this time, between the performance in 1603 and the quarto of 1605, that James dissolved the household of the Master of Revels and (in 1607) gave St. Johns's, the house and office attached to the position, to Lord Aubigny. Interestingly, not too long after, in 1621, Jonson was granted the reversion to the office of Master of Revels. Jonson's complex relationships here with the king, the king's favorite, the Revels office, and the Council may suggest the vulnerability of the independent author, but they also demonstrate no less effectively his ability to fly past many of the bureaucratic nets in a higher realm of royal and noble privilege. If he did have a brush with authority here, it seems to have been because he had superceded the usual court officers.

Similar political considerations surround Jonson's decision to remain independent of the Lord Chamberlain's company, probably because he regarded Pembroke as a friend and ally.

Pembroke's support of and interest in Jonson evidently went beyond the world of the theater, as can be seen in Jonson's dedication of the *Epigrammes* to him. In itself, this is a socially and professionally significant gesture that separates Jonson from the ranks of the players and moves him into the more aristocratic sphere of poetry. Indeed, it seems that Jonson was able to use this independent, nontheatrical link with Pembroke to separate himself still further from the usual professional ties and to cultivate his upward mobility, for soon after Pembroke became Chancellor of Oxford University in 1617 (having received his Master of Arts in 1607), Jonson was awarded an honorary Master of Arts degree.

The dedications, then, show Jonson's unique relationship to his art in the years from 1612 to 1616.[28] Relatedly, they tell us something about the nature of his art. As thanks for favors rendered rather than as pleas for patronage, they allowed him to retain his right to disregard popular opinion; the very fact that he had supporters demonstrates the legitimacy of his claims for his art and proves his case for the importance of art in the world of political reality. Ultimately, by the end of his career he narrowed his audience still further—to one: the king.[29] The Folio marks a major step in this narrowing process. Its dedications are to those who stood by him in the past. *Catiline* is the last of his plays to be given a dedication. The one play written before 1616, entirely his own but not included in the Folio, is *Bartholomew Fair*, which begins with an invitation to the king but remains otherwise undedicated. After 1616 Jonson abandons the public stage entirely for a decade, turning his attention to other activities and other forms, notably the masque and nondramatic poetry.[30]

The pattern of his career and his art is adumbrated in the Folio. The dedications begin with the plays and end with the *Epigrammes*—the collection of verses that takes the reader out of the world of theatrical illusion into the streets of London, the court, the tragicomic theater of the world dealing with real people and their illusions. Just as Jonson's drama after 1616 breaks the barriers between art and reality, so does the Folio: the distinction between play and patron dissolves with the recognition that all the dedicatees (including representatives from the Inns of Court, the universities, and the court) are absorbed into the *Epigrammes*. All the individuals are accorded epigrams further characterizing them and their relation to the poet. Critics have remarked on the drama of the epigrams, and it is the drama of history, a kind of docudrama, as those named and unnamed denizens originally outside the sphere of art are brought into it. The epigrams form a collection that subsumes into it not only the themes of the plays, but also the contemporary issues that Jonson hints at in the dedications themselves. The dedicatee of the *Epigrammes* is aptly chosen, by Jonson's criteria, since he himself embodies the quality of an epigram in integrity and moral purpose:

> I Doe but name thee PEMBROKE, and I find
>> It is an *Epigramme*, on all man-kind;
> Against the bad, but of, and to the good:
>> Both which are ask'd, to have thee understood.
>>>> (102)

Thus, instead of the dialectical relation between dedicatee and the work itself, where one comments on the other, the two are coextensive; the gap between poet and society, art and reality diminishes and ultimately suggests the inseparability of life and art.

Following the epigrams in the Folio are the barriers, masques, and entertainments, and they are all explicitly royal, court events.[31] Neither the section as a whole, nor the individual works has a dedication. The reasons for this are simple but important; there could be only one dedicatee—the king—and he could hardly be relegated to the back of a folio consisting mostly of plays dedicated to lesser figures. Furthermore, as royal entertainments, they belong to the royal audience, and so a dedication, giving the king what is by nature his anyway, would be doubly inappropriate.[32] And, as entertainments rather than plays, they are unique or nearly unique performances, recorded in the Folio but having their reality in the occasion of their performance. In this the masques are a kind of performed epigram wherein being and doing are one; the ideal suggested is much like that embodied in Pembroke. The entertainments are, then, an extension of the more democratic epigrams, a refinement of them and a narrowing of their *dramatis personae*. But they too are part of the real world of events—marriages, investitures, celebrations of real people, many of whom figure in the epigrams. Indeed, Lord Aubigny and the Earl of Pembroke both performed in the Lord Haddington masque of 1608. Consequently, the Folio moves from the world of art (the plays) into a world of reality imitating art, and ultimately, in the masques, into the world where art imitates the idealized perfected life of the court. From the fictional world of the play we progress to the artful world of play—the court of James, the art of which, by implication, exceeds even Jonson's. Jonson can dedicate his plays, but he cannot presume to dedicate the court masques.[33] It is no accident that the last masque, the final work of the Folio is *The Golden Age Restored*.

The absence of a dedication to any of the masques is the ultimate compliment to James. It suggests that James's court supplants Jonson's art. As Jonson says in epigram 95, "Although to write be lesser than to doo, / It is the next deed, and a great one too"; writing is part of the process of reform, and in an ideal world, like that hypostatically implied at the conclusion of the Folio, there would be no art or author, only being. The role of Jonson the artist dissolves in the golden age of artful order in the courtly milieu.[34]

The pattern outlined by the presence or absence of dedications, then, is one that iterates Jonson's view of art's relation to the world: one refining itself out of existence. It is also the pattern of his career as he leaves the theater for the court, and eventually imagines himself addressing the king alone. The dedications attest to a world of strife, patronage, politics and corruption. But in them we see those praised who have served the cause of bettering society through service to art. In them we also see Jonson at work elevating his own status, and that of his art, by freeing the poet-dramatist from a social station that is not only low but one of bondage. He negotiates his place into a world of court and courtiers, one imperfect but theoretically capable of reform. In publishing his Folio he places the work of playwrights on a par with that of poets, philosophers, historians, and theologians. To be free of a dedication (as the masques are) a work must be able to stand alone in a world that values its importance—a world, therefore, that no longer relies on power and patronage. This is largely the theme of the final masque, *The Golden Age Restored*. The concluding section of the Folio offers works that freely serve the monarch without being slave to him or needing to secure their precarious position through a dedication. Thus Jonson's dedications are part of the drama of the Folio itself—the drama of art involved in the struggle for power and social reform, finally projecting a very tentative vision of the golden age restored.

Notes

1. Michael Drayton, *The Poly-Olbion: A Chorographical Description of Great Britain* (London, 1612), sig. A; for this and the 1622 edition I have used the Spenser Society facsimile (New York, 1889; repr. 1970). Francis Bacon, *The Translation of Certaine Psalmes* (London, 1624). Useful surveys of the range of dedicatory writing are Clara Gebert, ed., *An Anthology of Elizabethan Dedications and Prefaces* (New York: Russell & Russell, 1933); Henry B. Wheatley, *The Dedication of Books to Patron and Friend* (London: E. Stock, 1887). Wheatley generalizes (pp. 9–10) that "In English literature the dedications written previous to the Restoration are mostly of a genuine character," but grants that there were many that were anything but "genuine." The naiveté of his generalization is evident, but his survey illustrates the uniqueness of each dedication in its manner of negotiating between text, context, and author. It is this individuality that makes the form so important for our understanding of the writer's attempt to establish authority over his work. For convenience sake, when discussing the Folio, I use here the Scolar Press facsimile of *THE WORKES OF Benjamin Jonson* (London, 1976). Except for indented quotations, I have normalized italic print to keep the text legible.

2. By political and spiritual economy, I mean the exchange that necessarily exists between a work's (and an author's) spiritual or imaginative integrity and judgment and the concessions that must be made to its patron or public. The dichotomy is a crux in Jonson studies; George Parfitt's *Ben Jonson: Public Poet and Private Man* (London: J. M. Dent, 1976) makes it the center of his analysis of the poet. Such metaphors (commercial and material) are increasingly common in Jonson criticism largely because Jonson uses them when discussing art and human affairs.

3. Among the best recent studies of Jonson's attempts to assert authority over his works are Richard C. Newton's "Jonson and the (Re-)Invention of the Book," *Classic and Cavalier: Essays on Jonson and the Sons of Ben*, ed. Claude J. Summers and Ted-Larry Pebworth (Pittsburgh: University of Pittsburgh Press, 1982), pp. 31–55; Richard Helgerson, *Self-Crowned Laureates: Spenser, Jonson, Milton and the Literary System* (Berkeley: University of California Press, 1983), pp. 101–184; Jonathan Goldberg, *James I and the Politics of Literature* (Baltimore: Johns Hopkins University Press, 1983), pp. 210–39; Joseph Loewenstein, "The Script in the Marketplace," *Representations* 12 (1985): 101–14; Annabel Patterson, *Censorship and Interpretation: The Conditions of Writing and Reading in Early Modern England* (Madison: University of Wisconsin Press, 1984), pp. 122–44. The current critical debates owe much to the originality of L. C. Knights's *Drama and Society in the Age of Jonson* (London: Chatto & Windus, 1937).

4. Wheatley, *Dedication of Books*, p. 67.

5. The Shakespeare First Folio poses many of the problems encountered in Jonson's work—and in very Jonsonian terms: throughout its prefatory apparatus it stresses the reader's need for understanding and judgment, thus emphasizing text rather than dramatic spectacle; it also reiterates the commercial nature of the covenant between reader and literature: "Judge your six-pen'orth, your shillings worth, your five shillings worth. . . . It is now publique, & you will stand for your priviledges wee know: to read, and censure" (*The Norton Facsimile: The First Folio of Shakespeare*, prepared by Charlton Hinman (New York: W. W. Norton, 1968), p. 7).

6. Drayton, *Poly-Olbion*, pp. 329–30.

7. As Wheatley points out (p. 3) Horace, Virgil, Cicero, and Lucretius (some of Jonson's favorites) were among the classical authors who established the precedent for dedicatory addresses. Jonson's dedication of *Volpone* offers a major definition of neoclassical satire; Drayton, describing *Poly Olbion* as "genuine, and first in this kinde," uses the dedication to Henry to make a statement about the originality of his work.

8. See, for example, Helgerson, *Self-Crowned Laureates*, pp. 21–24, and Patterson, *Censorship and Interpretation*, pp. 210–14.

9. Patterson, *Censorship and Interpretation*, pp. 159–202, discusses the politics of the revival of romance forms.

10. The phrase is, of course, Helgerson's and both he and Newton point to the persistent problems arising from Jonson's attempts at self-definition.

11. Such preliminary material is very common, but it is almost always preceded by a word from the author or publisher, whose eagerness to affiliate themselves with the text contrasts with the coolness with which Jonson bides his time and awaits his proper entry into the Folio.

12. See W. H. Herendeen, "'Like a circle bounded in itself': Jonson, Camden, and the Strategies of Praise," *Journal of Medieval and Renaissance Studies* 11 (1981): 137–67. Occasionally Jonson prepared individual presentation copies of masques, such as the British Library copy of the *Masque of Queenes*. This copy (C.28.g.5.) has an autograph letter to Queen Anne in which he states that he has printed the work to give it his "authority." And also, he goes on, because he had been asked to publish and annotate it by Prince Henry, to whom that copy is dedicated.

13. Considering Jonson's well-documented concern for the preparation of the Folio, and the uniqueness of Hole's frontispiece, it is safe to assume that Jonson had a hand in its design, or at least felt that it was an appropriate emblem for his work. Although not primarily concerned with the figure of Tragicomedy or her implications for the Folio, Lawrence Danson, in "Jonsonian Comedy and the Discovery of the Social Self," *PMLA* 99 (1984): 179–80 and 184, points out that she is the culmination of the other forms represented and develops a very interesting reading of the relationship between Jonsonian tragedy and comedy. The difficulty that remains is explaining her appropriateness at the head of the volume. For discussion of the engraved frontispiece in Renaissance England, see Margery Corbett and Ronald Lightbown, *The Comely Frontispiece: The Emblematic Title-Page in England, 1550–1660* (London: Routledge & Kegan Paul, 1979); see pp. 145–50 for a description of Hole's engraving. The modern tendency has been to blur the boundaries between romance and tragicomedy; this is largely the influence of the Shakespearean model and is not otherwise established on a historical basis. Jonson distinguished between them—as a rigorous classicist he found his unShakespearean model in Plautus and as a theorist he found in the Italian neoclassicists descriptions of the genre that distinguish it from romance.

14. The lines are paraphrased in *Discoveries* (2625–30), and originate in Heinsius, C. H. Herford and Percy and Evelyn Simpson, eds., *Ben Jonson*, vol. 11 (Oxford: Clarendon, 1925–52), p. 289. The subject is the similarity of tragedy and comedy; here, and also in the dedication to *Volpone*, Jonson reiterates his interest in mixed forms, although the title page is the only instance of the word *tragicomedy* in his works.

15. Allan H. Gilbert, *Literary Criticism: Plato to Dryden* (Detroit: Wayne

State University Press, 1962), pp. 512–13. See also pp. 520–28 where the discussion of Plautus and the effects of tragicomedy, comedy, and tragedy, resembles what Jonson has to say.

16. The language used by Guarini to describe the natural superiority of tragicomedy is very close to Jonson's discussions of sound structure and form in a play (*Discoveries*, 2654–2762).

17. Themes of the poet in society and the idealization of art appear in the early plays and the Folio's apparatus, as do themes of dehumanization through greed, of social involvement and apathy, of different kinds of servitude.

18. The exclusion of *Bartholomew Fair* (performed in 1614) from the Folio has always presented problems that scholars have resolved by accepting Herford and Simpson's theory that the typesetting for the volume began in 1614. This is unconvincing, partly because the play must have been written by 1614—time enough for inclusion in the *Workes*—and partly because at least one work written after 1614, notably *The Golden Age Restored* (1615), was included in the Folio. Evidence suggests, rather, that Jonson chose, probably for a number of reasons, not to include it. One reason might have been that Jonson thought of the play as experimental and wanted a marked break from the more homogeneous earlier work. Certainly the critical consensus is that *Bartholomew Fair* marks a turning point for Jonson. See, for example, Alexander Leggatt, *Ben Jonson: His Vision and his Art* (London: Methuen, 1981), pp. 23–44 and 66–72, and Anne Barton, *Ben Jonson, Dramatist* (Cambridge: Cambridge University Press, 1984), pp. 194–218; recent evidence presented by Kevin Donovan, in "The Final Quires of the Jonson 1616 *Workes*: Headline Evidence," *Studies in Bibliography* 40 (1987): 106–20, pushes the publication of the Folio to an even later date, further discrediting the explanation of Herford and Simpson.

19. William Herbert, Earl of Pembroke and Lord Chamberlain, the son of Henry Herbert and Mary Sidney (Philip's sister), is well known for his patronage of the arts; originally tutored at Wilton by Samuel Daniel, he remained loyal to the poet throughout his career. A more sinister figure is Esmé Stuart, Seigneur d'Aubigny (1574–1624), the younger brother of the second Duke of Lenox. Epigram 127 is addressed to him; *Forrest* 13 is a tribute to his wife; and *Under-wood* 75 is an epithalamion on his sister's marriage to Hierom Weston. For all Jonson's interest in Aubigny, the man remains a shadowy figure involved in some of the grimmer intrigue of James's life in Scotland. Although Aubigny is related to the king, Pembroke, an Englishman and a Sidney, is given the most prestigious status as recipient of the last two dedications.

20. Leggatt, *Ben Jonson*, p. 257. The quarto title page is also reprinted in the Folio.

21. The relationship between dedication and play, therefore, is similar to that which we saw in the case of *Every Man Out*.

22. Jonson often speaks of the violence and danger that are occupational hazards of his life (*Poetaster*, *Sejanus*, and *Catiline*, for example).

23. Gerald Eades Bentley, in *The Profession of Dramatist in Shakespeare's Time, 1590–1642* (Princeton: Princeton University Press, 1971), p. 288, argues conclusively for Jonson's unique independence: "By far the most distinguished of the unattached dramatists of the period was Ben Jonson, and his eclectic attitude towards the London acting companies, as well as his publication

patterns, are in sharp contrast with those of Shakespeare, Heywood, Fletcher, Massinger, Shirley, and Brome." Bentley's documentation of Jonson's unusual status in the profession adds a good deal of detail to my analysis of how and why Jonson cultivates this role. Following each play Jonson indicates the acting company, the genre (comical satire, for example), the performance date, the actors and company, and whether it had the Master of Revels "allowance." The companies include: The Lord Chamberlain's servants, The Children of Queen Elizabeth's Chapel, The King's Majesty's servants.

24. See Loewenstein, "The Script in the Marketplace," for a fuller discussion of the political implications of Jonson's manipulation of the book trade.

25. "I do not work so that the crowd may admire me, I am contented with a few readers" (Corbett and Lightbown, *The Comely Frontispiece*, p. 146). The epigraphs, which routinely dismiss popular disapproval and mock Jonson's rivals, underscore the way in which publication frees the playwright from the restraints of performance.

26. Jonson's "conservatism," as David Norbrook calls it in *Poetry and Politics in the English Renaissance* (London: Routledge & Kegan Paul, 1984), pp. 187–90, or "neoconservatism," as Loewenstein calls it ("Script in the Marketplace," p. 207) is a problematic quality that seems to run counter to other aspects of his character. In distinguishing here between an old-fashioned patronage system, such as that which Daniel exemplifies, and patronage in a more egalitarian commercial sense, I would suggest that Jonson's basically is not a conservative perspective.

27. This is a detail Jonson includes in the Folio whenever he can. For the changing role of the Master of Revels and an account of the dissolution of its offices and the gift of St. Johns's House to Aubigny in 1607, see E. K. Chambers, *The Elizabethan Stage*, 4 vol. (Oxford: Oxford University Press, 1923), 1, p. 101–2. It would appear that Aubigny's influence in such matters was great, and that of the Master of Revels increasingly symbolic.

28. Bentley, *Profession of Dramatist*, pp. 288–91.

29.

> Well, Gentlemen, I now must under seale,
>   And th'*Authors* charge, waive you, and make my
>   appeale
> To the supremest power, my *Lord* the *King*;
>   Who best can judge of what wee humbly bring.
> Hee knowes our weaknesse, and the *Poets* faults;
>   Where he doth stand upright, goe firme, or halts;
> And hee will doome him. To which voice he stands,
>   And prefers that, 'fore all the Peoples hands.

The Chorus, or Epilogue to the king at the end of *The Magnetic Lady*, Jonson's last complete play, culminates a pattern of isolation that begins to take direction in the Folio.

30. "An Execration Upon Vulcan" is Jonson's record of his intellectual interests during the decade when his only theatrical activities were masques. The works lost in the fire included his Grammar (later rewritten), poetry and drama, various theological and historical writings. After publishing the Folio, Jonson began his sabbatical with his walking tour to Scotland; he never again devoted undivided energies to the stage—the independence announced in the Folio is never lost.

31. Virtually every one of them explicitly states that it is a royal enter-

tainment, even if designed for someone less than the king (such as Lord Haddington's masque).

32. See Stephen Orgel's *The Illusion of Power: Political Theater in the English Renaissance* (Berkeley: University of California Press, 1975), especially pp. 59–89, for a discussion of some aspects of the decorum of masques and the protocol of the king's role in them.

33. Individual masques might be dedicated to the monarch, but not when they are gathered at the end of what could be regarded as a rather pretentious folio of plays and epigrams. Jonson was perceptive enough not to make the mistake of dedicating these works.

34. Naturally this vision is offered tentatively, as the praise of the court is in the dedication of *Cynthia's Revels*. Depending on one's view of the revision of the masque, the final compliment of the masque is more or less qualified.

Facts of the Matter: Satiric and Ideal Economies in the Jonsonian Imagination

Katharine Eisaman Maus

> For those of you who are interested in getting ahead, I have
> one suggestion: have a father who owns the business and
> have him die.
>
> —Malcolm Forbes[1]

In tragedy, characters die; in comedy, they do not. Though Jonson observes this generic rule scrupulously—Puntarvolo's dog, in *Every Man Out Of His Humour,* is his only real casualty—death nonetheless looms unusually large as a plot device in many of his comedies. In *Volpone* most of the characters are waiting for the hero to become a corpse, and he seems to comply at the beginning of the fifth act. *The Alchemist* is set in plague-ridden London, in a house that the master has vacated after the death of his wife—a bereavement that allows him to marry the desirable Dame Pliant, herself recently widowed, at the end of the play. In *Epicoene* Truewit suggests a plan to extract Dauphine's inheritance from his uncle Morose: "ha' him drawne out on coronation day to the *tower*-wharf, and kill him with the noise of the ordinance" (1.2.14–16; references are to act, scene, and line). In the same play the rich and titled Amorous La Foole informs us that the onset of his good fortune coincided with the moment when "it pleased my elder brother to die" (1.4.61); the prodigal Penyboy Junior, hero of *The Staple of News,* pays a similarly chilling tribute to his "loving and obedient" father: "a right, kind-hearted man / To dye so opportunely" (1.4.15–16). Jonson's characters revel in the possibilities opened up for them by the mortality of family members or associates, or plan to obtain such freedom by facilitating their demise.

This essay was first published in *English Literary Renaissance* 19 (1989): 42–64.

Mosca. But, what, sir, if they ask
       After the body?
Volpone.   Say, it was corrupted.
Mosca. I'le say, it stunke, sir; and was faine t' have it
       Coffin'd up instantly, and sent away.

                                        (5.2.76–79)

Mosca's highly charged combination of servility and aggression in this passage—the way he elaborates Volpone's plan with a little too much relish—is a reminder that the death of the patron hardly need imply the ruin of the parasite.

In Jonsonian comedy, death creates opportunities. The converse is also true: the conventional impossibility of death within the play makes ordinary comic rewards inaccessible for some of the characters. Because there is no generically appropriate way to eliminate that recurrent Jonsonian type, the bad husband, Celia cannot marry Bonario in *Volpone*, nor can Mistress Fitzdottrel marry Wittipol in *The Devil is an Ass*. Because Morose remains alive at the end of *Epicoene*, Dauphine cannot yet come fully into the inheritance that will ensure his prosperity. Because Volpone does not really die, Mosca cannot assume *clarissimo* rank and marry the avocatore's daughter.

Jonson's way of conceiving of death is very much at odds with the usual comic mode. As Northrop Frye observed in *The Anatomy of Criticism*, "an extraordinary number of comic stories, both in drama and in fiction, seem to approach a potentially tragic crisis near the end, a feature that I may call the 'point of ritual death.'"[1] In the cases Frye has in mind, the gratification of the comic characters depends upon overcoming or avoiding the threat of death; the audience applauds rather than regrets their survival. In Jonson, by contrast, the generic immortality of the comic characters seems not part and parcel with a comic emphasis upon gratification, but rather, a constraint upon that gratification.

The frustrated murderousness of Jonsonian comedy is, I shall argue, best understood in the context of his general assumptions about the forces of production, exchange, and consumption. A number of critics—L. C. Knights, Raymond Williams, Don Wayne, and Walter Cohen, among others—have discussed such issues in terms of Jonson's reaction to the nascent capitalism and moribund feudalism of the early seventeenth century.[2] My approach will differ from theirs in two respects. On the whole, I shall be less concerned with social causes than with literary effects. Moreover, I shall argue that the Marxist orientation of most criticism in this field has rendered a crucial issue invisible. Critics influenced by Marx tend to take the fundamental character of material life for granted: the economic relations between Jonson and his various audiences, or among Jonson's contemporaries in Jacobean London, provide what seems to them the proper interpretive framework for an understanding of Jonson's career. In my view, however, Jonson struggles with the problem of whether material life, however it may be defined, really possesses this priority, this hermeneutic privilege. The first part of the essay describes some of the ways such considerations manifest themselves in his comedies. The second section suggests some reasons why the economic axioms of Jonsonian comedy often seem suspended or reversed elsewhere in his oeuvre, especially in the masques and in certain celebratory poems. This suspension or reversal underlies the generic divisions that organize Jonson's own presentation of his writing and have, usually without explicit discussion, organized most writing about Jonson ever since. The last part of the essay briefly considers the impact of Jonson's economic assumptions upon the idiosyncratic conception of artistic production that makes possible his publication of the Folio *Workes*.

1

The fundamental principle of what I shall call Jonson's "satiric economy" might, anachronistically, be called the law of the conservation of matter. In the comedies and the satiric epigrams, he represents a world that contains a predetermined quantity of substance, a quantity not subject to increase. Jonson repeatedly singles out for ridicule the perpetual motion machine, the "Eltham-thing" that mysteriously derives something from nothing, not because anyone in the early seventeenth century has scientific grounds for dismissing such a phenomenon, but because it violates a basic intuition about the nature of the material world. Alchemy plays upon the same wishfulness, promising wealth and immortality for everyone at the same time with a blithe disregard for reality as Jonsonian comedy defines it.

Less fantastic methods for achieving real or apparent increase seem likewise out of the question. Jonson's comic characters typically produce nothing. Despite the illusion of social comprehensiveness produced by such plays as *The Alchemist* or *Bar-*

tholomew Fair, Jonson generally excludes from his comedies the artisan classes that populate Shakespeare's cities—the Athens of *A Midsummer Night's Dream* or the Rome of *Julius Caesar* and *Coriolanus*—and that occupy a crucial social place in such "city comedies" as Dekker's *Shoemaker's Holiday* or Middleton's *Trick to Catch The Old One.* The farmer Sordido, in *Every Man Out Of His Humour,* interests Jonson not as a producer of foodstuffs but as an entrepreneur plotting an illegal manipulation of the grain market. For Volpone, maintaining a distance from the processes of agriculture and manufacture is a matter of pride: "I gaine / No common way" (1.1.32–33). Even such "unnatural" forms of production as usury, the breeding of money from money—certainly a phenomenon which engages the moral imagination of many Renaissance playwrights—rarely figures significantly in Jonsonian comedy. In consequence, social life in Jonsonian comedy is a zero-sum game. What one person has, another cannot have. What one person acquires, another must forfeit.[3] Jonsonian comedy is not a form in which one or a few "blocking characters" attempt to prevent social communion, but one in which every character, at least potentially, is a "blocking character" to every other.

Jonson's characters are thus preoccupied with transferring objects and services: buying and selling, giving and stealing. But the "law of the conservation of matter" dominates more than commercial relations narrowly conceived. Jonson is fascinated with inheritance laws, which prescribe a way of managing one of the most significant forms of economic transfer: the reallocation of wealth after death of the owner. Theoretically such laws ensure the solidarity and continuity of the family by providing for the orderly conveyance of property from generation to generation. In Jonsonian comedy, however, they tend to become instruments of rupture and alienation. Perhaps it is not surprising that the rules of primogeniture give junior members of the family powerful parricidal incentives. But in Jonsonian comedy, their elders are at least as quick to perceive their gains in terms of their relatives' losses. "Shall my sonne gaine a benevolence by my death?" asks Sordido in *Every Man Out Of His Humour,* moments before his suicide attempt:

> Or anybody be the better for my gold, or so forth? No. Alive I kept it from 'hem, and (dead) my ghost shall walke about it, and preserve it; my son and daughter shall starve ere they touch it. (3.7.61–64)

"How I shall bee reveng'd on mine insolent kinsman" exclaims
Morose in *Epicoene*, as he plans to add to his family in order
to subtract from it: "This night I wil get an heire, and thrust
him out of my bloud like a stranger" (2.5.98–101). Corbaccio,
hoping to inherit Volpone's estate himself, disinherits his son.

The sexual destinies of Jonson's comic characters are subject
to the same constraints as their financial affairs. In most Renaissance plays, especially in those written for the adult acting
troupes, male characters far outnumber the female characters.
But Jonson's contemporaries rarely represent this discrepancy
as a serious source of frustration; in their plays, there are usually
enough marriageable young women to match with the suitable
men. In Jonsonian comedy, by contrast, the scarcity of women
almost always presents problems. If one character marries, then
another cannot; Lovewit's successful courtship displaces Surly,
Subtle, Drugger, and Face in *The Alchemist*, just as Winwife's
displaces Quarlous and Cokes in *Bartholomew Fair*, and Pol-
Martin's displaces Squire Tub, Chanon Hugh, Judge Preamble
and John Clay in *A Tale of a Tub*. Many of the women have
already been claimed before the play begins. Even Sir Epicure
Mammon, imagining himself surrounded by abundance of all
kinds, assumes that his sexual companions will be the wives
of other men, and that he will have to bribe the husbands to
permit his adultery. In almost all the plays widows, prostitutes,
and married women represent the main sexual opportunities
for unmarried men, and widows the best matches as far as
property is concerned.

These "second-hand women" are not the only commodities
that have been used before. In a world in which nothing new
can be created, everything anyone owns has necessarily had
an indefinite number of previous owners. In the first act of
Volpone, Mosca's Pythagorean play suggests that even the soul
is not a uniquely personal possession. Characters must appropriate setting and props. When Volpone wants to disguise himself
as a commendatore, he must go to elaborate lengths to obtain
a uniform; Mosca gets a soldier drunk and strips him, so that
somewhere offstage a naked and baffled man is presumably looking for his garments–a situation Jonson exploits to greater comic
effect in *Every Man In His Humour*. In *Epicoene* Truewit and
his friends plague Morose by "translating" LaFoole's noisy dinner party into his house. In *The Alchemist* the three schemers
take over a house left temporarily empty by the death of its
mistress and the flight of its master. In *Bartholomew Fair* the

fictional setting is as provisional as the actual setting, a play-house used at other times for bear-baiting. Hence the quarrels between Joan Trash and Lanthorn Leatherhead over the ground they have leased; hence the necessity for the temporary Court of Pie-Powders, or "Dusty-Feet," in which Adam Overdo so ineffectively dispenses justice among a transient population.

Jonson's most successful and exciting characters therefore tend to be masters of the inspired assemblage of haphazard materials, and they exercise their gift even when it is not required by circumstances. In *The Alchemist*, Subtle outdoes himself when Abel Drugger requests a sign for his shop.

> He first shall have a bell, that's ABEL;
> And, by it, standing one, whose name is DEE,
> In a rugg gowne; there's *D.* and *Rug*, that's DRUG:
> And, right anenst him, a Dog snarling *Er*;
> There's DRUGGER, ABEL DRUGGER. That's his signe.
>
> (2.6.19–23)

Subtle takes a name that suits its druggist owner perfectly, splinters it into meaningless bits, and then recompiles the scraps into a bizarre and fortuitous array.

It is not surprising that these jerry-rigged arrangements are constantly threatening to crumble or explode.[4] Even Jonson's geniuses of manipulation cannot manufacture something genuinely new, or something greater than its constituent parts. Those characters who take a satiric perspective upon the action or upon their fellow characters enunciate this principle clearly. For *Epicoene's* misogynists, women are baroque collections of alien materials, periodically reorganized. "All her teeth were made i' the *Blacke-Friers*: both her eye-browes i' the *Strand*, and her haire in *Silver-Street*," confides Tom Otter to his friends.

> Every part o' the towne ownes a peece of her. . . . She takes her selfe asunder still when she goes to bed, into some twentie boxes; and about next day noone is put together againe, like a great *Germane* clocke. (3.2.92–99)

In *The Alchemist*, Surly deploys a similar strategy for different ends, ridiculing the alchemists by listing their diverse ingredients:

> pisse, and egge-shells, womens termes, mans bloud,
> Haire o' the head, burnt clouts, chalke, merds, and clay,

Poulder of bones, scalings of iron, glasse.

(2.3.194–96)

This particular form of satiric rhetoric evokes a world made up of substances that stubbornly retain their original, inassimilable characteristics even as they are endlessly rearranged and forced into surprising and precarious juxtapositions.

The paucity of material resources in Jonsonian comedy and satiric epigram puts a premium on the ability to make several uses of the same thing.

> GUT eats all day, and lechers all the night,
> So all his meat he tasteth over, twise:
> And, striving so to double his delight,
> He makes himselfe a thorough-fare of vice.
> Thus, in his belly, can he change a sin,
> Lust it comes out, that gluttony went in.
> ("On Gut," Epigrammes 118)

Jonson represents Gut as a sort of bank, changing the coin of gluttony for the coin of venery. But the transformation is merely an apparent one. "It"—the twice-tasted meat, the raw material of gratification—is still identifiable after its transfer and re-use.

Related to Gut's perversely ingenious multiplication of pleasurable effects is the talent for swift circulation demonstrated by so many of Jonson's comic characters. For if one thing can be in two places at nearly the same time, then it is almost as if one thing had become two. Thus the alchemists double their effectiveness by doubling their roles: Face plays both the Captain and the Apprentice, Dol both the sister of a lord and the Faerie Queen. In *Volpone* Mosca admires his own ability to

> rise,
> And stoope (almost together) like an arrow;
> Shoot through the aire, as nimbly as a starre,
> Turne short, as doth a swallow; and be here,
> And there, and here, and yonder, all at once.

(3.1.23–27)

Thomas Greene cites this passage to support his argument that "*Volpone* asks us to consider the infinite, exhilarating, and vicious freedom to alter the self."[5] But mobility is not the same as self-alteration, and Mosca is really applauding here not his aptitude for metamorphosis but his ability to occupy more than one space at one time—to be "here, / And there, and here, and yonder, all at once"—and to create thereby a dizzying illusion of plurality. Epicure Mammon, more indolent than Mosca, plans to achieve the same effect with mirrors:

> glasses
> Cut in more subtill angles, to disperse,
> And multiply the figures, as I walke
> Naked between my *succubae*.
>
> (2.2.45–48)

The various forms of sexual fetishism in which Jonson's characters indulge are yet another way of creating spurious abundance; when Sir Voluptuous Beast, or Volpone, or Nick Stuff dress their wives or mistresses in various exotic attires they do so in order to fantasize multiple partners where there is actually only one.

The fact that things in Jonsonian comedy are not created but merely transferred also affects the imaginative lives of the characters in more subtle ways. When Mosca must persuade Corvino to prostitute Celia to Volpone, he invents a story about how Volpone has been temporarily revived by the application of the mountebank's medication. He elaborates the lie by describing the difference of opinion among Volpone's doctors about how the treatment ought to proceed:

> one would have a cataplasme of spices,
> Another, a flayd ape clapt to his brest,
> A third would ha' it a dogge, a fourth an oyle
> With wild cats skinnes.
>
> (2.6.29–32)

These treatments, according to orthodox Renaissance medical doctrine, work by soaking the infection out of the patient, removing it from the sufferer to the less valuable ancillary object—a process that renders especially horrible Corvino's willingness to donate his wife, "lustie, and full of juice," to the enterprise of reinvigorating Volpone. Mosca's delight in exposing the depths of Corvino's awfulness is obvious here and elsewhere, but it is less clear whether Mosca realizes that his fiction represents a disguised version of his own parasitic ambition to transfer Volpone's special attributes—wealth and social status—from their original source to a disgusting but supposedly beneficial attachment.

Even the characters' fantasies of plenitude founder on their unshakable awareness of actual scarcity. Jonson's comic voluptuaries do not share the complacency of their counterparts in Spenser and Milton—characters like Comus, who represents the world as generously, even over-generously supplied with the stuff of hedonistic consumption:

> Wherefore did nature powr her bounties forth
> With such a full and unwithdrawing hand,
> Covering the earth with odours, fruits, and flocks,
> Thronging the seas with spawn innumerable,
> But all to please, and sate the curious taste?
>
> (Comus, ll.710–14)

In Milton's masque, the Lady calls attention to the error in Comus's logic, the fact that apparent excess is achieved only by the deprivation of others. Volpone or Sir Epicure Mammon need no such interlocutor: they tend themselves to be perfectly explicit about how things were obtained and from where they were derived. Volpone tries to dazzle Celia with

> A diamant, would have bought LOLLIA PAULINA,
> When she came in, like star-light, hid with jewels
> That were the spoils of provinces.
>
> (3.7.195–97)

He cannot evoke the gorgeousness of the imperial concubine without recalling at the same time the vast spaces emptied by Rome's colonial predations. In The Alchemist, Epicure Mammon's gustatory peroration reaches a climax as he imagines himself dining upon the "swelling unctuous paps / Of a fat pregnant sow, newly cut off" (2.2.83–84). While it is usual to eat a piece of an animal, and not the whole thing, here this humdrum fact is made to seem unusually disturbing. Sir Epicure is typical of Jonson's characters in connecting consumption with despoliation, and with the competitive displacement of other claimants, the fetal piglets, for the same resource. Given what we already know about his temperament and preferences, his vivid evocation of the freshly mutilated animal seems positively matricidal.

At first glance it seems hardly in the interests of Volpone or Sir Epicure to dwell upon the conditions in which abundance is achieved. Why do they insist, then, upon the ruin they leave in their wake? Perhaps because in a world in which nothing is created and everything is endlessly recycled, the only definitive means of self-assertion is a form of consumption that destroys the article. Volpone offers Celia gems not to display but to eat, pearls not to wear but to "dissolve, and drink": "and, could we get the phoenix, / (Though nature lost her kind) shee were our dish" (3.7.204–5). The phoenix here represents the ultimate of desirable objects as the Jonsonian comic character conceives them. Because it is unproliferating it must be endlessly recycled, and though it cannot increase it is liable, at least in Volpone's mind, to destruction. Volpone does not deny scarcity, as Milton's Comus does, because by acknowledging that fact he has discovered a perverse compensatory pleasure.

2

In the masques and in many of the celebratory poems, the basic laws of the Jonsonian satiric economy seem to have been abrogated. "To Penshurst" celebrates a miraculous agricultural abundance, a landscape teeming with spontaneously generated edibles. "Earth unplough'd shall yeeld her crop, / Pure honey from the oake shall drop, / The fountaine shall runne milke," promises Pallas in The Golden Age Restored (163–65). In News From the New World the oft-ridiculed principle of perpetual motion once again makes its appearance, but this time it is invoked in earnest as an attribute of sovereign power.

> For he
> That did this motion give,
> And made it so long live,
> Could likewise give it perpetuitie.
>
> (349–52)

What has happened? How can the same person subscribe both to the view that seems to be Jonson's in the comedies and to the view that seems to be Jonson's in the masques and the poems of praise? The difficulty of answering this question is suggested by the history of Jonson criticism, which has tended to segregate itself rigorously by genre.[6]

Perhaps it is possible, however, to see Jonson's work in different genres as a series of strategies for representing possible relationships between desire and its objects, between demand and supply. Desire in the comedies is untrammeled but resources are scarce. Individuals struggle to accumulate all they can, but personal gratification proves incompatible with social justice in their world; even the most fortunate find that their desires outrun the available satisfactions. A better way of coping with scarcity, then, seems to be to restrain desire, to learn to be content with a little. This might be called a philosophical solution rather than an economic one, since it aims to change not the facts of the external world but the orientation of the perceiving subject. Its profound appeal to Jonson is evident in his poetry of resolution and self-denial, and in the rhetoric of his more admirable dramatic characters. Unfortunately it is a difficult course, requiring the virtual eschewal of sensual gratification. The other way to avoid an unpleasant discrepancy between demand and supply is, of course, to live in a world having the abundance to produce satiety.

The masques and many of the celebratory poems portray just such a world. But more than mere land-of-Cockaigne wishfulness informs these representations. In the idealizing genres Jonson draws upon a conceptual scheme available to him both in classical and in Christian political theory, which designates certain relationships and certain goods as beyond the economic order, exempt from the calculus of gain and loss. Such relationships involve not transactions but the cooperative realization of shared objectives, usually in a framework that recognizes a fundamental human affinity. A variety of relationships can be so described: for Aristotle, Cicero, and Seneca the privileged relationship is friendship; in Plutarch it is marital love; in Augustine it is the relationship among faithful Christians.

The kinds of goods realized in such relationships—love, virtue, skill, knowledge, peace of mind—are neither limited in quantity nor subject to private appropriation. In *The City of God* Augustine writes:

> The possession of goodness is by no means diminished if it becomes or remains a shared possession. On the contrary, the more harmonious and charitable are those who share it, the more the possession of goodness is increased. Thus he does not possess goodness who refuses to possess it in common; and the more he shares it, the more he acquires himself.[7]

In such circumstances the competitiveness that pervades social relations in Jonsonian comedy becomes pointless, or even self-

defeating. If one person becomes virtuous, knowledgeable, skillful, or loving, another person is not thereby forced to relinquish
those traits. Thus Jonson distinguishes true love from the "frequent tumults, horrors, and unrests" of "blind Desire":

> It is a golden chaine let downe from heaven,
>   Whose linkes are brighte, and even,
> That falls like sleepe on lovers, and combines
>   The soft, and sweetest mindes,
> In equall knots: This beares no brands, nor darts,
>   To murther different hearts,
> But, in a calme and god-like unitie,
>   Preserves communitie.
>
>   ("Epode," 47–54)

These chains and knots are not experienced as painful or coercive; the love is uncompetitive, nonoppositional, the combination of soft and sweet with soft and sweet.

In the masques and in many of the poems Jonson represents
these noncompetitive relations and goods as socially fundamental. He celebrates union, indivisibility, generosity, harmony—
between kings and subjects, between England and Scotland,
between bride and groom, between parents and children, between guest and host, between masquer and spectator, and even,
early in his career, between poet and stage designer. He "willingly acknowledges" Inigo Jones's contribution, he writes in
The Masque of Queenes, "since it is a vertue, planted in good
natures, that what respects they wish to obtayne fruictfully from
others, they will give ingenuously themselves" (705–709).

Some forms of human excellence, however, seem competitive
in their very essence. A certain kind of martial honor can be
won from or lost to another, as Shakespeare's Hal claims in
Henry IV, Part 1:

> Percy is but my factor, good my lord,
> To engross up glorious deeds on my behalf;
> And I will call him to such strict account
> That he shall render every glory up.
>
>   (3.2.147–50)

When Jonson treats such virtues in the masques, he consistently
minimizes or dissolves the element of rivalry. *A Challenge at
Tilt*, for instance, is structured as a chivalric contest. The masque
begins with "two Cupids striving the day after the marriage."

It emerges that one attends the groom and one attends the bride; each insists that the other is an imposter. To settle their dispute, they produce ten champions on either side who enter the lists and joust on the behalf of each. Eventually, however, Hymen appears to inform the rival Cupids that "this is neither contention for you, nor time, fit to contend." The argument turns out to have been misconceived: "you are both true Cupids." Moreover, not only is each Cupid legitimate, but they are necessary to one another's well-being: "your natures are, that either of you, looking upon the other, thrive, and by your mutuall respects and interchanges of ardor, flourish and prosper." In *A Challenge at Tilt* Jonson acknowledges the traditional knightly values of courage, strength, and martial skill, but he redefines them in terms of the cooperative virtues of marital harmony.

The communal emphasis of Jonson's "ideal economy" does not imply that all kinds of goods need be possessed in common. A confrontation in *Poetaster* clarifies Jonson's logic. The inferior Crispinus, hoping to be accepted into Maecenas's circle of poets, tries to ingratiate himself with Horace. Knowing no better, he assumes that Horace subscribes to the comic strategy of competition, appropriation, and displacement: "Let me not live, but I thinke thou and I (in a small time) should lift them all out of favour, both Virgil, Varius, and the best of them; and enjoy him wholy to our selves." The shocked Horace responds heatedly:

> Sir, your silkenesse
> Cleerely mistakes MECOENAS, and his house;
> To thinke, there breathes a spirit beneath his roofe,
> Subject unto those poore affections
> Of under-mining envie, and detraction,
> Moodes, onely proper to base groveling minds:
> That place is not in *Rome*, I dare affirme,
> More pure, or free, from such low common evils.
> There's no man greev'd, that this is thought more rich,
> Or this more learned; each man hath his place,
> And to his merit, his reward of grace:
> Which with a mutuall love they all embrace.
>
> (*Poetaster*, 3.1.248–59)

This conception of distributive justice is as old as Aristotle's *Politics*. Horace does not deny that some are thought more rich, some more learned; he simply denies that the perception of inequality interferes with mutual love. Indeed, in the traditional view a legitimate hierarchy of entitlements is not only an acceptable but virtually an essential feature of peaceful relations. For in that case "each man hath his place," whereas when all think themselves equal, or believe themselves to be denied equality by merely contingent factors, competition inevitably breaks out—between Mosca and Volpone, among the Collegiate Ladies in Epicoene, between Subtle and Face in The Alchemist.

The kinds of goods that are realized in the ideal sociopolitical realm ordinarily are immaterial ones. Thus in the tradition Jonson inherits, the ideal economy of "mutuall love" is always distinguished sharply from the economy of materialist expediency. Seneca writes:

> The foolish avarice of mortals distinguishes between possession and ownership, and does not believe anything its own which is held in common. But the philosopher judges nothing more fully his own than that which he shares with the human race. . . . When rations are distributed among a group of people, each one takes away only so much as is allotted to him. . . . These goods, by contrast, are indivisible . . . and they belong as much to everyone as they do to each person.[8]

Similarly in Cicero's De Amicitia, Laelius deplores those who

> value their friends as they do cattle or sheep, preferring those from whom they expect to profit most. Therefore are they cut off from the most beautiful and most natural friendship, which is desirable in and for itself.[9]

In both passages the nature of the ideal is rendered vividly apparent by its contrast with the quantifiable and limited material order, the world of money, grain, and cattle. Likewise Jonson repeatedly makes a distinction between the "sensual" people who evaluate everything in terms of the limited, allocatable goods of the material world, and the elite—philosophers, artists, scholars—who seem able to transcend and despise that order. He contrasts the "carcase" or "body" of the masque with its "spirit" or "soul" or "inward parts," reminding us that the former is traditionally torn apart by members of the audience as soon as the revels have ended. Like all "bodies" it can be dismantled, appropriated, redistributed, destroyed. But the latter is exempt by nature from depredation and change.

The consequence of this rhetorical strategy is that relations based upon material considerations must invariably figure as inferior to, and at best secondary to, at worst incompatible with, the cultivation of virtue.[10]

> Sonne, and my Friend, I had not call'd you so
> To mee; or beene the same to you; if show,
> Profit, or Chance had made us.
>
> ("*Epigram. To a Friend, and Sonne,*" 1–3)

Jonson's traditional convictions on the difference between the material and the ideal economy divide him from those moral philosophers later in the century and in the Enlightenment who try to found an ethics and a politics upon the material self-interest of the individual.[11] He sees clearly enough the connection between a social order that emphasizes material accumulation and such personal characteristics as egoism and acquisitiveness, but he has no way of representing such characteristics as sources of the virtues. In his distaste for a social system organized around competitive market forces, Jonson seems to resemble more recent critics of capitalism, but his antiacquisitive attitude has different motives and different consequences. It is preliberal rather than postliberal. For Jonson, virtue requires the minimizing or the repudiation of material motives and a material basis.

The relationship between the material economy and the ideal economy is not, however, merely a simple one of contrast. In a characteristic passage in *De Amicitia* (16.58), Cicero claims that friendship is not dependent upon need:

> It is indeed excessively sparing and meager to call friendship to a strict accounting, in order that debts might be balanced with receipts. It seems to me that true friendship is richer and more abundant. It does not watch stingily, anxious not to give more than it takes; nor does it worry that something might be wasted or spilled on the ground, or that more than the exact amount might be poured into the friendship.[12]

Cicero maintains that friendship ignores gain and loss, but his language, far from eschewing materiality, explicitly insists upon the analogy between friendly generosity and material abundance.[13] The relationships that are supposed to transcend economic considerations altogether, in other words, often seem to transcend merely the unpleasantness of scarcity. Jonson plays with this ambiguity in one of the poems to Celia in *The Forrest*. He invites his beloved to kiss him

> Till you equall with the store,
> All the grasse that *Rumney* yeelds,
> Or the sands in *Chelsey* fields,
> Or the drops in silver *Thames,*
> Or the starres, that guild his streames . . .
> That the curious may not know
> How to tell 'hem, as they flow,
> And the envious, when they find
> What their number is, be pin'd.
>
> ("To the Same," 12–22)

The mathematics of Celia's kisses are obscure. They vex the curious because they flow so fast that they cannot be distinguished, but they vex the envious because they are after all countable. They are both numberless and numbered.

In the poem to Celia, the difference between the infinite-in-principle and the infinite-practically-speaking seems inconsequential. But the politics of this difference can become significant. The moral value attaching to that which transcends material necessity is different from the moral value attaching merely to large material possessions. In "To Penshurst" the problem is vividly apparent. Jonson praises Sidney for hospitality and generosity, virtues he explicitly contrasts with competitive display and selfish consumption or "envious show." But he finds it difficult to specify the relation between the ideal and the material economy in the pastoral society he describes. On the one hand he asserts their radical incommensurability, and on the other hand he is unable to sustain a sense of the two kinds of reality as truly independent. When the tenants come to the great house with cakes and fruits, for instance, Jonson claims the gifts are superfluous.[14]

> But what can this (more than express their love)
>   Adde to thy free provisions, farre above
> The neede of such?
>
> (57–59)

"Free" here, as often in Jonson, is a highly charged word. It asserts that at Penshurst, transfers of goods neither impoverish the giver nor enrich the recipient. They are the sign and not the substance of the social bond; the loving relation of tenant and landlord seems liberated from the constraints of material necessity. But "free" also means "profuse." The tenants can bring gifts to the lord because they can easily spare them, the

lord does not need them because he is already plentifully supplied, and the guest can eat as much as he likes because there
is more than enough to go around.

Once again the language of the nonmaterial ideal collapses
into the language of material abundance. Though Jonson wants
to inscribe Robert Sidney's hospitality within the ideal economy,
that hospitality takes an emphatically material form:

> Here no man tells my cups; nor, standing by,
>   A waiter, doth my gluttony envy:
> But gives me what I call, and lets me eate,
>   He knowes, below, he shall find plentie of meate.
>
> (67–70)

If generosity depends upon an agricultural surplus, then virtue
seems unavoidably contingent upon a material order inferior
by definition. Unless, that is, the causal relationship is reversed,
and the wealth is a consequence of excellence, and not vice
versa: the Sidneys, in other words, are rich because they are
hospitable, rather than hospitable because they are rich. Jonson's
most effusive flattery of his patrons often takes this form. In
the dedicatory epistle to *The Masque of Queenes*, for instance,
he writes to Prince Henry:

> whether it be that a divine soule, being to come into a body, first
> chooseth a Palace fit for it selfe; or, being come, doth make it so;
> or that Nature be ambitious to have her worke aequall, I know
> not: But . . . both your virtue, and your forme did deserve your
> fortune. The one claym'd, that you should be borne a Prince; the
> other makes that you do become it. (7–14)

This strategy solves Jonson's metaphysical problem, but at the
cost of a grave implausibility. His own experience as an obese,
pockmarked, impoverished, but immensely gifted artist, makes
this position difficult for him to occupy long.[15]

In the masques, the allegorical character of the representation
provides another way of conceiving of the relationship between
the ideal and the material economy.

> The Machine of the Spectacle . . . was a MIKROKOSMOS, or Globe,
> fill'd with Countreys, and those gilded; where the Sea was expresst,
> heightened with silver waves. This stood, or rather hung (for no
> Axell was seene to supporte it) and turning softly, discovered the
> first Masque. . . . To which, the lights were so placed, as no one

was seene; but seemed, as if onely Reason, with the splendor of
her crowne, illumin'd the whole Grot. (*Hymenaei*, 668–672)

The gorgeous gold-and-silver globe stands without an axle, turns
without a mover, is lit not by ordinary lights but by "Reason,
with the splendor of her crowne." This mysteriousness is a
clue to the ideal nature of the representation—it expresses a
truth beyond facts of the material world. For the "sense" or
physical part of the masque, Jonson maintains, "doth, or should
alwayes lay hold on more remov'd mysteries." Like the flattery
in "To Penshurst" or in the prefatory epistle to Prince Henry,
allegory makes the material a consequence of the ideal, rather
than the other way around.

Yet even this solution to the dilemma fails to prove entirely
satisfactory. In Jonson's description, the miraculousness of the
represented plentitude is, of course, illusory. It *seems* "as if
onely reason, with the splendor of her crowne, illumin'd the
whole Grot," but what is actually being deployed here are the
engineering skills of Inigo Jones, master-carpenter. If this skill
is itself a kind of reason—a point I shall take up in the next
section—it is certainly not of a form that transcends the material.

So Jonson's sense of the two economies and their relation
to one another is never entirely settled. Materiality as he defines
it is so bleak and limited that it requires supplementation: he
must have recourse to another set of facts in order to account
for the full range of human experience. But his evocations of
ideal community turn out to be susceptible to reductive analysis.
In a well-known analysis in *The Country and The City*, Raymond
Williams accomplishes this kind of reduction for "To Penshurst," when he points out that Jonson suppresses the facts
of labor on the estate, massively misrepresenting the nature
of the rural economy. Jonson performs a similar demystification
himself, when he praises Sir Robert Wroth for his domestic
restraint:

> Nor throng'st (when masquing is) to have a sight
>   Of the short braverie of the night;
> To view the jewels, stuffes, the paines, the wit
>   There wasted, some not paid for yet!
> But canst, at home, in thy securer rest,
>   Live, with un-bought provision blest.
>   ("To Sir Robert Wroth," 9–14)

Here the court world becomes subject to precisely those laws from which Jonson exempts it in the masques. In order to execute this act of satiric subversion, however, Jonson must possess an alternative, a new locus of ideal social order—in "To Sir Robert Wroth," the pastoral world of "un-bought provision." Of course the pastoral world itself can be seen in terms of the satiric economy, too, but this emphatically is not in Jonson's interest at the moment.

The Jonsonian satiric vision depends upon the availability of an alternative economy, an economy that does not redeem material relations, but transcends them. The transcendent gesture in Jonson, however, tends to be actually or potentially compromised, and its insecurity has led some perceptive readers to minimize its seriousness or even to overlook it entirely.[16] Recent work on Ben Jonson has tended to concentrate upon his materialism, his emphasis upon the body in the plays and his almost corporeal presence in the poems.[17] But Jonsonian idealism is, I think, not so much halfhearted as beseiged, threatened not only by the instability of the tradition as he inherits it, but by the suddenly heightened interest in material relations characteristic of the early modern culture he inhabits.[18] It is not surprising that the political thinkers of the next few generations, in response to the massive social changes to which Jonson bears witness in his drama and poetry, should jettison the theoretical principles to which he still unsteadily adheres.

3

Throughout his career, Jonson strives vigorously to associate himself and his poetic vocation with the kind of social relationships that he portrays in the poems of praise and in the masques, and to ally the poet with the virtues that transcend the material economic order. But although many of his contemporaries conceive of rhetorical copia as in principle inexhaustible,[19] Jonson rarely represents the poetic gift in terms of the abundance that characterizes his ideal economies. The poet-character Asper, welcoming "attentive auditors" in *Every Man Out Of His Humour*, describes one version of Jonsonian *inventio*:

> For these, Ile prodigally spend my selfe,
> And speake away my spirit into ayre;

> For these, Ile melt my braine into invention,
> Coine new conceits.
>
> (Induction, 204–7)

The Jonsonian poet is a self-consuming artificer. Thus the prudent artist provisions himself thoroughly beforehand, for as Jonson writes in *Discoveries*, "exactnesse of Studie, and multiplicity of reading ... maketh a full man" (2482–84). The achievement of "fullness" not only guarantees the quality of the poetic product, but constitutes a kind of reinforcement for a "selfe" or "spirit" imagined as limited in quantity, dissolved and depleted by the act of creation.

Jonson's anxieties about the relative scarcity and nonrenewability of creative substance apply not just to himself, but to the entire artistic community. In *Epigrammes* 79, Jonson explains that Sidney was unable to beget a son because he expended the available resources in other endeavors:

> before,
> Or then, or since, about our *Muses* springs,
> Came not that soule exhausted so their store.
>
> (2–4)

In *Epigrammes* 23, "To John Donne," Phoebus and the Muses concentrate so much of their attention upon Donne that Jonson, both celebrant and rival, is left stammering and inarticulate, forced to end his poem because he is unable to find the proper words for it. In "To Shakespeare," Chaucer, Spenser, and Beaumont already crowd the available space for poets in Westminster Abbey. Here Jonson seems to invoke scarcity and competitiveness only to deny their relevance; for Shakespeare, he declares, is not the rival of these "great, but disproportion'd, muses." But actually the struggle has merely been removed to another arena. Jonson imagines the British champion confronting and overcoming the classical dramatists.

> The merry *Greeke*, tart *Aristophanes*,
>   Neat *Terence*, witty *Plautus*, now not please;
> But antiquated, and deserted lye
>   As they were not of Natures family.
>
> (51–54)

The latter-born son acquires his place in the literary canon by displacing the first-born. "He invades Authours like a Monarch," writes Dryden of Jonson, "and what would be theft in other Poets, is onely victory in him."[20] By asserting his own literary immortality, he necessarily excludes other possible claimants.

The poet as Jonson conceives him, then, seems linked more closely to the satiric than to the ideal economy. The creative faculty behaves like a material entity: it can be appropriated, reallocated, exhausted, competed for, stolen. The possibility of plagiarism distresses Jonson, almost alone among his contemporaries; he reviles Play-wright and Proule the Plagiary in the *Epigrammes*, and writes scenes of public humiliation for literary thieves into *Every Man In His Humour, Cynthia's Revels, Poetaster*, and *Epicoene*. Like the alchemists and the Bartholomew-birds of Jonsonian comedy, the plagiarist appropriates from others what he is unable to generate himself. But so, necessarily, does the "true" Jonsonian poet fashion what he needs from what he finds at hand, drawing upon his mind's carefully stocked treasury, converting "the substance, or Riches, of another Poet, to his own use" (*Discoveries*, 2467–69). And he possesses, moreover, a lively concern for the material form in which the artistic results are presented to readers, supervising the printing and publication of his collected work in a large volume the sheer expensiveness of which testifies to the kind of poetic significance Jonson wishes to claim for himself.

Needless to say Jonson does not treat his own poetic gift as the stuff of satire. How does he exempt the true artist from the reductive materialism of the comedies? Both the economy of Jonsonian comedy, characterized by a relentless competition for a fixed number of resources, and the economy of the masque, characterized by uncompetitive abundance, are economies of consumption rather than production. Jonsonian poetic theory brings back the term missing both from the otiose worlds represented in the masques and the country house poem, and from the sterile world of the satiric genres. The Greek word *poesis*, Jonson emphasizes, means "production" or "making." "A Poeme," he writes in *Discoveries*, "is the work of the poet: the end, and fruit, of his labour and studye" (ll.2375–76). That favorite Jonsonian word *work* refers to both process and product—a conceptual distinction he is always eager to elide. In the text of *Hymenaei*, he praises the set designed by his collaborator, Inigo Jones:

> that which . . . was most taking in the Spectacle, was the sphere of fire . . . imitated with such art and industrie, as the spectators

might descerne the Motion (all the time the Shewes lasted) without any Moover. (ll.668–72)

Jonson displaces our amazement from the mysterious self-sufficiency of the sphere to its actual dependence upon "art and industrie": to the very "Moover" its cunning construction seems to allow it to do without.

Thus reproductive sexuality, which Jonson is almost alone among dramatists in ignoring as a comic motif, figures largely in his metaphors of poetic production. In the *Epigrammes* poems are children, children poems. In *Every Man Out Of His Humour*, Asper describes himself as inseminated by appreciative spectators, who

> cherish my free labours, love my lines,
> And with the fervour of their shining grace,
> Make my braine fruitfull to bring forth more objects,
> Worthy their serious, and intentive eyes.
>
> (Induction, ll.135–38)

It is significant that Jonson tends to imagine the artist's creative role not as male but as female. In the defense of his satiric methods and motives appended to *Poetaster*, he refuses to apologize for his "long-watched labors," the plays he brings forth once a year:

> Things, that were borne, when none but the still night
> And his dumbe candle saw his pinching throes.

These poetic pregnancies differ significantly from the blissful unions celebrated in the marriage masques, from the painlessly knotted minds of "An Epode," from the pleasurable dalliance with Celia: not the ecstasies of sexual consummation but the difficulties of childbirth provide his metaphors for the poetic process. Thus Jonson's sexual metaphors for poetic production coexist with metaphors derived from other forms of toil: coining, ironworking, cloth production, agriculture, housebuilding, cookery.[21]

No matter how slow the style be at first, so it be labour'd, and accurate: seeke the best, and be not glad of forward conceipts, or first words, that offer themselves to us . . . the safest is to returne to our Judgement, and handle over againe those things, the easinesse of which might make them justly suspected. (*Discoveries*, ll.1705–8, 1721–23)

We seem a long way from the ethic of "To Penshurst," and its happy acceptance of things that volunteer themselves to be consumed.

Jonson's audiences in his own time and in ours have often wished him more spontaneous, less costive. But in Jonson's conceptual scheme, the pain and difficulty that attend creation are the signs of its genuineness. The laboriousness of artistic production seems to allow him to exempt himself both from the implausibilities of his ideal worlds, and from the reductiveness of his satiric ones.

Notes

I would like to thank Henry Higuera of St. Johns College for his advice on the Christian tradition of the "common good," and Robert Wiltenburg of Washington University for the opportunity to present part of this paper at the 1987 MLA Convention.

1. Northrop Frye, *The Anatomy of Criticism: Four Essays* (Princeton: Princeton University Press, 1957), p. 179.

2. L. C. Knights, *Drama and Society in the Age of Jonson* (London: Chatto and Windus, 1937), pp. 200–27; Raymond Williams, *The Country and the City* (New York: Oxford University Press, 1973), pp. 26–45; Don E. Wayne, "Drama and Society in the Age of Jonson: An Alternative View," *Renaissance Drama* 13 (1982): 103–29; Walter Cohen, *Drama of a Nation: Public Theater in Renaissance England and Spain* (Ithaca: Cornell University Press, 1985), pp. 292–301.

3. Of course Jonson is not alone in this insight. The extent to which one person's satisfaction necessarily precludes other people's satisfaction is a problem that emerges repeatedly in the literature of a society newly alive to material pleasures but still liable to severe scarcities of basic goods. Milton addresses the issue in *Comus*, Spenser in the second book of the *The Faerie Queene*.

4. Both Gabriele Jackson and Ian Donaldson have remarked upon the centrifugal quality of Jonsonian comedy on the level of plot: "The natural conclusion of Jonsonian comedy is complete fragmentation," writes Gabriele Bernhard Jackson, ed., in *Ben Jonson: Every Man In His Humour* (New Haven: Yale University Press, 1969), p. 7. See Ian Donaldson, "Language and Nonsense: 'The Alchemist'," *Seventeenth Century Imagery*, ed. Earl Miner (Berkeley: University of California Press, 1971), pp. 69–70.

5. "Ben Jonson and the Centered Self," *Studies in English Literature* 10 (1970): 337.

6. Critics who have addressed the problem have usually decided that Jonson is in some way of two minds, though they describe his dichotomies in a variety of ways. See, for example, Gabriele Jackson, *Vision and Judgment in Ben Jonson's Drama* (New Haven: Yale University Press, 1968); Arthur Marotti, "All About Jonson's Poetry," *ELH* 39 (1972): 208–37; Thomas Greene,

"Ben Jonson and the Centered Self," *Studies in English Literature* 10 (1970): 325–48; Richard C. Newton, "'Ben./ Jonson': The Poet in the Poems," *Two Renaissance Mythmakers*, ed. Alvin Kernan (Baltimore: Johns Hopkins University Press, 1977), pp. 165–95; and Alexander Leggatt, *Ben Jonson: His Vision and his Art* (London: Methuen, 1981). Though I share this view of Jonson as a deeply ambivalent author, I hope to demonstrate some connections between apparently contradictory attitudes, attitudes which I argue actually support and supplement one another.

7. "Nullo enim modo fit minor accedente seu permanente consorte possessio bonitatis, immo possessio bonitas, quam tanto latius quanto concordius individua sociorum possidet caritas. Non habebit denique istam possessionem qui eam noluerit habere communem; et tanto eam reperiet ampliorum quanto amplius ibi potuerit amare consortem." (*City of God* 15.5)

In *After Virtue* (Notre Dame: University of Notre Dame Press, 1984), pp. 190–91, Alasdair MacIntyre argues a modern version of the originally Aristotelian distinction between "external" goods such as fame, power, and money, and "internal" goods, intrinsic to a particular practice; for example, in chess, strategic imagination or a particular kind of analytic skill. "It is characteristic of what I have called external goods that when achieved they are always some individual's property and possession. Moreover characteristically they are such that the more someone has of them, the less there is for other people. . . . External goods are therefore characteristically the objects of competition in which there must be losers as well as winners. Internal goods are indeed the outcome of a competition to excel, but it is characteristic of them that their achievement is a good for the whole community who participate in the practice."

8. "Stulta avaritia mortalium possessionem proprietatemque discernit nec quicquam suum credit esse, quod publicum est. At ille sapiens nihil iudicat suum magis quam cuius illi cum humano genere consortium est. . . . Ex congiaro tantum ferunt homines, quantum in capita promissum est. . . . At haec individua bona . . . et tam omnium tota quam singulorum sunt." (*Epistulae Morales* 73.7–8)

9. "Amicos tamquam pecudes eos potissimum diligunt, ex quibus sperant se maximum fructum esse capturos. Ita pulcherrima illa et maxime naturali carent amicitia per se et propter se expetitia." (*De Amicitia* 21.79–80)

10. The precise relation of virtue to material goods is a hotly debated issue. Aristotle, in the *Nichomachean Ethics*, argues that moderate prosperity is a prerequisite for the exercise of virtue. But this is exactly the point at which the Stoic and later the Christian tradition diverges from Aristotle, as his position seems to make virtue dependent upon accidents of birth and fortune. Jonson, a syncretic classicist indebted to Roman writers who themselves preferred synthesis to rigorous consistency, inherits a traditional ambivalence. For a more complete account of the way inconsistencies in the classical tradition affect Jonson's assumptions about the nature of the material world and about the relationship of the material world to virtue, see Katharine Eisaman Maus, *Ben Jonson and the Roman Frame of Mind* (Princeton: Princeton University Press, 1984), pp. 24–29, 85–88, and 156–59.

11. For an account of this development in Hobbes, Harrington, Locke, Bentham, and others, see C. B. MacPherson, *The Political Theory of Possessive Individualism* (Oxford: Clarendon, 1962). Alasdair MacIntyre, in *After Virtue*, pp. 228–29, gives a concise account of the effect of these writers' nontraditional

social and political assumptions upon ethics. "It was in the seventeenth and eighteenth centuries that morality came generally to be understood as offering a solution to the problems provided by human egoism and that the content of morality came to be largely equated with altruism. For it was in the same period that men came to be thought of as in some dangerous measure egoistic by nature; and it is only once we think of mankind as by nature dangerously egoistic that altruism becomes at once socially necessary and yet apparently impossible and, if and when it occurs, inexplicable. On the traditional Aristotelian view such problems do not arise. For what education in the virtues teaches me is that my good as a man is one and the same as the good of those others with whom I am bound up in human community. There is no way of my pursuing my good which is necessarily antagonistic to you pursuing yours because the good is neither mine peculiarly nor yours peculiarly—goods are not private property."

12. "Hoc quidem est nimis exigue et exiliter ad calculos vocare amicitiam, ut par sit ratio acceptorum et datorum. Divitior mihi et affluentior videtur esse vera amicitia nec observare restricte ne plus reddat quam acceperit; neque enim verendum est ne quid excidat aut re quid in terram defluat aut ne plus aequo quid in amicitiam congeratur."

13. For an ingenious discussion of the analogies between philosophical thought and economic transactions in Plato and Aristotle, see Marc Shell, *The Economy of Literature* (Baltimore: Johns Hopkins University Press, 1978), pp. 21–48 and 89–101.

14. Gift giving, as writers from Seneca to Marcel Mauss have noted, is an ambiguous social act, a gesture of self-sacrifice in which self-interest plays a role. The gift thus occupies a position that seems to mediate between the materialist economy as Jonson conceives it, with its selfishness and scarcity, and the ideal economy of common goods. For Seneca's views, see *De Beneficiis* (an important text for Jonson); for Mauss, see *The Gift: Form and Function of Exchange in Archaic Societies* (New York: Norton, 1967). I would like to thank Stephen Greenblatt for alerting me to Mauss's work.

15. For a discussion of Jonson's evident discomfort with the strategies of praise in "To Penshurst," see William E. Cain, "The Place of the Poet in Jonson's 'To Penshurst' and 'To My Muse,'" *Criticism* 21 (1979): 34–48.

16. One example is Don Wayne, who in his excellent book *Penshurst: The Semiotics of Place and the Poetics of History* (Madison: University of Wisconsin Press, 1984) remarks that "the harmony and order which critics have celebrated in speaking of Jonson's nonsatiric work, verse as well as prose, are largely illusory" (p. 35).

17. See, for example, Robert M. Adams, "On the Bulk of Ben," *Ben Jonson's Plays and Masques*, ed. Robert M. Adams (New York: Norton, 1979), pp. 482–92; E. Pearlman, "Ben Jonson: An Anatomy," *ELR* 9 (1979): 364–94; Don Wayne, "Poetry and Power in Ben Jonson's *Epigrammes*: The Naming of 'Facts' or the Figuring of Social Relations?" *Renaissance and Modern Studies* 23 (1979): 79–103; Joseph Loewenstein, "The Jonsonian Corpulence; or, the Poet as Mouthpiece," *ELH* 53 (1986): 491–518. Wayne's argument resembles mine in its attempt to discuss Jonsonian materialism in terms of seventeenth-century political thought, but he associates Jonson with later writers, especially Hobbes, whereas I see Jonson as still participating in the tradition of political thinking against which Hobbes rebels in the next generation.

18. The period immediately following Jonson's career sees the virtual inven-

tion of economics as a separate area of inquiry in England in response to
the significant changes brought about by early capitalism and colonialism.
For an account of the origins of English economic thought in the years between
1622 and 1700, see Joyce Oldham Appleby, *Economic Thought and Ideology
in Seventeenth Century England* (Princeton: Princeton University Press, 1978).
C. B. MacPherson convincingly relates early modern political theory to social
conditions in mid- and late seventeenth-century England.

19. In *The Cornucopian Text: Problems of Writing in the French Renaissance*
(London and New York: Oxford University Press, 1979), Terence Cave describes
the figures of copia and cornucopia in a variety of sixteenth-century humanist
texts. For the writers Cave considers—Erasmus, Rabelais, Ronsard, and others—the problem is the management of plenitude, not (as with Jonson) the
problem of making a little go a long way. A number of recent critics argue
convincingly that the circumstances of Jonson's unprecedented literary profes-
sionalism lead him to a historically new conception of his writing as a form
of commodity. See, for example, Timothy Murray, "From Foul Sheets to Legitimate Model: Antitheater, Text, Ben Jonson," *New Literary History* 14 (1982–83):
641–64; Richard C. Newton, "Jonson and the (Re-)Invention of the Book,"
Classic and Cavalier: Essays on Jonson and the Sons of Ben (Pittsburgh: University of Pittsburgh Press, 1982), pp. 31–55; Richard Helgerson, *Self-Crowned
Laureates: Spenser, Jonson, Milton and the Laureate System* (Berkeley: University of California Press, 1982); and Joseph Loewenstein, "The Script in the
Marketplace," *Representations* 12 (1985): 101–14. Perhaps this alteration in
the writer's relation to his audience accounts for the difference in his theory
of artistic production. Of course, it would be possible for Jonson to demarcate
clearly between the process of artistic creation and the process by which
the finished works are conveyed to audiences, but he does not do so.

20. "An Essay of Dramatick Poesie," *The Works of John Dryden*, vol. 17
ed. Samuel Holt Monk (Berkeley: University of California Press, 1971), p.
57. Dryden's metaphor captures better Jonson's particular relation to his predecessors than do Harold Bloom's metaphors of filial struggle, because Dryden
is alert to the specifically proprietary claim made by the Jonsonian artist.

21. For an ingenious account of the culinary metaphor in Jonsonian poetics,
see Donald K. Hedrick, "Cooking for the Anthropagi: Jonson and his Audience," *Studies in English Literature* 17 (1977): 233–45. For a discussion of
the classical precedents for Jonson's preference for the laboured, see Richard
Peterson, *Imitation and Praise in the Poems of Ben Jonson* (New Haven: Yale
University Press, 1981), pp. 158–70.

Roman Ben Jonson

William Blissett

It is part of the definition of the city that its activities over the years should be complicated beyond all power of description, and if that is true of any city, how much more is it the case with Rome, where *urbs* is a synecdoche for *orbis*. It is part of the definition of the Renaissance that it should be conscious of itself as a new time resuming and reliving antiquity. As the Romans knew themselves and the Greeks, so the Renaissance knew the Romans (and the Greeks through the Romans) and themselves as something new.

A real freedom of the Latin language became a possibility in the humanistic schools, even in Shakespeare's grammar school in Stratford, certainly in Westminster School where Ben Jonson was taught by William Camden, who was to become England's first great historian. With *Latinitas* went *urbanitas*, a deep and prolonged familiarity with the history and culture of Eternal Rome. Shall *urbanitas* be translated as "Romanity"? *Romanitas* is not a classical word, and *urbanity* in English, and *urbanité* in French, have adopted a new meaning. Just as the word *literate* may be used for anyone who has profited by primary education and again for the most learned wit, so Ben Jonson was *latinate* in a basic and an advanced sense. As an inky schoolboy he would construe an oration for Murena or against Verres, a disquisition on friendship or on duties, absorbing and retaining Cicero's correct sentiments (easily reconcilable to the ethos of a good school, or an ordered polity, or even Christian ideas of the virtues of the private and the public man), Cicero's liveliness and boastfulness, and the great moment in his career—all to fall in place when in mature years he wrote his tragedy *Catiline*. Ben Jonson the satirist and poet and playwright could not have risen to what he achieved without further, more probing, self-directed studies in the Latin poets—Ovid and Virgil, of course, but in addition some others less central

to a school curriculum but temperamentally more congenial—
the epigrammatist Martial, the satirist Juvenal, the Greek "anato-
mist" Lucian, and most especially Horace.[1] Horace was, like
Jonson, a poet-critic, like him a soldier turned poet, a self-
disciplined artist, a patriot as private man. Close study of this
sharp observer of Roman life and manners helped alert Jonson
to the life and manners of his own city. From this latinity of
intermediate challenge Jonson distilled his "comicall satyre,"
Poetaster. The weightiest of his three Roman plays, *Sejanus*,
derives largely, in subject and tone, in "truth of argument" and
gravity of judgment, from a writer, Tacitus, who would never
have been anything but tough and resistant to the reader, even
in his own day, who taxed the latinity of the mature scholar
and rewarded it proportionately.[2] Jonson's latinity is thus directly reflected in three of the nine plays he so carefully prepared
for the Folio of 1616. *Poetaster* (acted 1601, published 1602)
was the last of the group of "comicall satyres"; *Sejanus* (acted
1603, published 1605) was next in composition but inaugurated
a new phase to which belong most of his acclaimed masterpieces; and *Catiline* (acted and published in 1611) was the last
play to be included in the Folio. The exclusion, for whatever
reason, of *Bartholomew Fair* (acted in 1614) greatly increases
the relative bulk and weight of the Roman third of the book,
which is in so many other ways as well classically designed.

Roman education was education in *urbanitas* and *gravitas*—
how through the ritual and political year to think, to argue,
to act like the Romans of the past. The "Roman myth" was
the curriculum.[3] The annals of fame and infamy, the records
of political and military engagements, were continually re-
counted, re-examined, distorted, regularized, as the politics of
amicitia, of patron and client, of local attachments, developed
into a politics of world power. Every politically ambitious man
of good family foresaw his own sculptured bust taking its place
among those of his consular ancestors—those "existing monuments that form an ideal order among themselves, which is
altered by the introduction of the new."[4] Clients and allies of
candidates for office, defenders and prosecutors alike, related
the men and events of now to the unfolding course of Roman
history. Absorbing folklore into annals, annals into history, the
Romans were a fully developed "historic people."

They remain so. It is remarkable how much Roman history
still lodges in our minds, what a procession of events, what
a throng of characters. Roman history was the school of Machia-

velli and Montesquieu, of Jefferson and Robespierre, of German liberalism and *reichsdeutsch Realpolitik,* of Mussolini and Harry Truman. Goethe casually throws out such a comment as this (in line with what we shall be finding in Jonson): "The Romans had advanced from a narrow, moral, comfortable, cosy and bourgeois existence to a wide expanse of world-rule, without losing their limitations; even that which has been called a 'sense of freedom' is in essence narrow-minded. They had become kings and they wished to remain fathers, husbands, and friends, as before; and the assassination of Caesar, the most tasteless deed of all, shows how little even the better men understood what it meant to be rulers." So speaks a mind magisterial but unprofessional; to this may be added the view of David Knowles, that Roman history "is a text book without rival for an historian in training, showing as it does the inexorable march of time and the sequence of wisdom and error and their consequences, in which every problem has been isolated and debated by some of the acutest minds of Europe for five centuries."[5]

Nor is this only discursive. Over and over again, the liveliest imaginations return, much as the Romans themselves returned, to take another look. Voltaire and Dumas and Ibsen (not to mention Stephen Gosson) all wrote Catiline plays, and Ibsen thought his most important work to be the immense ten-act, two-part world-historical drama *Emperor and Galilean,* about Julian the Apostate and a Third Empire beyond paganism and Christianity. The hugely popular nineteenth-century novels, *The Last Days of Pompeii* by Bulwer-Lytton and *Quo Vadis?* by Sinkiewicz, staked for Roman fiction a place it has never lost. Both Cardinal Wiseman and Cardinal Newman wrote Roman novels on the pagan-Christian theme, as in our day did Evelyn Waugh in *Helena.* Waugh's friend, Alfred Duggan, produced many historical novels, neat, compact and (several of them, ranging over the centuries from Romulus to Heliogabalus) very Roman. Robert Graves in *I Claudius* and *Claudius the God* achieved best-sellerdom (not unmixed with critical respect) in the 1930s and television's accolade in recent years. Thornton Wilder recreates the events of the *Ides of March,* and Gore Vidal in *Julian* returns to the theme that fascinated Ibsen. Marguerite Yourcenar, in *The Memoirs of Hadrian* (like Hermann Broch before her in *The Death of Virgil* and Walter Pater first of all in *Marius the Epicurean*) tries to achieve a revaluation of the Roman experience of the world from inside a Roman consciousness and sensibility. This is only a selection: the whole list would be like the description of a Roman triumph.

The Romanity that continues to our day takes shape at the beginning of the Renaissance when Petrarch exclaims, "Quis enim est omnis historia, nisi Romana laus?"[6] In England it is given its first permanently memorable expression by the dramatic poet Ben Jonson characterized as having but "small Latin and less Greek." The Shakespeare of *Julius Caesar, Coriolanus,* and *Antony and Cleopatra* stands in full imaginative possession of one rich and varied source, the parallel lives of Plutarch as translated, through the French, by Sir Thomas North in 1579. Not only in their strong general conception—the almost prepolitical "earliness" of *Coriolanus,* the crucial moments of Philippi and Actium in the other plays—but in their poetic details they are astonishingly Roman. Far outweighing such a lapse (*anachronism* is the word, its first recorded use in English being by Ben Jonson) as having a striking clock in Caesar's Rome, is the Romanity of Enobarbus's hope, by following a fallen lord, to "earn a place in the story," or the gasp of admiration for Cleopatra—"She's a most triumphant lady, if report be square to her," or young Octavius Caesar's marmoreal words of comfort to his sister abandoned by Antony:

> Be you not troubled with the time, which drives
> O'er your content these strong necessities;
> But let determined things to destiny
> Hold unbewailed their way.
>
> (3.6.82–85)

Ben Jonson, however, was immersed in classical studies, lived the classics, in a way that Shakespeare could not attempt. His own elegies and epigrammatic and lyric poems on classical models, his translation of Horace's *Art of Poetry* into English verse and of shorter passages of Ovid, Catullus, and Virgil, the adaptation of two Horatian satires in *Poetaster,* of Sallust and Cicero in *Catiline,* of Tacitus and Juvenal in *Sejanus* (with marginal annotations in the last case)—all this is unmatched in his contemporaries.[7]

It is significant that Jonson wrote no chronicle play—a genre monarchist, popular, Christian, full of pageantry. His English plays are up to the minute, with no roots in English history or lore (until the very late, unfinished *Sad Shepherd*). He makes a clean break with the past: parallels are permitted but not continuity. *Poetaster* takes a walk through a Rome in process of turning from brick into marble; *Sejanus* shows the human cost and consequences of the consolidation of absolute power in a Roman Empire unredeemable by its own political and moral resources; *Catiline* re-enacts the finest hour of Roman vigilance and resolution and celebrates a victory that playwright and audience know to be edged with ultimate defeat.

1

Jonson's first Roman play, *Poetaster*, a "comicall satyre," makes no pretence to that "truth of argument" the playwright held to be a prime requirement of tragedy.[8] It may be literary criticism, but it is not literary history. In the first act, young Ovid is a reluctant student of law, restive under his rich father's interdict on poetry as never having allowed anyone to get ahead in the world; in the last act, apparently no older, he and some other poets and the Emperor's daughter Julia are interrupted in an amusing but rather blasphemous charade of the gods and goddesses, and Ovid is banished from the court and Julia locked away. The real banishment occurred in A.D. 8 and involved the Emperor's granddaughter: Ovid was then over fifty and an established literary figure, so that this was for him a final metamorphosis, with a vengeance. Horace, whom Jonson represents as pleading for the delinquent, had been dead sixteen years. Jonson was a good scholar and it is unlikely that this radical telescoping of time is a simple error; why did he risk its being taken so? The historical conscience of the tragedian will be much more severe than it is here in the comical satirist.[9]

Poetaster is called a "comicall satyre," and while Jonson plays on the supposed connection between the satirist (often called the satyr) and the hairy goatish satyrs of the Roman forests, he may have known the real derivation of the word from Latin *satura*, a medley, a mixed dish, though this was not fully established by the great scholar Isaac Casaubon until 1605. The play itself is an odd mixture, like a book of Roman satires, dramatized, and given unity largely by the presence of the keen-eyed observer (here the poet Horace) and the place of action, the Rome of Augustus.[10]

It seems at the start that the Ovid plot will be dominant, that Jonson will amplify the theme of tension between the generations and the claims of poetry and of the world (the center of the Roman world, the law), even (puzzlingly) that Ovid, surely a major literary figure, will be the "poetaster" of the title. But this is a false lead, and the poetaster proves to be a minor poet and a minor figure in the play. Once Horace appears, the scene is his. He is the Roman "judging spectator" *par excellence*. It is Horace who puts down bad poetry—by making the bad poet bring it up: an emetic purges such barbarisms as *glibbery*, *lubrical*, *furibund*, *prorumped*, and *obstupefact*. The encounter of the true poet and the poetaster, of which this is the conclusion, begins when Jonson with great skill and verve dramatizes almost verbatim Horace's Satire 1.9, which tells of a long vain attempt by the poet to throw off an insistent yapping bore who tags along with him through the streets of Rome. Jonson's Horace too gives his rationale of satire—the distinctively Roman literary form[11]—in a free rendering of Satire 2.1, and in his praise of Virgil pays generous homage to a greater art than satire.

The play is obviously topical, and most commentary has had more to do with London than with Rome, but it is also a free imaginative reconstruction of a place and a historic moment. In writing it, Jonson chooses to locate his play, not in an abstract featureless Florence, as in the first version of *Every Man In His Humour*, or in an Italian island kingdom with St. Paul's Cathedral in its midst, as in *Every Man Out Of His Humour*, or in an Ovidian "Gargaphie," as in *Cynthia's Revels*, but in a city with real districts and streets, real magistrates and actors and lawyers and police spies and good-for-nothings, a real literary milieu of poets and pretended poets, some of them speaking their authentic works.[12] This effort qualified him for the close circumstantial look at Venice in *Volpone* and at London in the succeeding masterpieces of the Folio. The effort to imagine the details of a Rome he never saw may have opened his eyes to the London around him.

The Rome of *Poetaster* is not scenic, not a matter of local color, nor yet an effort to renovate the ruins of time. But it does leave the spectator or reader thinking Roman thoughts. What must seem, on balance, to the literary mind, harmless and amusing and needing at most a satirist or a stern literary critic—the charade of the gods and goddesses with Ovid as Jove and the Emperor's daughter as Juno—can hardly seem so to the incensed Emperor, set on by spies, informers, and jacks-in-office.[13] The authorities burst in upon the silly-clever scene and take it for subversive. Judgment is pronounced and is not revoked, though Horace himself pleads for his fellow poet. The best of rulers cannot, ex *officio*, understand the arts, and there are inequities in even the best policies having to do with morals and with art as reflecting or improving morals. Not only that: the artist, even that most social of private men, Horace, must be brought to see the stringent limits of his own political effectiveness.

2

In the "apologeticall Dialogue" appended to *Poetaster*, the Author in his own person, after some assertions of the power of satire and some pokes at the poetasters of the present, concludes thus:

> Leave me. There's something come into my thought,
> That must, and shall be sung, high and aloofe,
> Safe from the wolves black jaw, and the dull asses hoofe.
>
> (237–39)

We must take this something to be Ben Jonson's next play, *Sejanus*.

The wretched fall of Ovid had brought a moment of pity into a rather cool play otherwise full of serious or humorous literary discussion and social observation: these things, alas, will happen in the best ordered state. But the fall, like the rise of Sejanus calls into question the whole social order that needs and encourages such a man, then destroys him only to permit his replacement by another similar instrument of its will to power and death. The minimum of pity is involved here, but the maximum of terror—the terror of an emptiness at the heart of human affairs. The peace, order, and good government of Augustus yields to, or reveals itself as, the empire of Tiberius.

The reader of poems in the tradition of *The Mirror for Magistrates*, and the playgoer seeing the same tradition dramatized, is quite used to turns of the wheel of fortune—the rise of the great man, often the great evil man, his seeming invincibility, the generation of opposing forces, their consolidation, his fall. *Richard III* and *Macbeth* are examples that come to mind. The first audience of *Sejanus* must have failed its test by expecting simply this.[14]

Sejanus is a villain-hero and a creature of Fortune with a difference. He is the functionary or civil servant as villain-hero, and Fortune proves to be sufficiently embodied in the Emperor. Sejanus is resolute enough in mastering the complications of the city and the world, but he is and must remain the instrument of another. When the Emperor's son Drusus strikes him, he takes it with calculated restraint, contenting himself with winning Drusus's wife and her physician to a plot to poison his enemy. The turn of Fortune's wheel brings him wealth, revenge, all but total power; but his pride, even his insolence, remain servile, and for that reason he can never stand out as the representative human being who is the tragic hero.

If audiences were disappointed in this lethal bureaucrat as protagonist, they must have found the counterforces similarly unsatisfactory. Many perish offstage, appropriately enough, as victims of a civil servant's passion for anonymity. Silius, a military hero loyal to the family of Germanicus and openly disaffected with the regime, is denounced in the senate in a fine black-and-white scene—the darkness of tyranny setting off the white togas of high-minded old-Roman republican sentiment.[15] Subjected to a surprise show trial, he upstages his tormenters with a Stoic speech of eloquent correctness rounded out by a classic example of Stoic suicide. He stabs himself to color his rhetoric with a splash of blood and to show what freedom was, though Tiberius in turn upstages this *coup de théâtre* by expressing formal regret that he had been forestalled in his intended clemency. When the Roman occupation, politics, and the Roman art, rhetoric, have lost their effectiveness in the world of affairs, the Roman philosophy, Stoicism, defines and defends the last frontier of freedom.[16]

A second embodiment of old Rome is lured by a trusted senatorial colleague into making seditious statements while other spies, also senators, skulk in the eaves, taking it all down. Two other senators, Arruntius and Lepidus, frequently appear as disgusted or horrified commentators, almost a chorus, making well-phrased and high-minded comments with an impunity that insinuates to them and to us their irrelevancy to the main action, their futility.

The center of decision may seem to reside in Sejanus, but when we come to see that this is not so, we exclaim "I should have known it!"—always a sign of good dramaturgy. Tiberius is represented as dull, slow, old, apparently hesitant; but really he is always in full control of events, his timing dead right.[17]

According to Suetonius, his stepfather Augustus is said to have spoken the warning, "I pity Rome ground to pieces by his slow jaws," a phrase perhaps taken up by Andrew Marvell in referring to the "slow-chapp'd power" of devouring time; certainly, in this play Tiberius is a sort of hell-mouth into which everyone disappears. Sejanus tells his master of his suspicions of the Germanicus family and their followers and is allowed to think that some measured and discreet procedures against them would not be inappropriate, and so he liquidates them. When, however, he communicates his own desire to make himself more credible and effective in his master's service by a marriage alliance with the imperial house, he is told by Tiberius of possible difficulties with public opinion, but that the matter will nevertheless be taken under advisement. The Emperor then withdraws to Capri and after the third act is seen no more. The perpetuation of the reptilian mind in politics, its menace, its uncreating nullity, are best shown and exercised *in absentia*. Forum and senate, the old political life of the city on the human scale, have been swallowed by Leviathan. *Relegatio in insulam*—exile to an island, sometimes pleasant, sometimes hellish—had long been a measure taken against Romans of the highest rank; by imposing it upon himself, Tiberius seems to be saying, if Capri is a prison, then the world is one.

As his successors might push a button, Tiberius from a distance sends a long and wordy letter *(verbosa et grandis epistola)* to be read to the Senate, precipitating the great reversal of situation. The section of Tacitus's *Annals* that would have reported it is not extant, and so Jonson had to invent it. The ultimate in simulation and dissimulation, it is a rhetorical masterpiece, based on the utmost amplification of the trope of *litotes*, negative statement in positive words, positive statement in negative, a disorienting and spine-chilling mode of utterance.[18]

Jonson is sometimes faulted for combining material from the bright but sensational Suetonius and the somber and deep pondering Tacitus, as if he spread out their histories, and other sources as needed, and put together his play like a jigsaw puzzle. (Actually, it is estimated that not more than a quarter of the play is translated or closely paraphrased.) In his defence, these are the sources that must be used. Jonson himself said that Tacitus "wrote the secrets of the Councill and Senate, as Suetonius did those of the Cabinet [private chamber] and Courte"— both of them (he implies) real secrets.[19] The two sources also agree in large measure; and furthermore, the play makes the necessary choice and is finally concerned not to retail scandal like Suetonius but to deliberate like Tacitus and to come to a judgment of the Empire that includes and adds to his judgment. The plot line shows the resolution of Sejanus to "serve his time and feed his humour" (to quote the Jacobean translation of Suetonius).[20] But to apply to the whole imaginative construct implied by Jonson's sources, one would need as epigraph such a statement of Tacitus as this: "Never surely did more terrible calamities of the Roman people, or evidence more conclusive, prove that the gods take no thought for our happiness, but only for our punishment."[21] So one is bound to think during the long narrative of the fall of Sejanus (closely following Juvenal's Tenth Satire, "On the Vanity of Human Wishes"), recounting his dismemberment by the frenzied mob, the pulling down and melting of his statues, and the vile murder of his children.[22] When this overthrow, the very thing we have been waiting for, even in cold Stoical fashion praying for, is accomplished, the same Emperor continues the same public policies and the same private vices, to the same disapproving and futile comments of high-minded pagans with no more ground of hope for change than Tacitus himself had.

On this note the play ends in the theater, but I cannot believe that it allows the judging spectator to depart thinking only the thoughts of first- or second-century Rome. Tacitus noted in his *History* that, in Judaea, "under Tiberius all was quiet." Ben Jonson and his contemporaries can hardly have thought exactly so. Containing the lurid action of the play, containing the dark political wisdom of Tacitus, is a hidden epigraph, sternly unstated (as is only proper) and yet impossible to suppress, given the date of the action, 31 A.D.: the Prince of this world is judged.[23]

3

Ben Jonson returned to Rome a third time in 1611, after proving in highly successful plays a knowledge of London life and manners in some measure learned from and continuing his imaginative reconstruction of Rome. Galled at the failure of *Sejanus* in the theater, and doubtless also spurred by the success of *Antony and Cleopatra* in 1607 and *Coriolanus* in 1608, he resolved to try again, this time taking as his subject not a relatively unfamiliar story like that of Sejanus but one of the best known incidents in ancient history, familiar to every schoolboy—the conspiracy of Catiline and its discovery and frustration by Cicero. Not only was the material familiar, it even had a clear beginning, middle, and end and lends itself in many details to dramatic treatment.

At the very beginning of the action, the conspirators meet by night to plot the overthrow of all order and a saturnalia of vice and outrage and, according to report, take an oath or *sacramentum* in wine mixed with the blood of a slave killed for the occasion.[24] Theater!

Sallust interpolates a sketch of a woman supporter of the conspiracy, Sempronia, as if to provide Jonson with just his sort of bright, hard-edged satiric scene. I quote the 1608 translation of Thomas Heywood three years before the play:

> Amongst these was Sempronia, a Woman that had committed many virile outrages, above the creation of her sex. In birth and beauty commendable, in marriage and issue fortunate, well seene in the Greeke and Latine languages, and more curious-cunning in musicke and dancing, then well might stand with the reputation of honest. Adorned she was with many other qualities, but such, as were rather to be reckoned provokements unto Luxuria (yet more familiar unto her disposition) then either savoured of decency, or modest behaviour. It were harde to say, whether she were more prodigall, of her purse, or her honesty: so hot of constitution, that she woulde sooner graunt, then stay the asking of a question: beewraying the confidence of those that trusted her, and perfidiouslie dealing with those that credited her: Guilty of murder, and spent by Luxury, the fore-runner of povertie, without hope of recovery. Quicke Witted, a Versifier, frolicke, discoursive uppon any vaine, modest, amorous, or swaggering; whole given to jests and pleasaunt conceits.[25]

Sempronia having so sat for her portrait, Jonson has only to use this material and to add a scene in which she and another woman, Fulvia, discuss cosmetics and lovers and high politics. Fulvia it is who, more from jealousy of Sempronia than from a harlot's heart of patriotic gold, uses her blandishments to induce her conspirator-lover to pass on information to Cicero the consul and thus to precipitate the dénouement.

The great speech denouncing Catiline in the senate chamber is taken not from Sallust but from Cicero's own text. It must have been irresistible to Jonson, as Danton's call for audacity would be for a playwright of the French Revolution or one of Churchill's grand pronouncements for one looking back to the Second World War. Again, rhetoric being the language of conflict, the material is highly dramatic, but this time Jonson clearly misjudged its potential. Always ample and rotund, Cicero on that occasion had every reason to prolong the senators' suspense and Catiline's agony to the utmost, but in the Jacobean theater, where both the substance and the outcome of the speech would already be well known, five minutes of rhetorical aria would have been more effective than fifteen. It was probably here that the play failed in performance. This is unfortunate, for the arrest of the conspirators and the debate in the senate before their execution—including Caesar's speech for sparing their lives and the decisive speech of Cato against them—would have maintained dramatic interest in the last act, framed as they are by Catiline's oration to his army in a hopeless cause (a prefiguration of Milton's Satan) and the eloquent report of his death in battle.[26]

Strict unity of time is virtually impossible in a history play, but Jonson compresses his action into no more than three days, and *Catiline* has remarkable coherence and concentration on a single historical event, partly because his main source, Sallust, for the first time in Rome, is not an annalist but a true historian. Having defined its limits and established its historical center, the play allows the spectator or reader to reach behind and beyond them. The reach extends back to the long turmoil after the final defeat of Carthage, when Rome had to adapt the institutions of the city state to the demands of world power. Antecedent depth is given at the outset when the "Ghost of Sylla," victor in the first great civil war, wills the return of chaos. The historical Sulla, as *ferox* as he was *felix*, had something uncanny and horrid about him, and so he makes a convincing Senecan or Lucanic phosphorescent ghost from hell.[27] The mention of Pompey away on campaign and the presence of Crassus and especially of Caesar remind the historically informed of the next phase of the unfolding historical panorama. The figure of Caesar, encouraging the conspiracy but biding his time and refraining from implicating himself, is particularly fascinating, calling to mind Nietzsche's aphorism that "Catiline is the form of pre-existence of every Caesar."[28] Yet another frame of reference for Jonson's immediate audience is provided by the fresh memory only six years past (made more vivid by a date mentioned in the play, the fifth of November) of the Gunpowder Plot to blow up king and parliament—its betrayal and failure and the execution of the plotters. Jonson himself is thought to have played some part in foiling this attempt.[29]

Given all this richness of implication, why was the play a failure? One speech was too long, much too long, but that is only symptomatic of a deeper cause. Ben Jonson required his audience to think themselves back into republican Rome, to think republican thoughts. The comparable conspiracy in *Julius Caesar* displayed much incidental political rhetoric, but it was a conspiracy against a person, and that person was a usurper of power—a simple political paradigm. Here the conspiracy is against the senate and people of Rome. It challenges the constitution as understood by Cicero—power in the people, authority in the senate—and he confronted it with a coalition of all good men. Now, *potestas in populo, auctoritas in senatu* and *conjunctio bonorum omnium* are not among the maxims of English public life. A Jacobean audience accustomed to an anointed monarch with royal prerogative and a parliament representing the estates of the realm and used to debating the obedience and the liberty of the Christian man must have found the leap back to Cicero's senate and their own school desks too sudden. Perhaps it was too fatiguing to work out the maze of English and Roman parallels, holding king and lords temporal and spiritual and commons at the back of their minds and at the same time promoting to the front praetors and lictors and consuls and the ultimate decree of the senate.[30]

Jonson displays the Republic in its finest hour. The issue is clear—social order or anarchy. Cicero's dream of a unanimity and concerted action of all good men is for the moment realized; the authorities under this leader move decisively and effectively. And, delighting the heart of any Renaissance humanist, the statesman as orator rises to words that match the deed, deeds that match the words. Had the audience, the senate of Jonson's ideal Rome, been as alert and well informed as the playwright and taken this much in, they would have found that he had given more than this to ponder.[31]

The human fallibility of Cicero is a lesson any student of Roman antiquity comes to learn, in the lines and between the lines of Cicero himself, not to mention his contemporaries and later critics—from Cato the Younger, who referred in disapproving oxymoron to "our witty Consul," to Theodor Mommsen, who dismissed him as "ein Mann ohne Einsicht, Ansicht und Absicht." Cicero makes the form of modesty the substance of boast, the form of levity the substance of gravity: his self-deprecation contributes to a color of approbation, and on balance his self-acceptance is almost complete.[32] He is, with Horace in the next generation—and in another play by Ben Jonson—one of the first literary figures to present his own personality and its foibles with humor and the appearance of detachment. Effective as this is, as a lawyer's or politician's dodge, it was in Rome long delayed and severely controlled, doubtless because of the dominance of advocacy and prosecution in rhetoric, law and politics.

The habit had been formed of printing the vices and virtues of litigants or public men as all black or all white. Catiline's conspiracy was real enough, and the consul and the senate were in real danger, and yet there was an element of playacting, or courtroom drama, in Cicero's projection of himself as protagonist, and a maximum infusion of melodrama in the characterization of his antagonist, whose motto seems to have been *fiat iniquitas, ruat coelum*, precluding the insight of St. Augustine, himself a stern moralist, that "even Catiline did not love his own villainies."[33]

After making full allowance for the exigencies of the plot and for the parallels with English events, the Jacobean audience was required to grapple with certain stubborn facts. In a shining hour, acting through its best representative, the Republic employs renegades and spies and harlots, granting them immunity and reward, traps its enemies with ruses and betrayals, bribes the unreliable second consul with a rich province to pillage, and hustles Roman citizens off to execution after senatorial debate but without due trial, this last illegality being protested by that master of improvisation, Caesar, and defended by the strictest of constitutionalists, Cato. Clearly, *Catiline* is a political play for the mature mind, a mind that can distinguish the civil from the moral, that can accept the fact that advocates, prosecutors, and politicians, except when under oath, are not under oath, that can see that extreme measures may be forced upon moderate men.[34] This mature mind must meet a single proviso: it must have been formed and tempered by the study of Rome.

The play did not fail utterly. It continued to be admired and even performed in later years. From the time of the Commonwealth, and especially after the establishment of republics in America and France by students and enthusiasts of the Roman Republic, its categories of thought became more widely accessible. Nevertheless, its time, if it ever quite had a time, had passed. No matter how great the learning of a Renaissance humanist, antiquity must always be both an addition to and a simplification of his whole body of knowledge and experience: classicism is an art of omission. Ben Jonson omitted too little.

4

Rome is present in three plays of the Folio; mention must be made of some Roman absences. Most notable is the absence from the plays (though not of course from the poems) of what may be called the classical temper. However well ordered the construction of *Sejanus* and *Catiline* may be, the characters are often grotesques, gargoyles, their style only intermittently grand, their vision of life far from serene. Jonson is not a Mediterranean writer, and no scene of his could be pictured by Raphael or Poussin.

Again, Jonson's "twelve years a Papist" in his early maturity must surely have turned his thoughts toward Eternal Rome and its church, and yet Christian antiquity seems hardly to exist for him in either of its two idealized forms, the primitive church enduring persecution by the Empire or the undivided church as the Empire's instrument and successor, still less in its demonized form as incipient "Romanism."

What is even more surprising, the pugnacious Jonson never celebrates military Rome or presents a battle scene. In contrast to Shakespeare, all of whose Roman plays are martial, he is concerned entirely with policy and faction, with culture and anarchy, with Rome's idea of itself: he is civic and civil. His sense of dramatic propriety (and his experience as a soldier, doubtless) told him that while arguments on stage are actual, fighting is only virtual.

Finally, Jonson has little feeling for the ruins of Rome, that great perennial theme. He presents the Rome of Horace and Augustus, of Sejanus and Tiberius, of Cicero and Catiline, with hardly a thought of the present dilapidation of the scene. The closest he comes—and it is very far indeed from the plangent laments of Du Bellay and Spenser or the devouring time of Shakespeare's sonnets—is a passage near the end of *Poetaster*. After the judgment on Ovid and Julia, Augustus speaks to Mecoenas, Gallus, Tibullus, and Horace in praise of true poetry, as

> of all the faculties on earth,
> The most abstract, and perfect; if shee bee
> True borne, and nurst with all the sciences.

He who found Rome brick and left it marble is given this Horatian vision of the perdurability of art, the sculpture of rime:

> Shee can so mould *Rome*, and her monuments,
> Within the liquid marble of her lines,
> That they shall stand fresh, and miraculous,
> Even, when they mixe with innouating dust.
>
> (5.1.18–24)

Ben Jonson's Rome was not the travelers' Rome or the pilgrims': it was a country of the mind. This does not mean that it was a free invention. He worked hard at acquiring his Romanity, nor was he the first to do so. He belongs, of course, among the Renaissance scholars. But how many Latin writers themselves also must have first learned to be Romans in the Westminster Schools of their day—Virgil in Mantua, Catullus in Verona, Livy in Padua, Horace in Venusia, Cicero in Arpinus, Seneca and Lucan in Spain. Coming to Rome, they doubtless found they had much still to learn, perhaps to unlearn and relearn. Jonson submitted to a comparable discipline of revision in imposing "truth of argument" on his tragedies. In all three plays he presents great moments of Roman experience—the Republic consolidated for the last time, the golden age of literature in an Empire of hope, and the grinding away of Roman virtue in an Empire of despair. A Renaissance humanist has one permanent advantage over the Roman, whether of the Republic or the Empire: he knows that the Roman story is complete, however it may be reinterpreted. Its story fills the successive minutes of a full circle.

As well as the great extended speeches for which he is remembered, Cicero made a memorable short speech to the people, immediately after the execution of the conspirators. He spoke one word, *fuerunt*, "they have existed." Ben Jonson told his Scottish host that "he heth consumed a whole night in lying looking to his great toe, about which he hath seen tartars & turks Romans and Carthaginions feight in his imagination."[35] This shows how vivid and full-bodied his imaginings were; it also suggests that Roman history was a nightmare from which he was trying to awake. But his waking, appraising, judging mind can always see, and make us see, that "Rome has been," *Roma fuit*. Rome is finished, ended. Rome is finished, complete. Rome is finished, formed and polished in the historical imagination.

Notes

Everyone's first debt, mine included, is to the texts, notes, and criticisms of C. H. Herford and Percy and Evelyn Simpson in their edition of Ben Jonson, 11 vol. (Oxford: Clarendon Press, 1925–52). For Sejanus I am indebted also to the Yale edition of Jonas Barish (New Haven: Yale University Press, 1965) and for Catiline to the Regents edition (Lincoln, Nebraska: University of Nebraska Press, 1973) of W. F. Bolton and Jane F. Gardner.

1. For Martial, see Ian Donaldson, ed., Ben Jonson: Poems (Oxford: Oxford University Press, 1975), annotation and the sources, pp. 387–89; Douglas Duncan, Jonson and the Lucianic Tradition (Cambridge: Cambridge University Press, 1979); Kathryn A. McEuen, "Jonson and Juvenal," Review of English Studies 21 (1945): 92–104; Valerie Edden, "The Best of Lyrick Poets," in C. D. N. Costa, ed., Horace (London: Routledge and Kegan Paul, 1973), pp. 135–39, especially 139–48 on the approval of Horace by Erasmus, the study of him in higher forms of grammar schools and university, his small sales, Jonson's Ars Poetica as the first translation of Horace by a major English poet; Katharine Eisaman Maus, Ben Jonson and the Roman Frame of Mind (Princeton: Princeton University Press, 1984), pp. 11, 17.

2. Kenneth C. Schellhase, Tacitus in Renaissance Political Thought (Chicago: University of Chicago Press, 1976) traces the earliest reference to Tacitus, by Leonardo Bruni in 1403–4; the praise of his style by Linacre, Castiglione, and Elyot, though not by Cheke and Ascham; the great impetus to his reputation given by Justus Lipsius in his inaugural lecture at Jena (1572, published 1607), pp. 18, 102–3, 118. Henry Savile, tutor to Queen Elizabeth, in presenting his versions of the History and Agricola to her in 1591, said "He hath written the most matter with the best conceits in the fewest words of any Historiographer ancient or modern. But he is hard" (p. 157). Muret (1572) characterizes his style as asperum praeterea et insuavem ac spinosum—rough, harsh, and thorny; see P. Burke, "Tacitism," in T. A. Dorey, ed., Tacitus (London: Routledge and Kegan Paul, 1969), p. 151.

3. Michael Grant, Roman Myths (New York: Dorset, 1984).

4. T. S. Eliot, "Tradition and the Individual Talent," Selected Essays (London: Faber & Faber, 1952), p. 15.

5. Dom Adrian Morey, David Knowles: A Memoir (London: Darton, Longman & Todd, 1979), p. 40.

6. The followers of Petrarch took this to extremes, and Guicciardini called a halt: "The Romans ought not to be always on our lips."

7. I have discussed the "earliness" of Coriolanus in "Coriolanus and the Helms of the State," in Patricia Brückmann, ed., Familiar Colloquy (Toronto: Oberon Press, 1978), pp. 148–62, and the Romanness of Antony and Cleopatra in "Dramatic Irony in Antony and Cleopatra," Shakespeare Quarterly 18 (1967): 151–66. The Tragedy of Tiberius (1607; W. W. Greg, ed., Malone Society Reprints, London, 1914) is not a very good play, but the verse is competent and an organizing mind is at work, which is more than can be said for George Chapman's Caesar and Pompey (1631), a sad dégringolade.

8. See Joseph Allen Bryant Jr., "The Significance of Ben Jonson's First Requirement for Tragedy: Truth of Argument," Studies in Philology 49 (1952): 195–213; Ralph Nash, "Ben Jonson's Tragic Poems," Studies in Philology 55 (1958): 164–86.

9. He was not, of course, inerrant: his "Mecoenas" (for Maecenas) strikes one as odd (though it is not confined to Jonson), and he once cites Lucan as a character reference for Julius Caesar (*Masque of Queenes*, 453–54).

10. O. J. Campbell, *Comicall Satyre and Shakespeare's 'Troilus and Cressida'* (San Marino: Huntington Library, 1938) establishes the connection between Elizabethan verse satire on classical models and the plays of Jonson; Alvin Kernan advances the discussion in *The Canker'd Muse* (New Haven, Conn.: Yale University Press, 1959), pp. 54ff; see also Robert C. Elliott, *The Power of Satire* (Princeton: Princeton University Press, 1960). For the sense of the word *satura* see J. Wight Duff, *Roman Satire* (Berkeley: University of California Press, 1936), p. 13; Ulrich Knoche, *Roman Satire*, tr. Edwin S. Ramage (Bloomington: Indiana University Press, 1976), pp. 8–9 (also p. 15, on Casaubon's distinction, made in 1605, between Latin *satura* and Greek satyr-plays). Gilbert Highet, *Juvenal the Satirist* (Oxford: Oxford University Press, 1954), p. 47, speaks of the highlighting of brilliantly vivid pictures, to the neglect of structure, as a "tradition of Roman satire."

11. Quintilian, *Institutio Oratoria*, 4.1.93: *satura quidem tota nostra est*—satire is entirely ours. Horace refers to a certain "Italian vinegar" or sharpness—"*Italo perfusus aceto*," *Satires*, 1.7.32. An early acceptance of sharp laughter at personal oddity is reflected in a large number of family names, as F. R. Gowell points out in *Everyday Life in Ancient Rome* (London: Batsford, 1961), p. 150: "Ahenobarbus, 'red-beard', was applied to the Domitian clan; Balbus, a stammerer, Claudius, the lame, Plautus, flat-feet, Paulus, little, Crassus, fat. The names of animals were applied to others: Asinius, ass, Porcius, pig, Aper, boar, Vitellius, calf; while some had the names of plants: Cicero, chick-pea, Caepio, onion, Tubero, a truffle." He adds that "These soon ceased to be funny as people got used to them." Perhaps because there were so many (I can add Bibulus, Brutus, Caninius, Fabius, Flaccus, Furius, Gallus, Hybrida, Lentulus, Mus, Naso, Ofella, Piso, Pansa, Scrofa, Servilius, Spurius, and Verres), they seem not to have been much used in invective.

12. In Horace's satires, Rome is not in general "either terrifying or grotesque," nor is it very minutely described; see M. T. McGann, "The Three Worlds of Horace's Satires" in Costa, *Horace*, pp. 60–61.

13. Alexander Leggatt, *Ben Jonson: His Vision and His Art* (London: Methuen, 1981), pp. 93ff. on the banquet of the gods; on the character of Ovid, see Gabriele Bernhard Jackson, *Vision and Judgment in Ben Jonson's Drama* (New Haven: Yale University Press, 1968), pp. 20–30. Suetonius (70) says that Augustus took the part of Apollo at a banquet of the gods; Jonson either did not notice or could not use this: what a motive (but, alas, an unworthy motive) it would have given to his outrage at seeing Ovid upstage him as Jove.

14. J. W. Lever, *The Tragedy of State* (London: Methuen, 1971), distinguishes, perhaps a little too sharply, between Jacobean Roman plays and English History plays (p. 14) but asserts, convincingly, that *Sejanus* "amounts to a denial of the moral philosophy underlying such concepts as 'fortune's wheel'" (p. 68).

15. Jacob I. De Villiers, "Ben Jonson's Tragedies," *English Studies* 45 (1964): 433–42, on Silius the self-conscious "noble Roman"; see also Leggatt, *His Vision and His Art*, p. 142.

16. J. M. Rist, *Stoic Philosophy* (Cambridge: Cambridge University Press, 1969) carefully defines what Stoic *apatheia* is and is not (p. 25) and points

out that Seneca's defence of suicide was a new departure in Stoicism (p. 247). The theatricality of tyrannicide and of political suicide is discussed by Ramsay MacMullen, *Enemies of Roman Order* (Cambridge: Harvard University Press, 1966), pp. 70–71, 76.

17. Suetonius, "Tiberius," 21. Donald R. Dudley, *The World of Tacitus* (London: Secker & Warburg, 1968), p. 102: "None of his characters is more carefully stage-managed." This, applied to Tacitus's handling of Sejanus, carries over to Tiberius. R. H. Martin, "Tacitus and his Predecessors," in T. A. Dorey, ed., *Tacitus* (London: Routledge and Kegan Paul, 1969), pp. 135–56, on the way Tacitus modeled his Sejanus on Sallust's Catiline.

18. Tiberius earns honorable mention in Bacon's essay "On Simulation and Dissimulation." Daniel C. Boughner, "*Sejanus* and Machiavelli," *Studies in English Literature* 1 (1961): 81–100, argues that *Sejanus* 1.70–72 derives from *Prince* 7.2.31, and 3.637–46 from the *Discourses*. George Orwell might have cited the letter of Tiberius in his essay on "Politics and the English Language." It should be mentioned that many modern historians doubt the total depravity of Tiberius.

19. Herford and Simpson, *Ben Jonson*, 2:11 for proportions of derived material; 1:136, for Jonson on Suetonius and Tacitus.

20. Suetonius, "Tiberius," 61, in Charles Whibley, ed., Suetonius, *History of Twelve Caesars*, 1 tr. Philemon Holland (London: D. Nutt, 1899), p. 189.

21. Tacitus, *The History* 1:3 (tr. A. J. Church and W. J. Brodribb [London, 1864], p. 3).

22. The passage is discussed by H. A. Mason, "Is Juvenal a Classic?" in J. P. Sullivan, ed., *Critical Essays on Roman Literature: Satire* (London: Routledge and Kegan Paul, 1963), p. 113. Christopher Ricks deals with the culminating image of the play in "*Sejanus* and Dismemberment," *Modern Language Notes* 76 (1961): 301–8.

23. John 16:11. The hiddenness of sacred history within world history is a recurrent theme in the literature of Christendom. For an example congruent with this, see *Antony and Cleopatra* when Caesar Octavius says "the time of universal peace is near" (4.6.4).

24. Herford and Simpson, *Ben Jonson*, 2:117, for passages in *Catiline* taken from Sallust and Cicero. Plutarch (Life of Cicero 10.3) and Sallust both report the blood oath: see Charles Whibley, ed., *Sallust: The Conspiracy of Catiline and The War of Jugurtha*, tr. Thomas Heywood (1608) (London: Constable, 1924), p. 76.

25. Heywood, *Sallust*, 78. M. L. W. Laistner observes that Sallust's "personalities are graphically portrayed, but they are devoid of psychological subtlety. Their treatment reminds one of the 'types' familiar in the New Comedy and its derivatives." *The Greater Roman Historians* (Berkeley: University of California Press, 1947), p. 56.

26. There is, of course, something theatrical about a court of law: see J. Huizinga, *Homo Ludens* (London: Routledge and Kegan Paul, 1949), chap. 4; and Lily Ross Taylor, *Party Politics in the Age of Caesar* (Berkeley: University of California Press, 1949), p. 99: "The cases were divided into sections known as *actiones*, and the prosecutor was known as an *actor*." A. G. M. Nisbet, "The Speeches," in T. A. Dorey, ed., *Cicero* (London: Routledge and Kegan Paul, 1965), p. 62, discusses the "theatricality" of the Catilinarian orations; cf. Herford and Simpson, *Ben Jonson*, 2:124, where Jonson is seen as attracted

to the historical document and "truth of argument." "Sallust is the historian of decline and fall," writes Sir Ronald Syme, and his Catiline is "built up round a villain": *Sallust* (Berkeley: University of California Press, 1964), p. 56; and yet he did not regard the late Republic as "decadent" (16); it was Cicero who exclaimed "O tempora! O mores!"—more than anyone else saturating the vocabulary of republican thought with temporality and the ebb and flow of virtue and corruption, of which Bruce James Smith writes in *Politics & Remembrance: Republican Themes in Machiavelli, Burke, and Tocqueville*, (Princeton: Princeton University Press, 1984), p. 11. For the Satanic in Catiline and Caesar, see William Blissett, "Caesar and Satan," *Journal of the History of Ideas* 18 (1957): 221–32.

27. The ghost is praised by T. S. Eliot, "Ben Jonson," *Selected Essays*, 149–50. For the melodramatic character and appearance of the "morose dictator," see Arthur Keaveney, *Sulla The Last Republican* (London: Croom Helm, 1982), pp. 8–11, 88. The use of history in *Catiline* is first discussed by Lynn Harold Harris in his Yale edition (New Haven: Yale University Press, 1916) p. l–li and his articles, "Local Color in Ben Jonson's *Catiline* . . . ," *Classical Philology* 14 (1919): 273–83, and "Lucan's *Pharsalia* and Jonson's *Catiline*," *Modern Language Notes* 34 (1919): 397–402.

28. Joseph Bryant, "*Catiline* and the Nature of Jonson's Tragic Fable," *PMLA* 69 (1954): 265–77, especially for the balance and contrast of Cicero and Cato, Caesar and Catiline. Nietzsche's aphorism is in *Götzendämmerung*, no. 45.

29. B. N. De Luna, *Jonson's Romish Plot* (Oxford: Clarendon Press, 1967), pp. 35–36, 179.

30. For Jonson's demands on his audience, see De Luna, *Romish Plot*, 291; Angela G. Dorenkamp, "Jonson's *Catiline*: History as the Trying Faculty," *Studies in Philology* 67 (1970): 210–20: "It is in the choruses that the people 'learn their lesson,' the same one which Jonson would have us learn." (p. 218); A. R. Dutton, "What Ministers Men Must, For Patience, Use: Ben Jonson's Cicero," *English Studies* 59 (1978): 324–35: ". . . his audience is directly involved in (as it were) *creating* the play's scale of values" (p. 325). For Roman political categories of thought see Sir Ronald Syme, *The Roman Revolution* (Oxford: Clarendon Press, 1939), especially the trenchant discussion of Cicero, p. 153; Taylor, *Party Politics*, pp. 10–12 on *partes* as the two sides or parts of a case at law extended by Cicero to divisions in the state—*optimates* and *populares*; Donald Earl, *The Moral and Political Tradition of Rome* (London: Thames and Hudson, 1967), pp. 16–17 on the personal basis of Roman partisanship, and p. 23 on the social basis of Roman virtue.

31. Dutton, "Ben Jonson's Cicero," p. 335: "In *Sejanus* and *Catiline* Jonson surely envisages his own ideal audience as themselves members of a Senate—neither sycophants nor time-servers, neither rash nor improvident, but weighing the issues and the arguments, before arriving at a balanced and independent verdict."

32. See Dutton, "Ben Jonson's Cicero," p. 326, for various opinions of Cicero; Thomas M. Greene, *The Light in Troy* (New Haven: Yale University Press, 1982), p. 175, for the implications of the Renaissance debate on Ciceronianism.

33. Cicero, *Orator*, ed. and tr. H. M. Hubbell (London: William Heinemann Ltd., 1942): xxxvii.129: "I have always used a vigorous style, and by this kind of oratory I have often dislodged opponents. . . . The brazen Catiline was arraigned by me in the senate and was struck dumb." For Roman rhetorical

excesses, see Syme, *Roman Revolution*, pp. 149ff., Geoffrey Hill, "The World's Proportion: Jonson's Dramatic Poetry in *Sejanus* and *Catiline*," *Jacobean Theatre* (London: Arnold, 1960), p. 114. Augustine, *Confessions* 2:5.

34. See Nash, "Jonson's Tragic Poems," p. 173; Michael J. C. Echervo, "The Conscience of Politics and Jonson's *Catiline*," *Studies in English Literature* 6 (1966): 341–56. J. S. Lawry, "Catiline and 'The Sight of Rome in Us'," in P. A. Ramsay, ed., *Rome in the Renaissance: The City and the Myth*, Medieval & Renaissance Texts & Studies 18 (1982): 385–408.

35. Herford and Simpson, *Ben Jonson*, 1:141.

Ben Jonson and the Ideology of Authorship

Sara van den Berg

One of the primary metaphors of the Judeo-Christian tradition is the book, its content nature or human nature, its only author God. During the Renaissance this metaphor was significantly altered by the emergence of a new theory of human authorship supported by the philosophy of humanism and the technology of the printing press. The author who claimed to create unique fictions epitomized the humanist concept of the autonomous self. Sir Philip Sidney wrote *An Apologie for Poetrie* in part to refute antihumanist attacks on authors who dared create their own books, but it remained for Ben Jonson to become the first English writer to exploit the humanist concept of authorship by publishing his own collected works in folio.[1]

In "What Is an Author?," Michel Foucault argues that the humanist interpretation of literary texts as the acts of a unique person rests on four distinct definitions of the word *author:* first, a constant level of value in a body of texts; second, a field of conceptual or theoretical coherence in those texts; third, a stylistic unity in their language; and fourth, a historical or circumstantial identification of writing as the person's distinctive act.[2] Jonson's *Workes* (1616) establishes and investigates the new ideology. The frontispiece, the dedications and prologues to the plays, and the poetic collections in the Folio show Jonson working to reconcile the impersonal resources of genre and rhetorical mode with the personal resource of his own unique voice. The frontispiece announces not so much the content of Jonson's book as the power of his personal voice to negotiate the competing claims of timeless ideals and ephemeral commerce in which his art is situated. The semiotic design of architectural facade, allegorical figures, literary inscriptions, and publication data surrounds the central statement of title and author's name to portray a kind of force field in which the poet writes. The claim of authorship so prominent in the dedications is both affirmed and challenged in the poems of *Epigrammes* and *The Forrest*, which take as their major topic the interplay of language and identity. In *Epigrammes* Jonson fears, protests, and struggles to counteract the economic and ephemeral conditions of art by analyzing the public implications of reading and writing and the assumptions that underlie literary judgments. *The Forrest* envisions an alternative world for art, a private realm of intimate conversation and meditation. The poet adopts a public stance in *Epigrammes*, a private stance in *The Forrest*, and each permits a different enactment of authorship. The editorial arrangement of *Epigrammes* and *The Forrest* establishes relationships among the poems that both affirm and question the possible uses of the new ideology. Each criterion of authorship—value, vision, style, and biographical specificity—conveys a particular kind of authority. Each augments, but to some extent qualifies, the rest.

Criticism of Jonson's poetry often centers on one aspect of authorship, making the others subordinate, or sets one aspect in conflict with another. Many critics, for example, celebrate (or condemn) the conceptual unity of Jonsonian poetry manifest in reiterated ideas of self, society, language, and art, while others focus on the stylistic unity of Jonson's work—its distinctive syntax, rhythm, diction, its contours of sound, trope, and dramatic situation.[3] Both thematic and stylistic critics have often placed Jonson's work in the context of literary value, arguing that his aesthetic achievement should be measured against classical and aristocratic principles assumed to be universally valid. Jonson himself makes this claim for a constant level of value, or poetic excellence, declaring in the preface to *Epigrammes* that these poems are "the ripest of my studies" (1.25). He presumably culled these poems from a far larger number, consigning the rest to his bottom drawer. Although there is no preface to *The Forrest*, Jonson emphasized the constancy of poetic value he sought in that collection when, in the preface to *Under-wood*, he privileges both their variety and their excellence: "With the same leave, the Ancients call'd that kind of body *sylva* . . . in which there were workes of divers nature, and matter congested; as the multitude call Timber-trees, promiscuously growing, a *Wood* or *Forrest*; so am I bold to entitle these lesser Poems, of later growth, by this of *Under-wood*, out of the Analogie they hold to *The Forrest*, in my former booke, and no otherwise"

(8.126). Biographical critics have tried to describe Jonson's work as the enactment of his ideals, or have emphasized conflicts and tensions as its hallmark. Whether these conflicts are a matter of internal psychology or external class tensions between the poet and his audience, these critics argue that the rich particularity of phrase, line, and poem often disrupts the thematic and stylistic coherence of Jonson's poetry.[4]

Personal and cultural circumstances combined to occasion the 1616 Folio. By 1616 Ben Jonson had survived the failures of *Catiline* and *Sejanus* and was at the height of his public career. He had a substantial body of works, dramatic and poetic, that met his criteria of literary merit and conceptual coherence. The new dedications he prepared for these works redefine those classical criteria in contemporary terms. He justifies even failures like *Sejanus*, which "begot it selfe a greater favour than . . . [Sejanus] lost, the love of good men" (4:349), and *Catiline*, which had still to contend "against all noise of opinion" (5:431).[5] His professional success was matched by a political atmosphere in Jacobean London newly favorable to publication. By placing himself as author and authority at the center of *Epigrammes* and *The Forrest*, Jonson foregrounds the dramatic action of self in the matrix of present circumstance and past literary tradition. He also foregrounds the relationship between his identity as a unique person beyond the scope of words and his identity as an author charged with maintaining the power of the literary word. Jonson offers a third version of the poetic authority that John Guillory has traced in the careers of Spenser and Milton.[6] Unlike these epic poets, Jonson consistently chooses as the occasion for poetry those moments that clarify the double location of authorship in the golden world of art and the brazen world of circumstance.

The ideology of authorship rests on two major humanist assumptions: the autonomy of the individual and the primacy of texts as vehicles of human community. These humanist tenets, combined with the explosive growth of the printing trade and the number of available texts, led to the further assumption that some instances of language should be attributed to a single person. The new commodification of art, as Joseph Loewenstein has argued, would lead to the emergence of art as intellectual property, "owned" first by the printer but, according to later statutes, by the writer.[7] Jonson's 1616 Folio can serve as a paradigm of the tensions that can result when these assumptions about art as personal expression, vehicle of community, and lucrative commodity intermingle and conflict. Throughout *Epigrammes*, Jonson tests this nexus of competing values by explicitly addressing issues of language, writing, and reading. In *The Forrest*, he tries to develop his own program for poetry.

The portraits of Jonson that date from the seventeenth and eighteenth centuries testify to his success in shaping his own self-representation as author. These portraits, which offer a visual counterpart to Jonson's poetic self-representation, trace the emergence of a complex relationship between man and laureate. In their different versions of the relationship between the idea of autonomous personal identity and the idea of authorship, both portraits and poems enact the dynamic process of self-making and symbol-making that D. W. Winnicott finds common to childhood and cultural experience.[8] Analysis of Jonson's poetry and portraits reveals that the ideology of authorship offered him an aesthetic solution to the problem of identity that confronts the individual person in a culture of individualism; but, like all other solutions, his exacted its own price.

1

The multiple definition of the word *author* worked out in Jonson's Folio is implied in the iconography of the frontispiece.[9] Because Ben Jonson took such care with the preparation of his book, the title page can be considered a visual depiction of his personal ideology in relation to the general ideology of authorship available in his culture. The title, printed in block letters, and his name, printed in script, occupy the central box on the page. Two Horatian allusions are placed prominently in the design: one directly beneath Jonson's name, the other, as an inscription on a building, bisecting the page. As allusion, each quotation links Jonson not to the classical past in general but to the Roman poet he most admired and imitated. Moreover, the content of each quotation links Jonson to the coterie audience of humanist scholars and aristocrats who presumably shared his classical learning and values. The quotation beneath his name makes his purpose plain: "—neque, me ut miretur turba, / laboro: / Contentus paucis lectoribus" [I do not work so that I will be admired by the crowd, but am content with a few readers] (*Sermones*, 1.10.73–74).

The inscribed quotation that bisects the page makes explicit

the principle underlying the visual presentation of literary categories and historical circumstances: "SI[N]GVLA QVAEQV[E]
LOCVM TENANT S[O]RTITA DECEN[T]ER" [Let each particular
variety hold the place allotted to it] (Ars Poetica, 92). The architectural design is segmented into compartments or niches that
posit parallel and hierarchical relationships linking the motives
for art, the genres of drama, and the historical conditions of
staging dramatic works. The small portraits of Bacchus and
Apollo at the top of the page suggest both the disparate motives
for comedy and tragedy, the two sculpted figures that dominate
the page, and the two motives, at once opposed and intertwined,
that generate every work of art. These gods figure not only release and restraint but also emotion and intellect, pleasure and
instruction, and all the other dichotomies so prominent in aesthetic and moral theories of art.

The figures engraved on the facade of Jonson's temple of art
personify ancient and modern genres of drama: tragedy, comedy,
satire, pastoral, and, crowning the page, tragicomedy. Pastoral
and tragicomedy are not represented in Jonson's folio. Their
inclusion on the title page makes clear the ideal structure of
art within which he locates THE WORKES OF Benjamin Jonson.
The three figures grouped at the top of the facade—satire, pastoral, and tragicomedy—represent the fashionable new genres of
the Jacobean theater. By placing them on the shoulders, as it
were, of classical tragedy and comedy, Jonson outlines a theory
of the relationship between classical and contemporary literature reminiscent of that suggested by the windows of the cathedral at Chartres, which portray the writers of the gospels on
the shoulders of the Hebrew prophets.

Missing from the allegorical sculptures on the frontispiece
is poetry, the literary genre that permits Jonson to represent
directly his own speech and his own authority. He chooses
instead to include the words of another poet and his own name
in script. If there is a semiotic image of poetry on the title
page, it may be in these words rather than the indirect mode
of visual allegory. There is one other possibility: the theatrical
design of the page, which figures the Folio itself as a theater,
may find a microcosmic correlative in the structural patterning
of Epigrammes. The placement of Epigrammes just after the
plays serves at least two different functions. First, Jonson labels
his collection of epigrams a "Theater" (8.26), and thereby invites
us to consider the poems as moments of ethical drama. Second,

he emphatically reiterates acts of writing and reading—both his own and others'—and thereby emphasizes the transformation of his plays from stage to page.

The double language of Jonson's title page reinforces this claim. English words detail the particulars of Jonson's book—its title, author, and publication data—and anchor his ideal of art in the facts of commerce. The rest of the page is written in Latin: the allusions to Horace, the labels of different theatrical stages as PLAUSTRUM, VISORIUM, and THEATRUM. These Latin allusions and labels name the double character of the 1616 Folio as at once a collection of dramatic stage plays and a book of literature meant to be read. The transfer of stage works to the printed page is the crucial act of this publication. One step in this process is the depiction of three separate eras or sites of dramatic production: the original play-wagon of Thespis, the Greek theater (which Jonson, perhaps following Thomas Dempster, labels VISORIUM), and the Roman amphitheatre. The first of these, the PLAUSTRUM, is itself an amalgam of ancient and personal signification. The wagon, an emblem of early Greek theater, carries the victorious Thespis, who is presumably on his way to sacrifice to the gods the goat that trots alongside. Because the wagon is clearly of a common English design, Jonson may also intend an allusion to his own history as an actor, which Dekker mocked in *Satiro-mastix*: "Thou hast forgot how thou amble[d]st (in a leather pilch) by a play-wagon in the high way, and took' st mad Ieronimoes part, to get service among the Mimickes" (1.13). Jonson never forgave such mockery, and perhaps the play-wagon of victory is included on his title page in order to transform Dekker's gibe into an emblem of his own professional triumph in this book.[10] In support of this triumph, the title page is architecturally structured as a kind of theater that subsumes all possible dramatic genres and all prior conditions for playing. But this fourth theater, the printed page, transforms ephemeral stage work into eternal literature.

Although the entire book seems designed to exploit the possibilities of the new ideology of authorship in ways that would support Jonson's personal ambition, the 1616 Folio should be set in the context of the print culture newly dominant in Jacobean England. As Richard Helgerson argues, print culture was rife with contradictions and transgressions. The aristocratic assumption that print stigmatizes a writer remained in force despite the recognition that publication also certifies authorial power. In recognition of that power, James I chose to publish his works. Jonson could become the first poet to capitalize on the new medium of print partly because James, who published his works in folio in 1616, replaced the performative, theatrical mode of royal self-representation with the new literary mode of print.[12] Jonson emphasizes this link with James by praising the king as a fellow writer who will value a poet's book (*Epigrammes*, 4). Jonson's dedications to the different segments of the Folio, especially the preface to *Epigrammes*, clearly show that the professional poet did not share the aristocratic fear of print. However, because Jonson sought a coterie audience, he recognized a danger in the accessibility of print and the proliferation of his book as a commodity. Print revealed a writer to every reader and gave every writer an equal claim. The royal appropriation of the new medium of print was more than matched by the accessibility print afforded to dangerous or subversive ideas of the aristocratic opposition and, even more, to those of newly literate citizens from culturally marginal groups. King and poet might use print to confirm their political and aesthetic power, but the medium confers equal authority on every writer and every text. Print, therefore, because it enables a cacophony of texts, highlights the crisis in values, class identity, and the distribution of authority in Jacobean England.[13] It should perhaps be noted in this regard that the frontispiece of King James's *Workes* articulates an ideology of kingship based on religion and peace, figures who represent the divine source of royal power and the political goal of its exercise.[14] That political vision, dramatized so frequently in Jonson's court masques, was constantly under siege in the antimasque of actual circumstance. The crown and the crowd were often, at least implicitly, at odds in print, as they would be in the Civil War.

2

Reading, writing, and speaking are the dominant actions of *Epigrammes*. More than a book of names, *Epigrammes* celebrates language in all its guises.[15] Jonson emphasizes his own relationship to language; he not only writes, but writes about what he reads and how he is read. He reacts not only to what is said, but also to how it is said. For Jonson, language is identity in action, and he dramatizes acts of reading, writing, and speaking to clarify the relationship between language and identity. His own identity is enacted and dispersed in his diverse roles and relationships: as participant in discrete historical occasions, as aspirant to a place in literary tradition, and as writer who seeks a bond with his readers, both his contemporaries and later generations. What is true for the poet is true for those he portrays in poetry and those who read his work. Again and again, a person's use of language offers material for the poet's description and judgment. In the complimentary epigrams, the subject's language and the poet's language are reciprocal, in the satiric epigrams oppositional.

In the humanist model of identity, an individual can take as an ideal the status of an autonomous, unified subject. That Jonson subscribed to that model is inscribed everywhere in *Epigrammes*. Yet subjectivity is always contingent, associative, relational, and incompletely knowable in any one act or even in the aggregate acts of a person. Jonson himself admits failures of language and autonomy. In poems to friends and patrons, he often protests that he cannot say what he feels or fully express what he knows. Language is no more certain than identity. The discrepancy between language and all its referents—speaker, subject matter—is inevitable. The poet, despite his confident stance and humanist hope, is not really sure how to define himself. In the complex world of good and evil, "scarse one knowes, / To which, yet, of the sides himselfe he owes" (102.7–8).

Jonson's self-representation is keyed to the ideology of authorship from the very beginning of *Epigrammes*. The first few poems place the poet as author in four contexts: the classical literary tradition, contemporary society, practical economics, and personal vision. Most critics have noticed that Jonson models these poems on the opening section of Martial's collected epigrams, establishing a basis for his claim that he writes in "the old way, and the true" (18). "To My Booke" (2) introduces the nexus of society, money, and personal integrity that gives urgency and force to his classical art. The epigram divides neatly in half. The first seven lines concern what will be said of *Epigrammes* because he is its author. His catalogue of its supposed properties grows increasingly more anthropomorphic as he lists its (and his) supposed faults, until the book becomes not the stone a madman hurls, but the madman—the poet— himself. Lines 6 and 7 are the pivot of the poem: epigrams hurled by madmen "not caring whom they hit" mark the essential contrast between Jonson and the attitude wrongly imputed to him. He cares greatly whom he hits. Rather than hurl poetic

stones in the second segment of the poem, Jonson sets his book
and its well-tempered language against the "lewd, prophane,
and beastly phrase" of huckster poets who seek only the "loose
laughter" and "vaine gaze" of the carnival world. In the final
couplet, "He that departs with his owne honesty / For vulgar
praise, doth it too dearely buy," Jonson sets integrity against
economics by redefining the act of buying and selling his book
as his own purchase of an identity. By putting his redefinition
in the third person mode of proverb, Jonson lifts personal insight
to the level of abstract principle. He takes refuge not in his
personal worth but in the moral law that mandates proper self-
worth. He not only attacks the lawless world of madness, violence, display, and noise, but counters its "vaine gaze" with
a shrewd revision of his relationship to his book.

In the poem "To My Booke-seller" (3), Jonson probes what
it means to write for money; he seems initially to accept the
world of commerce, but finally protests it. He begins by accepting his own role as a commercial supplier, his book's character
as commodity, and the merchant's judgment of any book as
"good, or bad" according to the number of copies sold: "Use
mine so, too: I give thee leave." But having accepted all, he
tries to control its display and, therefore, his self-representation.
The twelve lines of the poem progressively qualify and deny
what he seems originally to accept. What bothers him most
is the marketing of his book to those who cannot understand
it, or who cannot even read. His only alternative is to insist
on its erasure, first by trying to keep it from such an audience,
finally by urging that it be sold for scrap paper rather than
aggressively ballyhooed. His language, if it carries no meaning,
logically has no value as a commodity, a condition that enables
the poet to reclaim it for himself. Jonson speaks to the bookseller
in the language of commodity and sales, but extracts his own
language from the arena of sales. By diminishing the commercial
value of his words, he contrives to preserve their value in non-
monetary terms of "good, or bad." The poet's shift from deference to defiance is clear in the reversal of "well" and "sell,"
the rhymes that open and close the poem. In the first couplet,
the poet seems to defer to the bookseller, who judges "wisely
well" whether or not a book will "sell." What seems wise marketing to the bookseller is finally condemned by the poet: "If, without these vile arts, it will not sell, / Send it to *Bucklers-bury*,
there 'twill, well." The real erasure of the poet's language is
achieved not by the author but by the bookseller, who would

presumably be quite content to sell any book as scrap paper, preferring a sure thing to the risk of literature. Jonson cannot wholly erase the condition of commerce in which he wrote and published his works, and perhaps he did not really want to do so. The fantasy of reclaiming his language from the remainder table and the scrap pile may be his way of countering his sense that to publish his work is to "crave / For the lucks sake, it . . . favour have." The real dilemma he faces is not just the situation of commerce but his reliance on the "favour" of readers. He began his book by appealing to readers to "reade it well" and "understand" (1), but in this poem he acknowledges a commercial definition of "wisely well" opposed to his own ideal of understanding.

Scattered through *Epigrammes* are poems that praise or deride different readers of his book. The set of complimentary poems addressed to John Donne and the Countess of Bedford exemplify the way Jonson uses acts of writing and reading to establish links between identity and language. Jonson initially portrays himself as an admiring reader of Donne's work (23) and Lucy Harington's character (84). Later, he praises both of them as ideal readers: the Countess reads Donne's satires (94), Donne reads Jonson's epigrams (96). In this strand of poems, all three people are variously depicted as writers, or written texts, or readers.

When language is considered an index to personal identity, originality or unique speech quickly becomes a key issue. Jonson savagely lampoons plagiarists—Prowle, Old-End Gatherer, Poet-Ape, Playwright—whose "small stock" of ideas betrays their own emptiness. Old-End Gatherer not only compiles a book of shreds and patches, but publishes it anonymously so he can claim himself as his own patron (53). If libel is a transgression (54), misrepresentation is even worse, making the plagiarist one with bawds and usurers (57) as Jonson implies by inserting a satiric quip against them in this series of epigrams about writers. The one positive example of a fellow writer and reader in this segment of *Epigrammes* is Francis Beaumont (55). What Poet-Ape takes, Beaumont gives—not ideas or words, but "indulgent thought[s]" and generous appreciation.

Jonson claims authorial status for himself by asserting, through his depiction of others, the importance of writing and reading. He both presents his subjects to themselves and presents himself to us and to himself as, above all, an author. Although his Folio honors the old claims of genre in its separation of plays, poems, entertainments, panegyres, masques, and barriers, the plays are arranged according to chronology rather than dramatic genre, and the entertainments, panegyres, masques, and barriers are not established in classical literary theory.[16] Moreover, the networks of verbal and thematic relationships that transcend generic differences mark the book as a crucial moment in the emergence of a new theory of language as the expression of an autonomous human person.[17] One way for Jonson to initiate such a radically new style is to seek validation for it in tradition, presenting himself not as an original but as a descendent, or even a copy. In this connection, the usual explanation of Jonson's classicism may need revision. That explanation holds that Jonson relied on classical tradition because it gave him a place to stand, exempting him from contemporary constraints of rank and economic status.[18] "I a *Poet* here, no *Herald* am," he declares (9). The very separateness of art is the source of the artist's power. At the same time, Jonson values literature because it reproduces the culture of the past and produces something new, his own authority in the present. He seeks a poetic voice that could dominate both the golden world of poetry and the brazen world of circumstance.

Not all epigrams are written in the first person. The alternation of poetic voice—the subjective first-person mode, the objective third—traces a process of dislocating and relocating the authority of voice. Direct personal statement could be considered the most assertive claim of authority, and the use of the third person mode might mark a slippage of personal power. On the other hand, Jonson's use of this mode may signify that he has the capacity to make impersonal or objective statements of general truth. The use of alternative modes of voice is not limited to the juxtaposition of different poems. Within a single poem, an impersonal description or portrait may end with a personal address. One example is the epigram on Don Surly (28). The poet, as well as his subject, seems to step out of the picture frame, moving from static description to dramatic action. The ending exposes the poet's personal motive for writing what had seemed an impersonal description. This shift reveals that the poem was occasioned by the poet's experience; he is implicated in the narrative. The Surly who judged the poet is now judged by the poet, who, as poet, takes revenge. Yet the weight of the poem remains with the impersonal account that itemizes Don Surly's rudeness. The personal last lines may not be entirely personal after all. The poet speaks for all those who have been abused by this man. The poem is not reduced to personal vendetta, but, by making the poet a spokesman for all Surly's victims, gives voice to their silent rage.

Throughout *Epigrammes*, Jonson plays with the capacity of language to carry more than one meaning. In the acrostic epitaph for Margaret Ratcliffe, for example, language inscribes meaning through the horizontal mode of syntax and the vertical mode of each line's initial letter (40). In satiric poems, dirty puns skewer bawds, lechers, alchemists, profligate heirs, aging ladies, and plagiarists. In poems of praise, the names of Edward Herbert, William Herbert, the Countess of Montgomery, Horace Vere, and other patrons prove to be complimentary puns that can be explicated by references to philology, mythology, history, or the Bible. Language and syntax can separate Jonson from those he condemns, creating a kind of verbal fork in the road, as in the epigram "To My Lord Ignorant": "THou call'st me *Poet*, as a terme of shame: / But I have my revenge made, in thy name" (10). The poet can appropriate and transform the language of his target: Court-Parrat, like My Lord Ignorant, is condemned "to praise me 'gainst his will" (71). In the complimentary epigrams, the reverse is true. Jonson's highest compliment to Camden, for example, consists of dramatizing the Camden in himself (14). Again and again, the poet merges his sensibility with that of men and women he admires.

Jonson repeatedly depicts other people in terms of their relationship with language. They seem, for the most part, disembodied minds in action. Even when they are shown in action— Goodyere hawking (85), the Countess of Bedford sending Jonson a deer (84)—he portrays people as interpreters of their own action. The actions he celebrates in the complimentary epigrams are most often related to language: Goodyere's reverence for books, Lady Bedford's appreciation of Donne's satires, the skillful translations of Savile, the writings of Camden, Beaumont, Donne, Sir Benjamin Rudyerd, and Sir John Roe. Sometimes the poet's praise sets up a network of writers: he summons the ghost of Caesar to praise Clement Edmondes, of Du Bartas to evaluate Josuah Sylvester, even of Sir Philip Sidney to evaluate the Countess of Rutland's poetic talent. Could Sidney read his daughter's works, Jonson declares, he would "better farre his booke" (79). The gentle jesting of the poet's tone disciplines the excess of his fantasies. In his complimentary epigrams, Jonson takes care to distinguish between aristocratic amateurs and his fellow professionals, but emphasizes writing and reading as modes of self-defining activity common to both groups. As he declares to the Countess of Bedford, Donne's ideal reader, "Rare poemes aske rare friends" (94).

Like the complimentary poems, many of the satiric epigrams are addressed to writers or readers. Jonson's satiric epigrams chastise professional hacks (Prowle, Old-End Gatherer) who plagiarize his work, men of no talent (Weake Gamester, Poet-Ape) who imitate it, amateurs (Fine Grand, Sir Annual Tilter) who appropriate it, learned or ignorant readers (My Meere English Censurer, Censorious Courtling, Groome Ideot) who, in different ways, misread it. Throughout *Epigrammes*, Jonson mocks those who seek to purchase or steal poetic fame. Opposed to Fine Grand's purse is the cornucopia of the poet's imagination, its bounty above all purchase: "*Item*, a tale or two, . . . *Item*, the *babylonian* song . . . *Item*, a faire *greeke* poesie . . . *Item*, an epitaph on my lords cock . . . [and] Fortie things more" (73). The question that underlies this vitriolic epigram is quite specific to the situation of Renaissance poetry and patrons: does a patron own the works he requests and buys? Jonson addresses that issue by denying the distinction between being and having. By itemizing increasingly vulgar poems, Jonson tars Fine Grand with their brush. What Fine Grand wants, and gets, defines him.

Readers who buy are no worse than rival writers who steal, who cannot tell that their shreds and patches, their attempts to fleece the public, will never be taken for a golden fleece. Men like Prowle and Old-End Gatherer lack the true poet's integrity and scope. To steal for gain is to admit a hollow core where imagination and vision should reside. Yet Jonson's attacks on such men acknowledge the commercial situation of his own art, a situation in which the new ideal of originality and personal attribution of a work has replaced the earlier ideal of anonymity or diffidence.

Only in the satiric epigrams does Jonson rely on physical specificity, reducing a person to a single feature or physical trait: Chev'ril's sweat, Person Guiltie's ulcers, Lady Would-Bee's handsome figure, Pertinax Cob's one good part, Sir Cod's foul odor, Gut's entire body, a "thorough-fare of vice" (118). But even these are relatively atypical. More often Jonson takes as his target a verbal tic or use of language: Lieutenant Shift's pet phrase, Brayne-Hardie's empty boasting, Lippe's histrionic attacks on the stage, the New Statesmen's wrongheaded whisperings, the Town's Honest Man's gossip-mongering, even Reform'd

Gamester's suspect discovery of the Bible, "the word / Quick in his lips" (21).

In the satiric epigrams, Jonson often mocks men and women by turning their own words against them or by transcribing their actions as a kind of speech. People speak what they are. "Language most shewes a man," Jonson argues in *Discoveries,* "Speak, that I may see thee" (2031–32). False speaking, hypocrisy, even silence can show a man. An incompetent lawyer like Chev'ril succeeds more by silence than by speech but gets paid for both (37). Don Surly argues, laughs, blasphemes, berates; all varieties of misspeaking are motivated by his overweening desire to have "the glorious name / Of a great man" (28). His words backfire; the world can judge language by norms not recognized or valued by the speaker. There is, for Jonson, a moral reality beyond the play or manipulation of language.

Language, however insufficient, remains an index to his subjects' being and to the poet's own identity. In the complimentary epigrams, questions of language and identity coalesce around the vexed issue of truth and flattery. Poems to Mounteagle (60), Cecil (63–64, 66), and Suffolk (67) assert Jonson's paramount need to protect truth from slipping into insincere formulaic praise. What must be maintained is the autonomy of the poet, his separation from the pressures of the patronage system; yet the claim to be separate is necessary to secure him real success in that system. The rage that erupts in "To My Muse" (65), originating in Jonson's disgust with his own mistaken judgment, spews in all directions—against the false lord, against his own errors, against poetry. Once focused on language, his anger occasions revision upon revision, until he concludes that the truth or falsehood of language finally reflects on its object, not on the language of encomium or on the poet. By recovering his faith in language, he recovers faith in himself.

The power of language transcends the poet's command of language. Jonson's distinctive voice is his great poetic achievement in *Epigrammes* and *The Forrest,* the presence in language that manifests and is supported by his humanist ideology, yet self-expression is not his primary goal. Writing gives to image the power to depict truth, and Jonson inscribes his unique ethical and aesthetic sensibility in order to affirm a common language greater than his own. The Jonsonian style and idiom are designed to show his own continuity with literary tradition, and it is perhaps a sign of his success that that style would prove both imitable and compelling for later writers from the Sons of Ben to Yeats and Auden.

The opening poems of *Epigrammes* define the book as the mirror of the poet, yet insist on the traditional distinction between the author and his book when he wants to claim his own authority to define authorship. The "I" that is dramatized throughout the book is not just ego but "subject": self represented to itself. This self-representation, precisely because of its condition of awareness, is grounded in alienation or separation as the defining trait of the subject. The solitude of identity is manifest in the inevitable discrepancy between "I" and any linguistic representation of "I." Any self-representation is inevitably a substitution for unmediated access to self. Conversely, any representation of another person both is and is not the person represented. The discrepancy between signifier and signified is the fundamental feature of symbolic thought in poetry. Moreover, because identity is only knowable as representation, it is always achieved in action and is therefore contingent, associative, relational, anecdotal. Because these necessary properties of identity frustrate its claim to stability and form, it becomes an undefinable object of desire. The poet may split himself between what he does in the poems and what he says as the poet who writes the poems, but his goal is to overcome that split or condition of self-separation. He splits himself, or limits himself to single acts, in order to seek an overarching, stable identity that can subsume all actions.

In these psychoanalytic terms, Jonson's book can be called a "transitional object": the me / not me in which self and other are reunited in an act of substitution or symbolic play.[19] Such play originates in response to the trauma of childhood, when the infant undergoes the intertwined processes of separation and individuation. The imaginary union with the mother is lost and mourned; the child substitutes symbolic equivalents and, simultaneously, develops a new desire for separate selfhood, for individuation. Those two desires—to merge and to separate—are mastered through the complex actions of creative play. For Ben Jonson, literature as transitional phenomenon could serve the twin needs of separation and individuation, of loss and gain. The ethical and aesthetic judgments enacted in the dyadic poems of *Epigrammes* and *The Forrest* are most often grounded in a relationship between the poet and one person. The poet uses the occasion of each relationship to affirm his own relationships with literary predecessors who are lost to him except in the substitutive mode of imitation and emulation, and with the general reader, who is likewise uncertainly knowable and whose response cannot be entirely controlled.

What is said of the poet can be said of readers as well. We can describe the pleasure of reading as losing ourselves in order to find ourselves. We may identify with the writer, but must at some point pull away, only to find that separation necessary to our progression from identification to identity.[20] Jonson's turn away from his readers, through the parodic mockery that ends *Epigrammes* and the private meditation that ends *The Forrest*, argues his trust that they share the double desire for separate identity and for merged understanding that pervades his book.

3

That desire is sheltered in a world of art as privileged as Penshurst or Durrants in *The Forrest*, which gathers together disparate poems Jonson composed or revised during his affiliation with the Sidney circle. Although the theme of reading and writing is less obtrusive and programmatic than it was in *Epigrammes*, Jonson uses the intimate modes of lyric and conversational epistle to enunciate his sense of a poetic career. He takes the measure of many kinds of writing; offers himself as a true mirror—norm, judge, and friend—of his subject; and, in a pair of epistles written ten years apart, records the different stages of his apology for poetry. Mirroring, the dominant metaphorical act of the epistle to Lady Katherine Aubigny, constitutes his final understanding of the poet's role.[21] This metaphor sums up the dialectic between self and self-representation, and between self and other, inherent in his poetry of personal relationship.

In *The Forrest*, far more than in *Epigrammes*, the poems are to or about women: Catullan lyrics to Celia, Horatian epistles to aristocratic brides. For Jonson, the world of privacy is emblemized by the life of women and its major actions of courtship, marriage, and motherhood. As a patriarchal poet, he invests women with particular importance as vessels of morality and virtue. "To the World," one of the most explicit statements of moral choice in the book, is even composed in a woman's voice (4). The one satiric epigram in the book, "To Sicknesse," takes the measure of self-absorbed, licentious wives. Mothers are especially important in the poetry of *The Forrest*. In the brief Anacreontic lyric that opens the book, Cupid's narrative of "MARS, and my *Mother*" sets up a network of desire linking gods and poets. This erotic model is countered by the idealized image of the Virgin Mary in the unnamed gentlewoman's lament (4), and by a succession of portraits of aristocratic wives. Lady Barbara Sidney is especially praised for teaching her children "the mysteries of manners, armes, and art" (2). The original ending of the epistle to the Countess of Rutland conveyed the poet's wish that she "bear a son," while the entire epistle to Lady Katherine Aubigny was designed to celebrate her impending motherhood.

Both Lady Aubigny and the poet value identity, the solitary way Jonson celebrates in moral language of judgment. Yet both of them also seek an ideal relationship that permits them to see themselves in another's eyes. The act of looking into a mirror to see oneself—and initially everything is a mirror—Jacques Lacan describes as the phase of the "specular I."[22] Modifying Lacan's theory of the mirror stage, D. W. Winnicott has declared that the first mirror is the mother.[23] That is to say, what a person sees offered by the mirror is the self initially offered by the mother. What the person continually seeks is a substitute for that 'true' mirror, a relationship of holding and valuing oneself.[24] Yet the "I" seen in the mirror will finally be recognized as forever different from the "I" who gazes therein; the "I" in the mirror is an idea never entirely coeval with the gazing "I." One way to cope with that dichotomy is to embrace symbolic substitutions, from transitional objects (teddy bears, blankets) to transitional phenomena (religion, politics, art) to personal relationships (marriage, parenthood). All of these have the capacity to offer the self to the self while maintaining their own integrity or otherness. They are, that is to say, dialectical. Lacan describes the end of the mirror stage as the moment that "inaugurates . . . the dialectic that will henceforth link the I to socially elaborated situations."[25]

Authorship is one way to recapture the ideal of the "specular I" and establish it as a condition of the "social I." It is as author, therefore, that Jonson regards himself as analogous to Lady Aubigny; both of them are alone by choice, both of them choose relationships with the few people they admire and who verify their ideas of self. Deference, however, requires that he offer not himself but his poem as a mirror in which Lady Aubigny can see "Your selfe but told unto your selfe": "No lady, but, at some time, loves her glasse. / And this shall be no false one." Repeatedly, he sets his poem against false mirrors, false sight, and the false sights of "spectacles, and showes." He derides those who "cannot see / Right, the right way," and warns her not to expect truth from the false world: "none askes / For truthes complexion, where they all weare maskes." The specular gaze in this poem belongs not to the poet but to the lady's loving husband. In lieu of the imaginary order of unmediated identity, which is emblemized in the relationship between poet and lady, Jonson offers her a poetic vision of a new order of identity, realized in the substitutive merging of a loving marriage: "Live that one, still." At the time Jonson wrote the poem, Lady Aubigny was pregnant with her first child; this poem tacitly assumes that she will be an ideal mother because she has first mothered herself, accepting both the solitary oneness of personal identity and the compensatory oneness of her marriage with Aubigny.

Winnicott, meditating on the distorted faces in the paintings of the modern British artist, Francis Bacon, emphasizes the importance of the face in human relationships. To see faces as distorted, Winnicott contends, reveals profound deprivation in the gazer.[26] An infant who cannot see, or is not given, itself in the mother's eyes will withdraw, he writes, if efforts to placate or win over the mother's face fail. Jonson consistently attacks the "studied arts" of the false world that "strut[s], and paint[s]" (4), and to counteract it offers the true book of the plain face, unadorned by paint and pretence. Those who accuse Jonson of misogyny often regard his metaphorical preoccupation with cosmetics as a sign of his dislike of women. "To Sicknesse" (8), a strongly gendered satiric epigram, begins by lamenting that smallpox attacks women and urges it to prey on men instead. But the poet reconsiders, and encourages the disease to prey on women who "at common game / Play away, health, wealth, and fame," and then waste exorbitant sums on "decoctions" like "spirit of amber" or "oile of Talke [talc]" to hold at bay the physical depravity that attends on their behavior. Overtly the poem posits a contest between the sexes, but covertly it depends on the disparity between moral and immoral women. If Jonson were a misogynist, one might expect his poem to depict the same women transformed from paragons to paramours. Instead, his focus remains an attack on specific kinds of behavior measured against the strong moral ideal he shares with worthy women. More important, the placement of this poem with others to and about women requires far more careful attention to Jonson's actual relationships with women. The covert moral compliment in this poem suggests that it may have been occasioned by the disfigurement of Lucy Harrington, Countess of Bedford.[27]

Although recent critics have argued that the juxtaposition of satiric and complimentary poems compromises the poet's act of praise, it can just as well be argued that each heightens the effect and the integrity of the other.[28] In this regard, the attack on promiscuous women in "To Sicknesse" augments the many compliments to women elsewhere in The Forrest. The poet's mirroring book becomes a kind of prism in which a reader can see what she is, what she might be, and what she is not. Equally important, in the mirror of women the poet can see himself.

In The Forrest, for the first time in the Folio, Jonson declares himself a Christian and explores the utility of words in the service of the Word—an essential component of humanist faith. It is remarkable that he does so only in The Forrest: in the epistle to Wroth, in the gentlewoman's complaint "To the World," and in the meditative lyric "To Heaven." It is tempting to say that he posits faith as an antidote to the sterile, confining framework of secular speculation, in which all relationships are reduced to a problematic relationship between self and an other who is somehow always a version of self. Faith does not prevent language but enables it. Without faith, the poet must finally fall silent, trapped in words that are no more than self-representation and therefore merit no other's interest.

Jonson's alternative to silence and bad faith is the defense of poetry articulated in the four Horatian epistles that loom above the other poems of The Forrest. His poems to Sir Robert Sidney and Sir Robert Wroth are meticulously detailed and specific, alternating between the language of fact and the language of metaphor, between literary model and immediate statement. This is the poetry of community, written in the languages of celebration and good counsel. His epistles to the Countess of Rutland and Lady Katherine Aubigny offer two quite different apologies for poetry. The first claims art as a universal timeless act of public statement. The second defends poetry as a private timely act of intimate conversation. The human love celebrated in the "Epode" (11) and dramatized in these two epistles is subsumed into the divine grace affirmed in the last lyric of The Forrest. The poet's act of faith in "To Heaven" (15) marks the last step in his poetry of dialectic. Surrounded by the gazes of a hostile world, he grounds faith in the fact of loss, self in the limited power of self, setting fault against grief as he seeks the salvation of his soul. He sets the loving, just "witnesse" of God against the staring, misjudging world that thinks him "sad for show." His faith in an absent, unknowable, but all-loving God is possible because of the child's experience of separation from a loving mother. This experience motivates subsequent religious quest, and, Winnicott suggests, is replicated in the visionary action of seventeenth-century religious verse.[29]

4

Jonson's ideology of authorship had to comprehend the paradoxical nature of language and its power as a mirror. On the one hand, language defines self; it is the way self presents self to itself. On the other hand, language is the 'not-self' as well, the vehicle of community, its meaning larger than any single speaker or speech act. To use language as a means of self-definition is to be used by language. The opposition of self and language is made plain in the paradoxical definitions of *subject* common in English. The word can denote a position of weakness, what is governed or perceived or studied. This is the most common use of the word in Jonson's poetry, whether to designate the king's subjects (*Epigrammes*, 35, 36, 51, 94) or the subject of the poet's art (*The Forrest*, 10, 12). *Subject*, in other words, can designate either the gazer or the person gazed upon, the person who studies or who is studied. The subject as object is subjected to the power of the acting, gazing subject.

Ben Jonson is virtually invisible in the 1616 Folio. There is no portrait (as there had been for Daniel in 1601 and would be for Drayton in 1619 and for Shakespeare in 1623).[30] The poems in the Folio offer no description of his appearance or personal quirks. Instead of seeing the poet, we hear his responses and judgments. He is mind, feelings, principles, and values, embodied entirely in a language of assertion and judgment. It is only later, in the poems of *Under-wood*, that Jonson tries to address the corporeality of the self by using his body as subject matter and metaphor in a series of poems about visual and verbal self-representation. The most well known is his lament to Sir William Burlase, "With one great blot yo'had form'd me as I am" (*Under-wood*, 52). For a man of language, the best vehicle for self-representation, albeit idealizing and selective, is not the canvas but the page. Jonson's preference is especially evident in "My Picture Left in Scotland," which sets the poet's "sweet" language against his "mountaine belly" and "rockie face" (*Under-wood*, 9).

Yet throughout the poems of the 1616 Folio Jonson gives new urgency to the traditional theory of *ut pictura poesis* by exploiting the metaphor of the face as a primary text of self-representation.[31] As he declares in *Discoveries*, "Man is read in his face" (522). His satirical poems delineate his rage at faces that fail to represent truly the person or the poet. Throughout *Epigrammes*, he lashes out against the false faces of society's masquerade: Something's "great face" (11); Don Surly's "tympanies of businesse, in his face" (28); the "Blowne up" (90) face of Mill's aging lover; the "slight faces" made by the Ripe Statesmen (92); the Town's Honest Man's constant "shifting of it's faces" (115); Mime's frenetic activity until his "face doth hit / On some new gesture, that's imputed wit" (129). In the preface to Pembroke, Jonson describes court life as a kind of funhouse of unsatisfactory mirrors and masques, acceptable only if those who inhabit it acknowledge their masquerade: "I would rather know them by their visards, still, then they should publish their faces at their perill, in my *Theater*" (8.26). Jonson later reversed the direction of the metaphor in his epistle to Lady Aubigny, defining a true book as a true mirror. This version of the metaphor recurs in a later poem, which defines a good book as a mirror which wicked and foolish men avoid: "an ill man dares not securely looke" on such a book, "but will loath, or let it passe, / As a deformed face doth a true glasse" (*Ungathered Verse*, 24).

What holds for men in general is especially true of the poet himself, and the sequence of portraits of his face dramatizes how that symbolic book was revised in the course of his career. The changes in Jonson's relationship to the ideology of authorship can be traced in these paintings and engravings. In all these works, the locus of authority seems hard to discern. The poet is subject to the gaze of the painter, and subsequently, to that of anyone who sees the portrait. Conversely, the poet's evasion of or confrontation with the viewer enables him to retain or reclaim authority.

The most important portrait of Jonson, and the source of many copies and adaptations, has been attributed to Gerrit van Honthorst, but is now thought to be the work of Abraham van Blijenberch, a Dutch painter resident in London from 1617 until 1620. Along with Paul van Somers and Daniel Mytens, van

Blijenberch introduced into England a melancholy, or introspective, Dutch style of portraiture that quickly replaced the Elizabethan style of lavish display. Jonson's enormous head and shoulders fill van Blijenberch's canvas, the rough brush strokes conveying a sense of the man as somehow larger than life. His intense, huge eyes seem to turn away from the painter and inward in search of himself. This portrait gives us only the poet, without any classical ornament.[32] Van Blijenberch's portrait was the basis for Robert Vaughan's engraving for the 1640 Folio of Jonson's works, but Vaughan places on Jonson's head an ill-fitting laurel wreath. The awkwardness of the image suggests something of a disparity between Jonson's ineluctable reality and the constraints of the public idea of the poet. The transformation of man to laureate is complete in William Marshall's engraving of a classical bust of Jonson in the duo-decimo edition of the poems in 1640.

In a later portrait, the painter and current location of which are unknown, Jonson is surrounded by the trappings of classical art and the tools of his trade—paper, pen, and books. Herford and Simpson have dismissed this painting, which once belonged to Booth Tarkington, as a mediocre eighteenth-century work; David Piper speculates that it might date from the mid-seventeenth century.[33] The likeness seems to be taken from the van Blijenberch portrait but extended and amplified in the style of William Dobson, who portrayed several Caroline courtiers against similar backdrops of drapery, statuary, and books.[34] The portrait may have been a memorial image created after the poet's death. In any case, Jonson's stance of power and achievement in this portrait does not square with what is known of his later years.

The poet's straitened circumstances are portrayed in only one portrait, which David Piper rightly describes as unprecedented and unique.[35] In this "begging portrait," the poet holds up the manuscript of some Skeltonic verses imploring John Burgess, clerk of the Exchequer, to forward his overdue pension (Underwood, 57). The poem and the painting are at once a rueful joke, a plea, and an act of rage, as the poet is forced to admit the constraints on his autonomy that accompanied his decline from preeminence. The figure of Fortune that decorates his inkstand, placed in the lower lefthand corner beneath the manuscript, underlines the diminished condition of the poet and the humiliation that attends it.

If writing as an institution manifests the values of other in-

stitutions in its society, each writer nevertheless develops a
personal ideology never entirely congruent with the general ideology. This conflict between the general and the personal is
a prominent feature of Jonson's poetry. It has often been inter-
preted as a sign of his personal psychological conflict; he has
even been labeled "an artistic schizophrenic."[36] However, the
conflict is not simply a matter of one man's psychology. To
understand the way Jonson finally locates authority in the drama
of personal and poetic relationships, it is not sufficient to attend
only to literary tradition, or to Jonson's moral and aesthetic
thematics, or his stylistic traits, or to his biographical circumstances. All of these prove crucial to his ideological understanding of himself as an author. The conflicting models of authorial
identity that were possible to him derived less from his personal
psychology than from the culture in which he lived. That is
not to say that psychology can be eliminated in favor of a contest
between competing ideologies. The acts of self-making and
symbol-making that Winnicott and other psychoanalysts have
described are reenacted in the face of the poet and in his book.
His language of self-representation is his own, as he confronts
not only his identity but his isolation. All the patterns of ordering his poems—juxtaposition, sequence, thematic or dramatic
reiteration—can be read as insoluble conflict, paralyzing paradox, or bracing multiplicity. The possibility of these mutually
exclusive interpretations testifies to autonomy as a condition
that is necessarily provisional.

The painting of van Blijenberch portrays Jonson as an unique
autonomous human person. When the van Blijenberch likeness
is overlaid with a laurel wreath (in Vaughan's engraving) or
surrounded by professional accessories (in the Booth Tarkington
portrait), the relationship between the new ideology of authorship and the ideology of the free human subject seems less
congruent than might be supposed. The Tarkington portrait,
whether painted in the seventeenth or the eighteenth century,
prettifies the intense work of van Blijenberch and subdues the
poet's personal presence to a system of literary practices and
honors. The public ideology epitomized in Marshall's engraving
becomes so powerful a tool of defining the man that at least
one eighteenth-century engraver published as Ben Jonson a toga-
clad and laurel-wreathed portrait now known to be derived from
a miniature of Peter Oliver painted by his father, Isaac Oliver.[37]
The "begging portrait" offers an image of the poet both trapped
and freed by writing, an image that goes beyond even the inten-

sity of van Blijenberch's painting. In this portrait, as in so many poems of Under-wood, the poet who had designed the 1616 frontispiece to minimize the commercial nature of his book now puts his self-representing art to the service of his own economic need. The majestic 1616 Folio has been reduced to a single page. The autonomy of the author has been compromised by the dependency of the man.

Notes

1. See Richard C. Newton, "Jonson and the (Re-)Invention of the Book," in Classic and Cavalier: Essays on Jonson and the Sons of Ben, ed. Claude J. Summers and Ted-Larry Pebworth (Pittsburgh: University of Pittsburgh Press, 1982), pp. 31–58. See also Sir Philip Sidney, "An Apologie for Poetrie," in Elizabethan Critical Essays, vol. 1, ed. G. Gregory Smith (London: Oxford University Press, 1904), pp. 148–207. On the new technology of print, see Elizabeth Eisenstein, The Printing Press as an Agent of Change, 2 vols. (Cambridge: Cambridge University Press, 1979).

2. Michel Foucault, Language, Counter-Memory, Practices: Selected Essays and Interviews by Michel Foucault (Ithaca: Cornell University Press, 1977), pp. 113–38.

3. On Jonson's theme of selfhood, see Thomas Greene, "Ben Jonson and the Centered Self," Studies in English Literature 10 (1970): 325–48; on society, see Hugh Maclean, "Ben Jonson's Poems: Notes on the Ordered Society," in Essays in English Literature from the Renaissance to the Victorian Age, Presented to A. S. P. Woodhouse, ed. Millar Maclure and F. W. Watt (Toronto: University of Toronto Press, 1964), pp. 43–68, and contra Maclean, Raymond Williams, The Country and the City (New York: Oxford University Press, 1973), pp. 26–34. On Jonson's language and style, see Wesley Trimpi, Ben Jonson's Poems: A Study of the Plain Style (Stanford, Calif.: Stanford University Press, 1962); Judith Kegan Gardiner, Craftsmanship in Context: The Development of Ben Jonson's Poetry (The Hague: Mouton, 1975); and Richard S. Peterson, Imitation and Praise in the Poems of Ben Jonson (New Haven: Yale University Press, 1981).

4. See Arthur Marotti, "All About Jonson's Poetry," ELH 39 (1972): 208–37, and Stanley Fish, "Authors-Readers: Jonson's Community of the Same," Representations 7 (1984): 26–58.

5. For additional self-justifying statements, see Jonson's ode to himself (Under-wood, 23).

6. John Guillory, Poetic Authority (New York: Columbia University Press, 1983), pp. 21–22.

7. Joseph Loewenstein, "The Script in the Marketplace," Representations 12 (1985): 101–14.

8. D. W. Winnicott, Playing and Reality (London: Tavistock Publications, 1971).

9. My analysis of this design builds on information provided by Margery Corbett and R. W. Lightbown in The Comely Frontispiece: The Emblematic

Title-Page in England, 1550–1660 (London: Routledge & Kegan Paul, 1979), pp. 145–52. See also the provocative analysis of the Folio title page and catalogue in Timothy Murray, *Theatrical Legitimation: Allegories of Genius in Seventeenth-Century England and France* (New York and Oxford: Oxford University Press, 1987), pp. 23–104, esp. pp. 65–76.

10. I am indebted to Jennifer Brady for this suggestion.

11. Peter Stallybrass and Allon White, in *The Politics and Poetics of Transgression* (Ithaca: Cornell University Press, 1986), pp. 27–79, argue that Jonson embraced an "elevated" concept of authorship "in opposition to the theatre and the fair" (p. 77). On Jonson's attitude toward his audience, see Peter Carlson, "Judging Spectators," *ELH* 44 (1977): 443–57, and John Gordon Sweeney III, *Jonson and the Psychology of Public Theater* (Princeton: Princeton University Press, 1985).

12. Richard Helgerson, "Milton Reads the King's Book: Print, Performance, and the Making of a Bourgeois Idol," *Criticism* 29 (1987): 1–25, esp. pp. 2–8.

13. Helgerson, "Making of a Bourgeois Idol," pp. 3–8; J. W. Saunders, "The Stigma of Print: A Note on the Social Bases of Tudor Poetry," *Essays in Criticism* 1 (1951): 139–64. Annabel Patterson reads *Under-Wood* in light of Caroline political crises in "Lyric and Society in Jonson's *Under-wood*," in *Lyric Poetry: Beyond New Criticism*, ed. Chaviva Hošek and Patricia Parker (Ithaca: Cornell University Press, 1985), pp. 148–63.

14. Corbett and Lightbown, *Comely Frontispiece*, pp. 137–45.

15. On *Epigrammes* and the theme of naming, see David Wykes, "Ben Jonson's 'Chast Booke'—The *Epigrammes*," *Renaissance and Modern Studies* 13 (1969): 76–87; and Edward B. Partridge, "Jonson's *Epigrammes*: The Named and the Nameless," *Studies in the Literary Imagination* 6 (1973): 153–98.

16. Jonson's own comments in *Discoveries* show the continuing power of literary genres and rhetorical modes in literary practice, but he reserves his strongest writing for his opinions of specific authors.

17. See Hanna Gray, "Renaissance Humanism: The Pursuit of Eloquence," in *Renaissance Essays*, ed. Paul O. Kristeller and Philip Wiener (New York: Harper and Row, 1968), pp. 199–216, and Richard A. Lanham, *The Motives of Eloquence* (Berkeley: University of California Press, 1976).

18. See Don Wayne, *Penshurst: The Semiotics of Place and the Poetics of History* (Madison: University of Wisconsin Press, 1984), and Katharine Eisaman Maus, *Ben Jonson and the Roman Frame of Mind* (Princeton: Princeton University Press, 1984).

19. D. W. Winnicott outlines this concept in "Transitional Objects and Transitional Phenomena" (1951), in *Playing and Reality*, pp. 1–25.

20. On the processes of separation and individuation, see Margaret Mahler, *On Human Symbiosis and the Vicissitudes of Individuation* (New York: International Universities Press, 1968), pp. 7–31; and Margaret Mahler, Fred Pine, and Anni Bergman, *The Psychological Birth of the Human Infant: Symbiosis and Individuation* (New York: Basic Books, 1975). On reading and pre-oedipal pleasure, see James Strachey, "Some Unconscious Factors in Reading," *International Journal of Psychoanalysis* 11 (1930): 322–31, and my discussion of reading in "Reading and Writing Dora: Preoedipal Conflict in Freud's 'Fragment of a Case of Hysteria,'" *Psychoanalysis and Contemporary Thought* 10 (1987): 45–67.

21. For another interpretation of the theme of mirroring in the epistle to

Lady Aubigny, see William Cain, "Mirrors, Intentions, and Texts in Ben Jonson," *Essays in Literature* (Macomb, Ill.) 8 (1981): 11–23.

22. Jacques Lacan, "The mirror stage as formative of the function of the I," *Ecrits*, tr. Alan Sheridan (New York: W. W. Norton and Co., 1977), pp. 1–7.

23. D. W. Winnicott, "Mirror-role of Mother and Family in Child Development" (1967), *Playing and Reality*, pp. 111–18.

24. Winnicott describes the importance of the "holding relationship" in "The Theory of the Parent-Infant Relationship," *The Maturational Processes and the Facilitating Environment* (New York: International Universities Press, 1965), pp. 37–55. For an extended clinical example, see *Holding and Interpretation: Fragment of an Analysis*, ed. M. Masud Kahn (New York: Grove Press, 1986).

25. Lacan, *Mirror Stage*, p. 5.

26. Winnicott, "Mirror-role of Mother and Family in Child Development," pp. 111–18, esp. p. 117.

27. See Jonson's related epigram on smallpox (*Under-wood*, 34). In *Conversations with William Drummond* (348–49) he comments on the smallpox that disfigured Sidney's mother. *The Forrest* 8, however, may have been occasioned by his sympathy for another smallpox victim, the Countess of Bedford, who withdrew from public life after her face was ravaged by the disease in 1614, just about the time Jonson was readying his *Workes* for the press. She was also a member of the Sidney circle, and is singled out for special mention in the epistle to the Countess of Rutland (*The Forrest*, 12). See Barbara Lewalski, "Lucy, Countess of Bedford: Images of a Jacobean Courtier and Patroness," in *Politics of Discourse: The Literature and History of Seventeenth-Century England*, ed. Kevin Sharpe and Steven N. Zwicker (Berkeley, Los Angeles and London: University of California Press, 1987), pp. 52–77, esp. pp. 58–59.

28. Annabel Patterson emphasizes compromise or contamination in "Jonson, Marvell, and Miscellaneity?" in *Poems in Their Place: The Intertextuality of Poetic Collections*, ed. Neil Fraistat (Chapel Hill and London: University of North Carolina Press, 1986), pp. 95–118. For other interpretations of poems and placement, see Fraistat, "Introduction: The Place of the Book and the Book as Place," pp. 3–17, and Earl Miner, "Some Issues for Study of Integrated Collections," pp. 18–44. Richard C. Newton, "Making Books from Leaves: Poets Become Editors," *Print and Culture in the Renaissance*, ed. Gerald P. Tyson and Sylvia S. Wagonheim (Newark: University of Delaware Press, 1986), pp. 246–64, reads *The Forrest* as a unified "critical collection."

29. Winnicott, *Playing and Reality*, p. xi.

30. Richard Helgerson, *Self-Crowned Laureates: Spenser, Jonson, Milton and the Literary System* (Berkeley, Los Angeles and London: University of California Press, 1983), p. 255.

31. See also Mary L. Livingston, "Ben Jonson: The Poet to the Painter," *Texas Studies in Literature and Language* 18 (1976): 318–92.

32. The portraits discussed here are described by Herford and Simpson, *Ben Jonson* 11:591–92. The van Blijenberch portrait is discussed by David Piper in *The English Face* (London: National Portrait Gallery, 1978), pp. 88–89, plate 34.

33. See Herford and Simpson, *Ben Jonson* 11:591–92, and David Piper, "The

Development of the British Literary Portrait up to Samuel Johnson," *Proceedings of the British Academy* 54 (1968): 51–106, esp. p. 58. This painting is reproduced as plate 9.

34. See Malcolm Rogers, *William Dobson 1611–46* (London: National Portrait Gallery, 1983), the catalogue of an exhibition held from 21 October 1983 to 8 January 1984.

35. Piper, "The Development of the British Literary Portrait up to Samuel Johnson," pp. 57–58. The portrait is reproduced as plate 8.

36. Marotti, "All About Jonson's Poetry," p. 209.

37. This miniature was probably misidentified because the costume—toga and laurel wreath—seems so appropriate for England's first successful classical poet. See Herford and Simpson, Ben Jonson 11:592.

Classicism and Neo-Classicism in Jonson's *Epigrammes* and *The Forrest*

Stella P. Revard

In selecting and ordering the nondramatic verse for the double volumes of the 1616 Folio—*Epigrammes* and *The Forrest*—Jonson displays the disposition of a Renaissance Neo-Latin poet. Not only has he chosen to call his folio *Workes* in emulation of the Neo-Latin poet's *Opera*, but he has also chosen the genres of poems most favored by the Neo-Latin school—the epigram, the ode, the epistle, the mock-epic, and the silvan epode. The overall layout of poems in double volumes with a large group of *epigrammata* followed by a miscellaneous group of *silvae* also pays homage to the design of the Neo-Latin book.

Further, while Jonson writes in English for an English-speaking audience, he has chosen, like the Latin humanist poet, to root his poetry firmly in the classical style with avowed imitation of classical Roman and Greek authors, choosing his models from such Roman poets as Martial, Horace, Catullus, Statius, and Tibullus. Although there are some traces of Anacreon and the Greek Anthology in the poems of the 1616 Folio, Jonson betrays an overwhelming Roman debt, reserving his courtship of the Thespian Muses and his imitation of Pindar, Alcaeus, and other Greek poets for the fireside days of his semiretirement. His espousal of Martial and Horace as models connects him both with these ancient Roman poets as primary sources and as secondary with the humanist poets of Italy, France, and the Netherlands, whose books he has been reading and whose lead he has been following in the imitation of the classics. Those writers—Politian, Sannazaro, Marullus, Secundus, to name a few—not only rescued classical poetry from neglect, rediscovering such writers as Catullus and Pindar, but also initiated the serious practice of imitating the best of the Roman and Greek poets in their own Latin verse.

138

Thus, when we consider Jonson's imitation of the classical genres and poets, we must keep in mind that Jonson is imitating both directly and indirectly. When he creates his book of epigrams, for example, he has in mind not only the original verse of Martial and the writers of the Greek Anthology, but also the epigrams of Neo-Latin stylists such as Marullus. When he writes love lyrics in imitation of Catullus, he is well aware that Pontano, Secundus, and many others had imitated the same lyrics. When he adopts Horatian tones for his poems of rural retreat in *The Forrest*, he recognizes that Horace was a favorite model for Neo-Latin poets. In appraising Jonson's debt to his great Latin originals, we must not forget that he also owes a great deal to those Neo-Latin poets before him who had much to teach about the art of classical imitation.

Jonson's library attests both to his classical and neoclassical taste. Although only a small number of books (about 206 inscribed with his name and motto) survive from the substantial library that Jonson owned before the 1623 fire, these few give us a clear notion of Jonson's reading.[1] Major Roman and Greek authors are represented, many in individual copies, some only in large anthologies such as Roviere's. There are three separate editions of Horace, three of Martial. Although all copies of Martial have publication dates after 1615, by which time Jonson had already written most of his epigrams, the copious annotations of these books, particularly of the 1619 Scriverius edition, testify to Jonson's continued interest in and reading of Martial. Side by side with the older classical writers, Neo-Latin poets are well represented, both in single and multiple author editions and in anthologies. Besides Gruterus's Anthology are collections of Secundus with his two brothers, of Secundus with Marullus and Angeriano, of Pigna with Ariosto and Calcagnini, as well as single editions of Melissus and collections of ancient epigrammatists by Pithou and of Neo-Latin epigrammatists by Quercu. Quercu's anthology is particularly important in that it includes more than seventy poets, some classical, but most of them the leading Neo-Latin epigrammatists of the fifteenth and sixteenth centuries, plus a good selection of minor epigrammatists. All poets except one (the Scottish Latinist Buchanan, given to Jonson by Drummond) are continental writers—Italian, French, German, Belgian, Polish—most of them sixteenth-century writers whose work ranges from love lyric to epigram, mock encomia, fable, and religious meditation. The number and range of these writers represented tell us that Jonson's knowledge of Neo-Latin poetry was broad and his taste eclectic.

Neither in his library nor in his poetic borrowings does Jonson incline to English humanist poets; his epigrams owe little to the line of native Neo-Latinists from More to Owen.[2] He makes considerable use, however, of the Renaissance Latin writers of the continent; when imitating a classical writer on the one hand, Jonson is often borrowing from a continental neoclassical writer on the other. For example, the "Charis" sequence in The Underwood adopts the figure of the older lover from the original Greek anacreontea, but it also employs material from Girolamo Angeriano's Erotopaegnion; a volume Jonson owned contains Angeriano's poetry bound with Secundus and Marullus.[3] Similarly, the song, "That Women are but Mens Shaddowes," has a composite heritage. Inspired, reputedly, by a conversation between the Earl of Pembroke and his Lady, its theme of the fleeing lover turned pursuer is common to poetry by Sappho, Catullus, and Martial. Its most substantial debt, however, is to a Neo-Latin poem by Barthemi Aneau.[4] In assessing the influences on Jonson's poetry, therefore, we must take care not only to look at classical sources, but also to pay attention to contributing influences from neoclassical poetry.

Few critics would deny that Martial is the strongest influence on Jonson's epigrams. Jonson claims him as his model in the preface to the Epigrammes, though he does reassure a modern Cato that he has avoided Martial's scurrility and that a reader may enter Jonson's theater without fear of scandal. Jonson adopts the tones of the Roman epigrammatist in lecturing his reader, his book, and his bookseller; even while he denies emulating Martial's flattery of Domitian, he addresses James and courts his favor in accents that resemble Martial's. In number, order, and arrangement, Jonson's book of 133 epigrams resembles a book of Martial's. Each of Martial's twelve books of epigrams contains roughly one hundred poems.[5] The epigrams of these books range from distichs, triads, and quatrains to semiepistolary poems of thirty to forty lines, the average epigram falling into a middle range of between eight and fifteen lines. Like Martial's, Jonson's epigrams range from the distich to the epistolary, with the usual epigram of moderate length allowing for an introduction, elaboration, and snappy close. The likeness between Jonson and Martial is strongest in the satiric epigrams of the first half of Jonson's book, where the English writer seems determined to create a gallery of London types to stand beside

Martial's Roman collection. After the first sixty or so epigrams, however, Martial's influence wanes. Commendatory epigrams begin to outnumber the satiric, and in the final third of Jonson's book, in which the commendatory epigram dominates, the Renaissance mode of complimentary epigram overshadows the satiric Roman mode.

Even in the satiric epigrams Jonson is following Martial loosely rather than slavishly. Only a relatively few epigrams are close copies of Martial's. Jonson is keenly aware of the difference between his own society of playhouses, gaming establishments, and hothouses and Rome's bathhouses and banqueting halls. James's court, moreover, is not Domitian's. The characters who walk the boards of Jonson's epigrams more resemble the characters of his own comedies than those of Martial's epigrams. Of course, both Jonson and Martial favor certain stock satiric types, drawn from a common body of satiric literature older than either poet. Lawyers, doctors, usurers, undertakers, and bawds have long been the butt of epigrammatical and comedic wit. Martial derived them from the Greek Anthology and from the Roman writers before him; Jonson could have drawn them from Martial's sources or from Martial alike. Martial has a pretty fellow (1.9), an alchemist (1.92), a spendthrift (3.10), a miser (1.98), a patronizing patron (2.67), a glutton (3.22), an old busybody (4.78), and a pretentious lawyer (5.51). It is hardly surprising that Jonson creates ready counterparts for these in his affectedly dressed English Monsieur, his alchemist, his spendthrift lieutenant, gamester, usurer, surly lord, debauched courtier, quack doctor, and tricky lawyer. Yet these are fully developed counterparts of Martial's types, not merely Roman citizens wearing English dress.

Jonson and Martial differ in their treatment of the satiric types that inhabit their epigrams. Commenting on the absurdities of his idle, self-indulgent society, Martial affects a detached moral equanimity. Jonson aims at correction and can rarely refrain from moral comment. Both say they attack the vice and not the person, but Martial's epigrams often seem to be personal attacks. He dwells on the peccadillos of human behavior, the particular follies of particular persons. He jeers at the balding man who tries to cover his head with a few hairs (10.83); he slyly pricks the pride of the antiquary in his ancient possessions by inquiring if he has nothing new (4.39); he laughs at the young lady with the pretty face who attempts to hide her ugly body by bathing in her underclothes (3.3). Martial is the master of the put-down. How many of his epigrams deal with the secret follies or secret vices (often of a sexual nature), secret, that is, to all but the exposer Martial? He makes fun of ladies who paint themselves, who use false hair and false teeth (5.43, 6.12) or of the ancient dame who, hoping to win a young lover, continues to depilate like a girl (10.90). The moral laxities of others provoke his ridicule rather than his scorn. He tells the much-married Roman matron that she is an adulteress by order of law (6.7); the cuckolded husband, he remarks, owns everything but his wife (3.26). He can joke about the chaste wife who went to Baiae a Penelope and returned a Helen (1.62) or tease the jealous husband that he merely provokes a crowd of lovers by setting an armed guard on his wife (1.73). He rarely does more than wag his finger at girls of easy virtue. He quips that he likes a girl of the middle sort, neither too easy nor too difficult— he hates being sated or crucified (1.57). He tells a girl to keep refusing him, for it provokes his desire, but not to refuse too long (4.38). When he chides a girl, it's not for her indiscretions but only for revealing them; even a whore keeps quiet (1.34). Martial holds these characters up for our inspection and destroys them with a final witty dismissal. Even when he deals with sexual practices of homosexuals or heterosexuals that he finds unsavory, he does no more than slyly sneer or snigger.[6] To expose the fornicator, adulterer, or pederast is enough; Martial does not lecture. Often he appears only quietly amused, as, for example, when he narrates the case of the much abused Cinna and the flagrantly unfaithful Marulla, who has filled her husband's house with bastard sons fathered by Cinna's servants. One child resembles the cook, another the bailiff, another the baker, Martial ironically comments, and Marulla would have had as many children as Niobe, had not some of her husband's servants been eunuchs (6.39). Clearly, Martial has spun out this tale of adultery not to make a moral point, but so that he can spring the final joke on us. Often, for Martial, the joke is all.

Some epigrammatists of the Renaissance imitate Martial's satiric types, his jokes, and his casual manner closely. Johannes Secundus, for example, has some light-hearted epigrams that exist purely for the joke. He has a painted lady, a lady with false hair and teeth, an old woman reduced to buying a lover, suitors of a married woman who dupe her old husband by buying him fine clothes in which to tour the town.[7] In each, Secundus examines the humor and not the morality of the situation. Jonson does not subordinate the morality of the case by

merely laughing at the vices of women or the venality or venery
of men who exploit them. In a volume that contains epigrams
commending ladies such as the Countesses of Bedford and Montgomery and the daughters of Robert and Philip Sidney and of
Edward Carey, he cannot afford leniency to erring wives and
exploiting husbands. Fine Lady Would-Bee, the court lady, who
aborts her unborn children in order to remain fashionable at
court, is a foil to these ladies of virtue, wit, and beauty. She
earns Jonson's outrage at her teeming barrenness, for she has
made her "wombe, / Of the not borne, yet buried . . . the tombe"
(62). Similarly, Sir Voluptuous Beast provokes Jonson's anger
and not his laughter; like Martial, Jonson exposes Beast's con-
duct; unlike Martial, he does not shrug it off.

> Then his chast wife, though BEAST now know no more,
> He'adulters still: his thoughts lye with a whore.
>
> (26)

Only when the case does not involve a serious moral issue
will Jonson take the jest and let the moral go. He can joke
about the perfumed Sir Cod wooing "with an ill sprite" (19)
or the whore of the cashiered Captain Surly keeping him in
cash (82) or about the "one good part" of Pertinax Cob (69).
Or, in a style that truly emulates Martial, he can spin out an
anecdote for the joke in the final line. He does so in the epigram
on Giles and Joan, a poem that probably takes its suggestion
from a triad of Martial's on the compatible incompatibility of
warring spouses:

> Cum sitis similes paresque vita,
> Uxor pessima, pessimus maritus,
> Miror non bene convenire vobis.
>
> Since you are alike and equal in disposition,
> The worst of wives, the worst of husbands,
> I marvel that you don't get along better with one another.
>
> (8.35)

Jonson begins by posing a query analogous to Martial's: "WHo
sayes that GILES and IONE at discord be?" (42). He continues
by dramatizing a miniature domestic comedy, where, with the
neighbors observing, Giles and Joan alike repent their marriage,
avoid each others' company, and yearn to be released from one
another. Like Martial's Cinna, Giles has a household of children

not his own, and like Martial, Jonson makes a joke of it.

> The children, that he keepes, GILES sweares are none
> Of his begetting. And so sweares his IONE.

In the final summary three lines, Jonson, inverting Martial's paradox, marvels not at the discord of this ill-matched pair, but at the concord that their discord involuntarily produces.

> If, now, with man and wife, to will, and nill
> The selfe-same things, a note of concord be:
> I know no couple better can agree!

While now and then Jonson follows Martial's lead in creating satiric portraits, he frequently imitates his master when he talks of poets, poetry, and poetasters. In Martial, Jonson found a fellow spirit, and both poets were peculiarly obsessed with their poetic reputations. In poem after poem they defend their epigrammatical style and pay in full any invidious imitator, slanderous critic, unappreciative commoner, or vile poetaster who might not praise their genius or who might dare to contest with them their supremacy in the art of poetry. Often Jonson directly echoes Martial's views, echoes them, I believe, both because he profoundly agrees with them and because he wishes to set himself up as the kind of witty arbiter of poetry that Martial was. He hopes for his *Epigrammes* the approval Martial won for his; he hopes for himself the enduring reputation of the Roman poet.

The proems or introductory epigrams of most of Martial's twelve books discuss and defend the aims of his poetry. Claiming precedent from the best poets of the past, Martial argues for the license with which he writes and warns against anyone trying to rewrite or tone down his poetry. Assuming that he composes not only for a contemporary but also for a future audience, Martial proclaims that he wishes to please both himself and his readers. Repeatedly, almost self-consciously, Martial returns to the subject of his poetry and defends this or that aspect of his art (1.1–5, 2.86, 3.2–4, 4.23,29, 11.2 for example). He courts both present popularity and future fame; he is piqued at followers who praise him but do not buy his book (1.117). While assuming nonchalance, he fears that the same audience that courts him now may reject him and cast off his books to suffer the degradation of other cast-off books—to become in some market, wrappings for fish (3.2; 4.86). While enjoying on the one hand his popularity, he fears on the other that because he is a prolific writer widely read for entertainment he will gain no lasting fame. He numbers himself with Catullus, Virgil, Ovid, Menander (5.5) and sees himself as a successor to the Greek epigrammatists (4.23), but fears that others may not esteem him so. Martial wants adulation both now and later. As he tells a friend in an early epigram—to ashes, glory comes late ("cineri gloria sera venit" 1.25.8).

Jonson could easily identify with this literary testiness, for it is clearly so like his own. While bragging of the superiority of his book, he too fears, like Martial, that its pages might be dismembered to become market wrappings at Bucklersbury (3). Like Martial, he takes pains to defend the style of his epigrams, claiming that he writes in a new and totally different way. His epigrams are honest and blunt like Martial's, though never, he asserts, coarse and offensive (2). He has as little patience with critics as Martial did, and a good number of his epigrams hold the critics up to ridicule. Although he can submit himself, he says, to the judgment of a learned friend (17), he cannot bear the invidious criticism of rivals. He scorns the playwright who accuses him of lacking salt (49). As Martial railed at those who read his works badly or who lacked proper appreciation, Jonson complains of the censorious courtling who renders faint praise (52) or the "Groome Ideot" whose ignorant reading mutilates his verses. For imitators and plagiarists alike he has no time. He convicts Proule the Plagiary (81) and the plagiarizing playwright who like a sheep stealer filches fleeces from him (56) and the court lord who "borrows" his verse (73). He excoriates even those who merely steal the limelight from him, chaffing at Court-Parrat (71) and Court-ling (72) and their would-be wit. Fool and Knave alike he avoids, those who "stroke" or "strike" (61). Although he does not speak in his volume of epigrams of his claim to lasting fame—he merely asserts that he has written honestly and well—he is not above seeking comparison with ancient poets. His attachment to and emulation of Martial proves this. In The Forrest he speaks more directly. Echoing Horace (4.8.11–32) in his "Epistle to Elizabeth, Countess of Rutland," he says:

> It is the *Muse*, alone, can raise to heaven,
>   And, at her strong armes end, hold up, and even

The soules, shee loves.

(12)

Like Martial, Jonson hoped for lasting fame.

Jonson's imitation of Martial, however, goes beyond mere adoption of the Roman poet's literary sentiments and stances. As epigram 112, "To a Weake Gamster in Poetry," demonstrates, Jonson ventures at times almost line-by-line paraphrase. Although he creates a different frame for his words to the over-zealous imitator—Jonson imagines that he is playing at primero with a weak gamester—the center lines of Jonson's twenty-two-line epigram march both to the tune and stride of Martial's twelve-line poem. Martial is typically succinct:

Scribebamus epos; coepisti scribere: cessi,
    aemula ne starent carmina nostra tuis.
transtulit ad tragicos se nostra Thalia cothurnos:
    aptasti longum tu quoque syrma tibi;
fila lyrae movi Calabris exculta Camenis:
    plectra rapis nobis, ambitiose, nova.
audemus saturas: Lucilius esse laboras.
    ludo levis elegos: tu quoque ludis idem.
quid minus esse potest? epigrammata fingere coepi:
    hinc etiam petitur iam mea palma tibi.

We were writing an epic; you begin to write; I cease
    lest our songs stand in rivalry with yours.
My Thalia transferred to tragic buskins;
    you also fitted to yourself the long tragic robe.
I moved the strings of the lyre plucked by Calabrian Muses;
    you seize my newly acquired plectra from us, ambitious man.
Should we venture satire, you labor to be Lucilius.
    I play with light elegy; you also play the same.
What lesser thing can there be? I begin to fashion epigrams;
    My palm is already sought by you even in this.

(12.94.1–10)

Martial's entertaining narrative is mimed by Jonson, line by line, genre by genre, point by point with scarcely a variation:

I cannot for the stage a *Drama* lay,
 Tragick, or *Comick;* but thou writ'st the play.
I leave thee there, and giving way, entend
 An *Epick* poeme; thou hast the same end.
I modestly quit that, and thinke to write,
 Next morne, an *Ode:* Thou mak'st a song ere night.
I pass to *Elegies:* Thou meet'st me there:
 To *Satyres;* and thou dost pursue me. Where,
Where shall I scape thee? in an *Epigramme?*
 O, (thou cry'st out) that is thy proper game.

(112)

The joke is, of course, that Jonson's fawning poetaster does not more slavishly imitate Jonson than Jonson himself has imitated Martial. Jonson, in turn, would claim the prerogative of the skillful follower, and as Jonson's epigram illustrates, he has learned his lessons well. Here is Martial's balanced line, his deft hand at turning and re-turning a phrase, his rapier swiftness at thrusting a point home. These are the qualities that Jonson wishes to imitate here and elsewhere in his "translated" English medium.

In language and poetic technique Jonson's epigrams illustrate the profit with which he studied Martial and pay compliment to his Roman master. When Don Surly tilts his "Rhinocerotes nose" (28), Jonson both effects a complimentary echo of Martial's youths and old men with their rhinoceros noses (1.3.5–6) and shows that he well understood how a poet with a single vivid word could convey the air of "sneering superciliousness." Jonson also learned the art of the insinuating question from Martial. Martial puts down the would-be artist of Venus, who in his heart preferred Minerva (money) by coyly asking, "Do you wonder that your work displeases?" "et miraris opus displicuisse tuum?") (5.40). He rebukes his stingy host who offers magnificent bathing but poor dining accommodations by querying, "Since I dine so badly, why should I bathe so well?" "tam male cum cenem, cur bene, Flacce, laver?" (1.49). Jonson in a similar way turns the question against the subject of his epigram. Of the Old-End Gatherer (53), who compiles his books out of others' works, Jonson queries:

 For, but thy selfe, where, out of motly, 's hee
  Could save that line to dedicate to thee?

Or of the histrionic preacher, Lippe, who sermonizes against plays, Jonson asks:

> Though *LIPPE*, at *PAULS*, ranne from his text away,
>> T'inveigh 'gainst playes: what did he then but play?
>>> (75)

Martial is the master of few words, of the quick turnabout, often effected with a deft repetition. The wit of one of his most famous epigrams (imitated popularly in the English verses to Dr. Fell) depends upon the repetition of both "non amo te" (I do not like you) at the beginning and at the end and a centrally poised "possum dicere" repeated in the negative and the affirmative:

> Non amo te, Sabidi, nec possum dicere quare:
> hoc tantum possum dicere, non amo te.
>
> I do not like you, Sabidius, nor can I say why;
> But so much can I say, I do not like you.
>> (1.32)

In 5.13 he puts down a rich pretender by neatly reversing a phrase at the end of the epigram, "What I am you cannot be, but what you are anyone can be." Similarly, the simple exchange of meus (mine) and tuus (yours) in the epigram on the inept reciter of verses drives home Martial's point with an understated economy:

> Quem recitas meus est, o Fidentine, libellus:
> sed male cum recitas, incipit esse tuus.
>
> It's *my* book you recite from, Fidentinus,
> but when you recite badly, it begins to be *yours*.
>> (1.38)

Several of Jonson's distichs imitate this technique of repetition with reversal. In his epigram on the "cashierd Capt. Surly," Jonson contrasts *old* with *new* while he works a turn on the word *keep:*

> Surly's old whore in her new silkes doth swim:
> He cast, yet keeps her well! No, shee keeps him
>> (82)

In his epigram "To Fine Grand" he drives his point home in

a Martial-like way by quipping, "pay me quickly', or Ile pay you" (73). Jonson's reversal in the epigram "On Gypsee" updates a joke that Martial employed in his poem on the doctor turned undertaker: "quod vispillo facit, fecerat et medicus" (what the undertaker does now, the doctor practiced before) (1.47). Of Gypsee, the whore turned physician, says Jonson, "For what shee gave, a whore; a baud, shee cures" (41). For Jonson the epigram is more than a character in verse; it is an opportunity for display of versatility in word games. As Martial created a tour-de-force in his epigram on the gladiator Hermes (5.24) by repeating Hermes's name at the beginning of each of the fifteen lines, so Jonson in his epigram on the prodigal Lieutenant Shift repeats at the end of each couplet the phrase that Shift uses to deflect his creditors, "God payes" (12). From Martial Jonson learned these tricks of the epigrammatist's trade—the provocative opening, the daring use of repetition, the under- stated put-down, and the art to bring an epigram full circle round to a stinging conclusion.

But Jonson does not merely admire Martial for his satirical epigrams or for his mastery of the tricks of the epigrammatical trade. He can imitate the Roman poet in his more congenial moods. A case in point in Jonson's close adaptation of several of Martial's invitation epigrams (5.78, 10.48, 11.52) for his own epigrammatical invitation of a friend to dinner (101). In this epigram Jonson is all warmth and good humor. Adopting the self-deprecatory tones of Martial, Jonson invites his friend to his "poore house" for a simple supper. Jonson not only echoes Martial's words of invitation, he even copies, so far as he can, the Roman's menu and promised entertainment. Like Martial, all he has to offer is a modest fare (salad, eggs, olives, fruit, cheese), moderate drinking, simple entertainment, and honest company. Like Martial, he regrets that he cannot offer more, and jests that to entice the friend, he is tempted to lie and promise a more sumptuous meal. Like Martial, also, he promises not to recite his own verses. Jonson's witty adaptation of Martial tells us as much about Jonson's own aspirations for himself and his poetry as it does about his penchant for classical adapta- tion. Assuming the role of the congenial poet-host at his own board, Jonson tells us he aspires not only to wit and position as the poetic arbiter of his time, but also to the congeniality and popularity that Martial enjoyed.

Jonson's imitations of Martial extend beyond those epigrams of the first book, where Jonson clearly signals to his reader that he is following a Martialian model. In the odes, songs, and epistles of The Forrest and in the funerary and commendatory epigrams of the first book, traces of Martial are to be found, sometimes in a word, a phrase, a line, sometimes in a relatively extended passage. Jonson will silently follow Martial, without acknowledging his source, for in these poems different models preoccupy him, and it is these he wishes his readers to recognize. Although Martial has many moods, he is known primarily as a satirist, not as a lyric or elegiac poet. Hence, when Jonson writes his series of epitaphs—on his son (45), his daughter (22), the child actor, Salomon Pavy (120), Margaret Ratcliffe (40), and Elizabeth L.H. (124)—he treats them as inscriptional pieces, updated elegies in the mode of the sepulchral verses of the Greek Anthology, where either tones of simple lament or pious hope for salvation dominate.[8] The Greek epigrams often open with inscriptional indications—here lies, this stone marks, this tomb contains—or call upon a passer-by to stop and read and to lament. Following this model, Jonson begins each of his epitaphs with a simple exhortation: "HEre lyes to each her parents ruth" (22), "WOuld'st thou heare, what man can say / In a little? Reader, stay" (124), "WEepe with me all you that read / This little storie" (120). Like the Christian epigrammatists of the Anthology, Jonson expresses hope for the soul that has departed from earth and gone to heaven. The child, S. P., "being so much too good for earth, / Heaven vowes to keepe him" (120); Jonson's daughter Mary is safe in heaven with "heauens Queene" (22); Jonson's son has escaped earth's miseries (45). Yet each of Jonson's epigrams expresses not only Christian piety, but also Roman stoicism, and a few have as sources the affecting tributes that Martial wrote on the death of young women not unlike Elizabeth L. H. and Margaret Ratcliffe or young children not unlike Jonson's own son and daughter and Salomon Pavy. In 5.34,36 and in 1.88 Martial laments with great tenderness the death of a little slave girl and a little slave boy; in 1.114 he expresses a father's grief for his daughter. That Jonson knew and admired epigrams such as these, he silently attests to when in the final line of the epigram on his son, "As what he loves may never like too much" (45), he directly echoes Martial's stoic lament (6.29.7–8) for a favorite slave-boy, "Quidquid ames, cupias non placuisse nimis" (Whatever you love, desire that it not please too much). Without calling attention to Martial, Jonson once more betrays a debt to Martial's artistry.

Similar borrowing occurs in "To Penshurst" and "To Sir Robert

Wroth," where Jonson adopts a predominately Horatian mood, but employs descriptive phrases and touches from some of Martial's country epigrams: on Licinianus's Spanish retreat (1.49) and on Faustinus's Baean villa (1.45). In "To Penshurst" Martial's "picta perdix" become Jonson's native "painted part-rich"; the country maidens who supply the liberal board at Faustinus's villa become nubile Kentish farm girls who carry baskets of fruit and cheese. Although Jonson models scenes on Wroth's estate on descriptions of the Spanish countryside in Martial's 1.45, he does not openly adopt Martial as his Roman counterpart. He reserves that honor for Horace, whose Epode 2 ("Beatus ille") he alludes to in the first line, "HOW blest art thou, canst love the countrey, WROTH" (3). Horace's Epode 2, a poem Jonson translated for The Under-Wood as "The praises of a Countrie Life" (85), was the bible for the Renaissance on the joys of rural living. For both "To Penshurst" and "To Sir Robert Wroth" it serves as a general and a particular model.[9] Jonson, however, is not the first to employ Horace as a model for poems extolling the delights of country life. Imitations of Horace begin with Martial and Statius and continue with Neo-Latin poets from the fourth century on. Hence Jonson may look back not only to Horace but to Horace's Latin and Neo-Latin followers when he designs his poems on country life.

Neo-Latin imitation begins in the late classical era when writers such as Ausonius, the fourth-century Christian poet, espouse the Latin of the golden age for their poetry rather than the late Latin of their own eras. These early Neo-Latinists, together with the humanist writers of the fifteenth and sixteenth century who follow their practice, not only adopt the distinctive vocabulary and style of classical Latin, but also its favored genres of poetry: ode, epigram, eclogue, elegy, epistle. While imitating the language and genres of classical Rome, the Neo-Latin poet adapts those for quite different ends. He uses the epigram, for example, more often as a medium for serious address to friends and royal patrons, than as a satiric form. He may begin a love elegy or lyric by employing an Ovidian or a Catullan argument, but he usually freely elaborates to persuade his Neaera or Stella. And while using Horace's techniques in a rural idyll or ode, he aims to describe not the Roman poet's but his own retreat. As a Renaissance man, Jonson is often more in sympathy with the aims and interests of the Neo-Latin poet of the past century than with the Latin poet of the first century B.C. Such, I believe, is the case with Jonson's country estate poems, his love lyrics, and his familiar epigrams.

Jonson certainly knew many of the Neo-Latin imitations of Horace's Epode 2. Important among them is the long poem on the beauties of the Moselle that Ausonius wrote in the fourth century A.D. to celebrate his native Gaul. Concentrating in it on topological description of a specific setting, Ausonius virtually invents the country-estate poem that, as Herford and Simpson note, Jonson and his fellow seventeenth-century poets find so agreeable a medium.[10] Ausonius is only the first in the line of Neo-Latin poets to write such poems; as Carol Maddison points out, this kind of poem becomes popular among the humanist poets of the fifteenth and sixteenth century.[11] Some poets merely praise the rural idyll; others, joining Horace's Ode 4.12 to Epode 2, invite friends to share the rustic entertainment. Pontano urges Sannazaro to come to Baiae; Flaminio invites Cardinal Farnese to leave Rome; Secundus exhorts his tutor to attend him in the country. Other Neo-Latin poets praise their own and not others' estates. Flaminio imagines his return to his paternal villa, reciting his pleasure at visiting once more his trees and fountains and entertaining his own rustic muses there; Du Bellay imagines leaving Paris to return to the countryside of his youth and to grow old there.[12] Pietro Crinito celebrates the joys of rural retirement at the Silva Oricellaria, the country place that the Italian humanist, Bernardo Ruccellai, the cousin to Lorenzo de' Medici and like Lorenzo a patron of the arts, built as a retreat for himself and his poet and scholar friends. There Ruccellai played the part of a latter-day Maecenas, or perhaps more fitting, the Italian counterpart to noblemen like Sidney and Wroth, who gathered poets at their country estates. Employing the Horatian phrase, "beatus ille," Crinito extends the implications of country retirement to include the cultivation of the muses as well as the cultivation of crops and farm animals.

> Et illum beatum, qui sub antiqua ilice
>   Liventis expers ambitus
> Vel sacra vatum curat, aut doctum otium
>   Curis solutior fovet.

> Blessed is he who beneath an ancient oak,
>   Taking no part in envious ambition,
> Either cares for the sacred arts of poets

Or, free from care, fosters learned leisure.[13]

For Crinito the city man does not merely, like the original spokesman of Horace's epode, the usurer Alfius, long for retreat to the peace of the country, while he continues to heap up money in town. The poet-spokesman wishes to escape from the court of intrigue and ambition so that he may devote himself to poetry and learning in a community of scholars and humanists. Further, he criticizes the life of the city, where man pursues riches and high position, rather than virtue and learning. Crinito's commendation of Ruccellai looks forward directly to Jonson's praise of the Sidneys and the Wroths.

In "To Penshurst" and "To Sir Robert Wroth" Jonson combines directly Horatian with modified Renaissance motifs. The outline of Horace's famous epode is discernible in "To Penshurst" and "To Sir Robert Wroth"; both Horace and Jonson praise an idealized rural estate, where the landowner, far from the cares of city and court, occupies himself with the supervision of a large farm. Overseeing the cultivation of trees and vines and the tending of cattle and sheep, enjoying the changes of the seasons, he reaps the fruits of country life—tangible fruits, such as the ripened pear and grape, and the spiritual fruit of perfect contentment. The country idyll provides both Horace and Jonson the opportunity to describe the beauty and variety of landscapes in different seasons of the year and to praise the activities and sports that man enjoys in field, stream, woods, and fountain. Moreover, the idealized estate affords more than recreation and retreat; it encourages ideal domestic life with wife and children and ideal compatibility with the servants and tenants of the estate and its surrounding countryside. Horace praises the chaste wife ("pudica mulier"), who tends the hearth of her lord and master and who cares for the loving children she has borne to him. Moreover, to illustrate how the perfect balance of man and nature also fosters the balance in relationships of man to man, Horace concludes his country idyll with a bountiful feast, where the lord, surrounded by his wife, children, servants, and neighbors, enjoys the produce of his own land.

Jonson in "To Penshurst" particularizes Horace's picture of country contentment. With references to Sidney's oak or Gamage's copse, with Kentish scenes of wandering sheep, bullocks, kine, and calves on the banks of the Medway, with praise of local fishing and hunting, Jonson gives an English color to the Roman scenes he inherited from Horace. "The blushing apri-

cot, and woolly peach" ripen on Penshurst's stone walls, recalling the ripening fruit of Horace's epode, and like Horace, Jonson
gathers neighboring tenants and farmers for a great country feast.
But, most of all, Jonson, like Horace, places at the center of
his poem on country contentment a lord, matched with a lady,
who is "noble, fruitfull, chaste" and who has given him children
he "may call his own." The companion poem to Wroth, although
different in emphasis and detail, also looks back to Horace.
Jonson creates another idealized country retreat, where "'Mongst
loughing heards, and solide hoofes: / Along'st the curled woods,
and painted meades, / Through which a serpent river leades,"
a lord may find a cool shade he may call his own. Here too
we have mowed meadows and green copses, where Pan, Sylva-
nus, the nymphs, and the Muses might find a home; here too
dwells a lord, mated with a noble spouse, who enjoys the sports
of the country and who welcomes his neighbors to shearing
and harvest feasts. Yet the poem to Wroth is not all idyll. Like
the Renaissance poets who wrote in the Horatian mode, Jonson
is aware of the city that the country lord has left, for he includes
a long section where he denounces the pursuit of wealth and
position. Unlike lawyers and usurers, Jonson tells us, Wroth
does not seek gold; unlike courtiers who flatter vice and pursue
great place, Wroth has made his peace and is happy to enjoy
his country service.

Like other Renaissance poets, Jonson promotes a nostalgia
for a return to a rural past, where virtue may be and where
the good life may be shared with friends. The city-bred Jonson
finds at Penshurst, as Crinito found at the Silva Oricellaria,
friends with whom he enjoys not only country, but poetic pleasures. Here is the Renaissance community of poets, scholars,
patrons, and friends realized in rural England. Jonson comes
to Penshurst as a guest who commands the liberality of the
board as though it were his own; at Wroth's country estate
he accepts the nobleman's grace of welcome, sharing the happiness of a friend who has achieved the Juvenalian "body sound,
with sounder minde" and is content to grow old in the country.

> Thy peace is made; and, when man's state is well,
> 'Tis better, if he there can dwell.

Although Jonson inherits the country estate poems from Horace,
the Renaissance poets who cultivate this mode influence Jonson's attitudes toward the genre. For them the country estate

poem was a means for making a statement about the ideal poet-scholar's life; they did not merely dream of country pleasures. Jonson's hopes for the Jacobean era were expressed in his praise of Sidney and Wroth. When he passes on this genre to Carew, Herrick, Waller, Marvell, and Denham, he passes on a classical exercise with very definite neoclassical implications. If he read the odes of Casimire Sarbiewski that were becoming popular in the 1630s, he might have observed that the Horatian poem of rural retreat continued its popularity with Neo-Latin writers of the continent. Casimire's ode of retreat from Rome to the country estate of Paolo Orsini, the Duke of Bracciano, stands beside Jonson's poems as an imitation of Horace and, like them, expatiates on the delights of a country farm and praises the lord and patron who has found his contentment there.[14] It illustrates also the vitality throughout the seventeenth century of this classical mode that Renaissance poets had so much made their own.

Other poems from *The Forrest* benefit both from Latin and Neo-Latin tradition. Jonson's three lyrics to Celia are originally inspired by two famous poems of Catullus to Lesbia (5, 7) and by a series of prose passages from the *Epistles* of Philostratus.[15] Yet while a Latin or Greek original may provide Jonson with his subject matter and with a rough plan for narrative development, other influences shape Jonson's attitude and lead him to assume a tone quite different from Catullus's or Philostratus's. To Martial as a reviser of Catullus he owes the curt flippancy of his tone; to several Neo-Latin love poets, most notable among them Secundus, he owes a sensual playfulness. Catullus's original lyric (5) is an impassioned exhortation to live and love free from the envious grudging of elders; in Jonson's free translation this becomes a lascivious invitation to prove the "sports of love," while deluding the watchfulness of "household spies." The difference in tone may partly be accounted for by dramatic context; Jonson's first song is adapted by the lecherous Volpone to press his suit on the unwilling Celia. An impassioned pleading sincerity would be out of place in Volpone's decadent Venice, but the assumption that a lyric of classical antiquity can serve the voluptuous pleasures of another age is quite appropriate. In the second lyric Jonson replaces ardent evocation of distant climes—far-off Libya and its innumerable grains of sand, the far-flung heavens with unnumbered stars that look down upon lovers—with places closer to his English home: Runnymede with its leaves of grass, Chelsea and its sands, Thames and its water-drops. The stars that conclude the list shine in an English sky, closer to home for Jonson's audience. Jonson's suggestion that one steal a few kisses on the sly is also mundane beside the sometimes physical, sometimes metaphysical yearnings of Catullus's original lover.

But Jonson is not the first to bring Catullus's lyrics down to a more common level. One of Catullus's first imitators, Martial, in an epigram that offers a slightly flippant answer to the mistress's question, "How many?," takes an arch view of the whole proceedings. Responding to Diadumenus, Lesbia's stand-in in this poem (6.34), Martial offers a different list of unnumber-ables: sea waves, shells on the Aegean shore, bees from Cecropia, only to cap the quantity with an insinuating compliment to Caesar that not all these could equal the applause of hands and voices when Caesar appears unexpectedly at the theater. Undercutting the transcendence of Catullus's attempt to number, Martial puts the impractical love poet in a practical perspective by finally remarking: he who can number them wishes for few ("pauca cupit qui numerare potest") (6.34.8). Yet throughout his poetry Martial takes a sceptical view of Catullus's sublime "basiationes" (kissings), for when he uses this Catullan word it is to put it down, as when in 7.95 he complains of Linus's "hibernas basiationes" (wintry kissings) or rejects Posthumus's offensive "basiationes" (2.23). Jonson's tone in the first two lyrics to Celia has more in common with Martial's than Catullus's, in spite of the fact that he closely translates many of Catullus's lines. For as Martial enjoys topping Catullus by offering a practical answer to Lesbia's question, Jonson in the conclusion of the second lyric sneers at the curious and envious who might pry into his love affair:

> That the curious may not know
> How to tell'hem, as they flow,
> And the envious, when they find
> What their number is, be pin'd.

> (6)

Renaissance Latin poets take another way with Catullus's kissing, intensifying both the sportiveness and the eroticism. They too have their effect on Jonson. Pontano, Navagero, Du Bellay, Celtis, and Secundus warmly exhort mistresses who render kiss for kiss; these playful kisses, nippings, and nuzzlings make explicit the implied eroticism of Catullus's plea for innumerable kisses. The Renaissance poet urges not one but multitudes of kisses on his mistress (see Joachim Du Bellay, "Voti Solutio"; Conrad Celtis, "De Nocte & Oscuto Hasilinae, Erotice"; Andrea Navagero, "Nox Bona").[16] Amid these osculatory exercises, some poets glance over their shoulders at their great Latin predecessor (newly rediscovered in the Renaissance) and render an account to this first of poets who demanded hundreds and millions of kisses. We find unmistakable references in both Pontano and Secundus. Invoking the Muse whom he courts in hendecasyllabic verse, Pontano alludes to the amorous play that she inspires:

> Quod uos en pretium: aut manet uoluptas?
> Inter lacteolas simul puellas:
> Inter molliculos simul maritos:
> Ludetis simul: atque prurietis
>
> What reward or pleasure awaits you?
> Sometimes among milk-white girls,
> Other times among tender husbands,
> You play and are wanton. . . .
>
> (14–17)

As the boy touches the girl and she responds to his caress, as the two begin to play, Pontano asks his Muse the Catullan question, "Quot? quot oscula? morsiunculasque? / Quot? quot enumerabitis duella? / Quot suspiria: murmura: & cachinnos? (How many? how many kisses? and little bites? how many struggles will you enumerate? how many sighs? murmurs? laughs?" 25–27). But he does not pause to enumerate, for with his question he has suggested the love play between the two; in a sense he leaves enumeration to his Dutch successor, Johannes Secundus, whose erotic *Basia,* a sequence of nineteen numbered and differentiated kisses, summed up for the Renaissance the art of osculation. Basium 6 and Basium 7 play the Catullan numbers game, the first in lanquid pleading elegiacs, the second in sprightly glyconics.[17] In the other Basia Secundus employs hendecasyllables; this short line, so popular with Neo-Latin poets, may find its English equivalent in the octosyllabics of Jonson's Catullan invitation, a verse form he passes down to later English love poets.

Secundus opens Basium 6 by complaining, as Catullus did, about keeping too strict accounts:

De meliore nota bis basia mille paciscens,
  Basia mille dedi, basia mille tuli:
Explesti numerum, fateor, iucunda Neaera,
Expleri numero sed nequit ullus amor.

Bargaining for two thousand kisses of better sort,
  I gave a thousand; I took a thousand kisses.
You have filled up the number, I admit, delightful Neaera,
  But no love is able to be fulfilled by number.

                                                    (1–4)

Secundus continues with his own version of the Catullan list of innumerables. Does Ceres keep track of ears of grain or leaves of grass? Does Bacchus count the grapes or honey bees he grants to the farmer? Or Jove the drops of water with which he irrigates the fields? Neither then should Neaera count, or if she does count, Secundus asserts, making a final turn on the number game Catullus began, she should give innumerable kisses for the innumerable tears she has caused: "Et mihi da, miseri solatia uana doloris, / Innumera innumeris basia pro lachrymis" (And give me, as a vain release from wretched sorrow / innumerable kisses for innumerable tears) (25–26). Here are all the Catullan elements, reshuffled and played out again with a bittersweet wit.

  Basium 7 is pure game that begins with a recollection of the hundred and thousand kisses that Catullus attempted to number—here in Secundus's version with drops of the sea and stars of the sky.

> Centum basia centies,
> Centum basia millies,
> Mille basia millies,
> Et tot millia millies,
> Quot guttae Siculo mari
> Quot sunt sidera coelo . . .
>
> A hundred times a hundred,
> A hundred times a thousand kisses,
> A thousand times a thousand kisses,
> And so many thousand thousands,
> As many as drops in the Sicilian sea,
> As many as stars in the sky . . .

                                                    (1–6)

This almost sing-song repetition in the bright glyconics of

Secundus's meter reduces the game of counting to child's play and gives birth in the second part of the poem to yet another competition—a second trial of the impossibles. For attempting to gaze with his eyes upon Neaera as he bestows innumerable kisses with his lips, his lips become the rivals of his eyes for his love's favor, and he finds himself caught in another interminable game.

With a sprightly sense of invention Secundus reinvents Catullan formulas and passes on to the generation of Latin and vernacular poets that followed him a gentler, more sporting Catullus. It is perhaps this sportfulness that Jonson urges in the first lyric to Celia or the breathless game of kiss on kiss that he plays in the second lyric: "KIsse me, sweet . . . / Kisse again: no creature comes. / Kisse, and score up wealthy summes / On my lips, thus hardly sundred, / While you breath. First give a hundred, / Then a thousand, then another / Hundred, then unto the tother / Adde a thousand, and so more" (6). The Jonsonian accumulation of grass, sands, drops, and stars in the second lyric more suggests the bright abundant living nature of Secundus's poem than the distant stars and sands of Catullus's original.

The sensuous persuasions of Secundus's Basium 4 may also contribute something to Jonson's lyric art in "Drink to me only with thine eyes." Many lines of this lyric are exact translations of Philostratus's prose; the first line exactly renders Philostratus's "ἐμοὶ δὲ μόνοις πρόπυνε τοῖς ὄμμυασιν." However, the kiss that Jonson asks Celia to leave in the cup owes something to the little kiss that Secundus first asks from Neaera—a nectared kiss, smelling of spices, that has the power to confer immortality:

> Non dat basia, dat Neaera nectar,
> Dat rores animae sua veolentes,
> Dat nardumque, thymumque, cinnamumque,
> Et mel. . . . .
> Quae si multa mihi uoranda dentur,
> Immortalis in iis repente fiam . . .

> Neaera does not give kisses, she gives nectar,
> She gives the sweet-smelling dew of her soul;
> She gives nard, thyme, and cinnamon,
> And honey . . . .
> If I were given much of this to consume,

I would suddenly become immortal . . .

(1–4, 8–9)

As Secundus conflates the drink and the kiss, so does Jonson, making the kiss, moreover, inspire a thirst that draws forth the soul. The nectared kiss in Secundus's lyric confers immortality; Jonson calls for a "drink divine" he would not trade for Jove's nectar. Secundus imagines himself sharing the banquets of the gods, but quickly adds that he does not wish to be a god without Neaera. To the prose of Philostratus's narrative the sensuous transforming quality of Secundus's lyric adds a kind of rapturous poetry.

Other Neo-Latin lyrics stand beside Philostratus's narrative and provide different perspectives on the wreath of flowers that takes its immortality from Celia. Writing of the violets that his mistress sent him, Politian tells us that the flowers retain the scent of his lady and breathe forth her odor. So fortunate are they, moreover, that they take a second life from her, serving as consolation for the rejected love they symbolize.

> Quam dulcem labris, quam late spirat odorem?
>   En uiolae in uobis ille remansit odor.
> O fortunatae uiolae, mea uita, meumque
>   Delitium, O animi portus & aura mei.

> How she breathes forth a sweet scent from her lips;
>   That scent remains in you, Violets.
> O fortunate violets, my life and my delight,
>   O haven and breath of my soul.[18]

(27–30)

The Neapolitan poet Girolamo Angeriano (Hieronymus Angerianus), whose works Jonson owned and whose *Erotopaegnion* Jonson imitates in his Charis sequence, sends a crown of flowers to his Caelia with a different sentiment. As Jonson tells Celia that he sent the rosy wreath, not so much to honor her, but with the hope that in her presence "It could not withered bee" (12), Angeriano tells his Caelia that he wishes to give her such a gift so that while the garland lived, then for a little while beauty might also live: "Si quaeris, donum quid vult sibi tale: corolla / Vt viret haec, paruo tempore forma viret" (Angerianus, *Poetae tres Elegantissimi*, p. 23r). Once more, Renaissance poetry supports and diversifies a motif that Jonson has taken primarily from an ancient source.

In Jonson's commendatory epigrams and epistles, Renaissance sources attain ascendancy over the classical. Although the commendatory poem has its roots in ancient literature, not until the Latin poetry of the fifteenth and sixteenth centuries does it achieve full development. As Jonson himself notes in *Epigrammes* Martial wrote epigrams to Domitian, epigrams, however, that Jonson puts aside as models for his to James. Sometimes, however, in the balanced phrasing of Martial's epigram to Caesar on assuming the name Germanicus, cadences may be recognized that Jonson adopts for his epigrams of praise.

> Creta dedit magnum, maius dedit Africa nomen,
>> Scipio quod victor quodque Metellus habet;
> nobilius domito tribuit Germania Rheno;
>> et puer hoc dignus nomine, Caesar, eras.

> Crete gave a great name, Africa a greater
>> The one that the victor Scipio, the other that Metellus holds;
> a nobler yet Germany bestowed at the Rhine's conquest;
>> and worthy of this name you were, Caesar, though still a boy.
>>>> (2.21–24)

Surely Jonson's opening praise of Clement Edmonds on his translation of Caesar's *Commentaries* owes something to the way Rome praised her conquering Caesars.

> NOt *CAESARS* deeds, nor all his honors wonne,
>> In these west-parts, nor when that warre was done,
> The name of *POMPEY* for an enemie,
>> *CATO*'s to boote, *Rome*, and her libertie
>> All yeelding to his fortune, nor, the while,
> To have engrav'd these acts, with his owne stile
>>>> (110)

Further, it is not just Martial's praise of conquerors that Jonson finds fit model for emulation in his epigrams on Jacobean lords and literati. To a degree Jonson learned how to open an epigram with a choice epithet of praise from the opening of Martial's epigrams, such as his to Quintilian.

> Quintiliane, vagae moderator summe iuventae,
>> gloria Romanae, Quintiliane, togae . . .

> Quintilian, highest governor of errant youth,

Glory of the Roman toga, Quintilian. . . .

(2.90.1–2)

Jonson's propensity to begin his epigrams of praise with the name of the honoree, followed by an apt epithet describing him or her, is just the kind of rhetorical device that he and other Renaissance poets might have learned from Martial. How many epigrams begin in just this way: "DONNE, the delight of PHOEBUS"; "CAMDEN, most reverend head"; "JEPHSON, thou man of men"; "LUCY, you brightnesse of our sphaere." Even when he disclaims Martial as the model for his moral and commendatory epigrams, Jonson cannot escape being influenced by the Martialian style.

But, though there are Roman models for the commendatory epigram, the art of graceful commendation belongs more to the Renaissance than to antique Rome. It is a humanist art, practiced particularly by a community of Neo-Latin poets who wrote for each other and for the royal patrons who supported them. It was the very kind of community that Jonson in the early Jacobean era hoped for and for which he wrote as he assembled and arranged the epigrams of the first book and the commendatory pastorals and epistles of the second. In his collection of Neo-Latin poets, Jonson could look back on Renaissance models for the kind of poetry and the kind of society he attempted to fashion. One model of humanist epigram and verse epistle was Marullus, whose poetry Jonson read and whose volumes he had collected for his library.

Michael Marullus (1453–1500), highly celebrated in Europe for his elegant Latin *epigrammata,* followed the Greek or the Catullan model and not the Martialian one, his wit being Attic and his penchant for the mythological rather than the satiric mode.[19] Sharing the love tradition with Pontano and Secundus, he wrote epigrams to Neaera, even one on a stolen kiss. Unlike Secundus, who occasionally enjoyed a Martial-like joke and wrote epigrams on faithless wives, old or painted courtesans, and cuckolded husbands, Marullus confined his witty epigrams to Vulcan confronted by a wheedling Venus or Apollo losing Daphne to a laurel. A resident at various times in Rome, Naples, and Florence, Marullus wrote commendatory epigrams to Maximilian Caesar, Lorenzo de' Medici, King Charles of France, and to nobles at the different Italian ducal houses. His literary friends were Pontano, Sannazaro, and Politian, all of whom he wrote verse to. Closely connected to the Scala family, of which both

Bartolomeo and Alessandra were poets, he married Alessandra sometime after 1494. The legacy of commendatory epigrams that he left range from relatively brief to long epistolary verses and even semi-odes and are written to kings and noblemen, poets and learned friends, noblewomen and learned ladies. As such, they are important models for Jonson, whose own range of acquaintance and of poetic genres are comparable.

Making use of the Greek Anthology and employing the epi-gram as a means of familiar address, as humanist poets had begun to, Marullus raised the epigram to a serious art form and made it possible for poets who followed and ultimately for Jonson himself among them to transcend the merely satiric or inscriptional aspects of epigram writing. As Jonson was to, Marullus defends the morality or "chastity" of the epigram. Addressing himself to Quintilian (1.62), he affirms that Phoebus and the Muses approve chaste poetry and that there should be no war between probity and wit; let obscene license be far from us, he says, "Sit procul a nobis obscoena licentia scripti: / Ludimus innocuae carmina mentis opus" (15–16). Yet in this he is not narrow-minded; in a congenial epigram to Sannazaro, he tells his friend that a good poet is a rare bird, and because Virgil and Catullus suffered lesser talent, so should Sannazaro (2.26). But Marullus did not merely write of poetry in his serious epigrams; taking a wide view of the world about him, he wrote of national and international affairs, of the wars within and without Italy. Addressing both Charles VIII of France, whom he advised to attend more to the political affairs in his country than to hunting, and Maximilian Caesar, whom he urges to bring peace to Europe, Marullus, an exiled Greek from Constantinople, never tires of urging those in power to oppose the Turk and reinstate the Greek rule. Marullus's political epigrams could serve as models for Jonson, who takes the liberty to ask James I to reestablish law in England after the public upheaval that plague and political plotting have worked against the state (35, 51).

Yet it is the personal and not the political epigrams of Ma-rullus that are far more important as models. He writes to literary men not only as fellow poets but as friends. He addresses Giovanni Pico, the Platonist, as the delight of the Muses, "deli-tiae novem sororum" (3.7), just as Jonson was to address Donne as the "delight of PHOEBUS and each Muse" (23), and he writes a laudatory epitaph on Pico's death, alluding not only to his nobility, genius, grace and rare spirit, but to the sunset of Socratic studies at his departure (4.31). With similar generosity, Jonson writes to Beaumont, to Edward Alleyn, to Josiah Sylvester, to Thomas Overbury, to Clement Edmondes, and to the composer Alphonso Ferrabosco. These tributes to writers and men of accomplishment, written in the Renaissance style, stand side by side with those carping Martialian epigrams on poet-apes, mimes, and would-be wits and playwrights and plagiaries.[20]

Jonson's person often enters his poetry; the personal approach to life and morality is part of his poetic stance. In this too the Renaissance mode in the epigram, particularly those of Marullus, is exemplary. Marullus's epigram on his dead brother, written in imitation of Catullus, and his epitaph for his father introduce the note of restrained but personal grief into his poetry. He can write feelingly to Antonio Petrucci, to whom he looked not only as a protector but as a father ("non ut patronum, sed pium ut decet patrem / nimirum amasque solus et tibi constas"). In these, Renaissance poetry joins with ancient poetry in furnishing Jonson with models for his epitaphs to his son and daughter and in providing a model for the filial verses he wrote to Camden, who, like Petrucci to Marullus, was patron and father figure.

Marullus also at times stretches the epigram into the epistle, providing a model for Jonson. In the verses on his exile, in the consolatory lines to Andrea Matthaeus Aquavivius on the death of his father, in the semiepistolary poem to Franciscus Ninus the Elder, Marullus discourses on the times, offers moral and political comment, makes personal observations on his own and others' trials, and even includes digressions on how poetry provides sustenance and consolation in all this. Marullus does not invent this semiepistolary mode; other humanist poets before and after employ it. But we may find in these precedents for poems such as the epistles to the Countess of Rutland and Katherine, Lady Aubigny, in the second volume, or some of the longer epigrams of Jonson's first book, such as that to Sir Henry Savile. In this epigram to Savile, Jonson not only compliments Savile on his translation of Tacitus, but also expatiates on how Savile might become a man to speak "the intents, / The councells, actions, orders, and events / Of state, and censure them" (95). In this Jonson moves beyond the Martialian mode. Similarly, the epistolary poems of The Forrest start with epigrammatical intent but accomplish more. They not only address and compliment the ladies, but also address Jonson's concern about the abuses at court, friendship cracked, merit neglected. Like Marullus, Jonson retains the belief in the power of poetry to transcend all, and like Marullus, Jonson appeals to the mythological past to assert it.

Finally, the set of epigrams that Marullus writes to Alessandra Scala surely has its effect on the tone and manner of address that Jonson adopts for such learned ladies as the Countess of Bedford, Lady Mary Wroth, and the Countess of Rutland. Alessandra Scala came from a family of humanists and poets and was herself accomplished in verse. In 3.4, Marullus compares Alessandra to Sappho and says that the muses now, as before, have increased in number with the new poet. In another epigram (3.41) he tells her that, though young, she has surpassed even the accomplishments of her father. He wonders at her beauty, as well as her muse-like talents, and concludes she is a goddess (4.17). In one of the longest of the epigrams (4.4), he mounts still more mythological connections and Alessandra moves from being Sappho to muse to Pallas. Jonson uses similar devices in his commendatory epigrams. Cupid is struck by the beauty as well as the virtue of Philippa Sidney. In 105 Jonson compares Lady Mary Wroth's accomplishments in verse with those of her famous uncle, Philip Sidney; in 74 he makes similar comparisons in addressing Elizabeth, Countess of Rutland. In 105 Jonson begins by calling Lady Mary Wroth "a *Nymph*, a *Muse*, a *Grace*," and then proceeds to accumulate more mythological identities for her as the poem progresses: Ceres, Flora, Venus, Diana, Juno, and Pallas. Lucy, Countess of Bedford, becomes in one epigram (94) the "Life of the *Muses* day," both morning-star and evening-star, and in another (76) the epitome of that kind of creature a poet might most wish to honor, love, and serve. Compliments to poetic ladies are assuredly as old as the Greek Anthology, which contains laudatory epigrams to Sappho as well as to accomplished queens, such as Berenice. But for the graceful use of mythological reference, the Elizabethan age looked to Italy and to the humanist poets.[21] Though Jonson, unlike Marullus, did not marry any of the ladies he lauded, he follows in the humanist tradition that revived mythological compliment to pay tribute to learning as well as beauty.

Jonson's double-volumed book of poems included in the 1616 Folio would not have been written in the modes nor have been collected in the groups and order that they were without the example of the humanist poets before him. Like them, he valued classical influence; like them, he adapted the classical poems to his own age. Both the emphasis that he places on being master of the miscellany in the English *sylva* and the high value that he places upon epigram as the maturest of forms looks back to the taste of Neo-Latin masters such as Pontano, Marullus, and Secundus, who displayed their versatility in writing in the miscellaneous modes and had raised the epigram to the art form that Jonson so assiduously cultivated for his English audience.

Notes

1. See David McPherson, "Ben Jonson's Library and Marginalia: An Annotated Catalogue" in *Studies in Philology* 71 (1974): 3–106.

2. For a recent discussion of the sixteenth-century epigram tradition in England see Mary Thomas Crane, "*Intret Cato*: Authority and the Epigram in Sixteenth-Century England," *Renaissance Genre: Essays on Theory, History, and Interpretation*, ed. Barbara Kiefer Lewalski (Cambridge: Harvard University Press, 1986), pp. 158–186; Ann Baynes Coiro, *Robert Herrick's Hesperides and the Epigram Book Tradition* (Baltimore: Johns Hopkins University Press, 1988), pp. 78–104.

3. See McPherson, *Ben Jonson's Library*, p. 94. Also see Raymond B. Waddington, "'A Celebration of Charis': Socratic Lover and Silenic Speaker" in *Classic and Cavalier: Essays on Jonson and the Sons of Ben*, ed. Claude J. Summers and Ted-Larry Pebworth (Pittsburgh: University of Pittsburgh Press, 1982), pp. 121–38, for a discussion of influences on the Charis sequence.

4. See O. Wallace, *Notes and Queries*, 3.8.187. Also see "Commentary" on *The Forrest* in Ben Jonson, *Complete Works*, ed. C. H. Herford and Percy and Evelyn Simpson (Oxford: Clarendon Press, 1952), 11.38.

5. Citations of Martial's poetry will be from Martial, *Epigrams*, 2 vol., ed. and trans. Walter C. A. Ker. (Cambridge: Harvard University Press, 1968, rev.). Translations, unless otherwise noted, are my own.

6. McPherson discusses Jonson's habits as an annotator, noting that Herford and Simpson "avoid mentioning the half-dozen annotations in which Jonson discusses an epigram that deals with oral sexual intercourse" (11–12).

7. *The Love Poems of Johannes Secundus*, ed. F. A. Wright (New York: E. P. Dutton, 1930). I have consulted Jonson's copy of Secundus (Folger Shakespeare Library), *Poetae tres Elegantissimi* (Paris, 1582).

8. Jonson owned a copy of the Greek Anthology printed in Heidelberg in 1603. See item 68 in McPherson's catalogue.

9. Horace, *The Odes and Epodes* (Cambridge: Harvard University Press, 1927, rev.).

10. "Commentary," 11.33.

11. Carol Maddison, *Apollo and the Nine* (Baltimore: Johns Hopkins University Press, 1960), pp. 88–91.

12. Modern anthologies that include these poets are the following: *An Anthology of Neo-Latin Poetry*, ed. and trans. Fred J. Nichols (New Haven: Yale University Press, 1979); *Poeti Latini del Quattrocento*, ed. Francesco Arnaldi, Lucia Gualdo Rosa, Liliana Monti Sabia (Milan and Naples: Riccardo Ricciardi,

1964). For Pontano, I have also used *Pontani Opera* (Venice: Aldus, 1505); for Flaminio, *Carmina* (Venice, 1558); for Secundus, *Poetae tres Elegantissimi* (Paris, 1582).

13. Petrus Crinitus, *Poematon* (Leiden, 1543), 1.8.

14. Matthias Casimire Sarbiewski, *Lyricorum Libri IV. Epodon Lib. Vnus* (Lyrics, Epodes, Epigrams) (Antwerp, 1632).

15. See Herford and Simpson, "Commentary," 11.39.

16. See Nichols, *Anthology*.

17. See Wright, *Love Poems of Johannes Secundus*. Also see Caspar Barth, *Erotopaegnion* (Frankfurt, 1623), pp. 117, 124, 126–27 (Jonson's copy, British Library). Numbers 10, 20, and 25 are imitations of Catullus, 5 and 7.

18. Politian in Arnaldi et al., *Poeti Latini del Quattrocento*, pp. 1020–22.

19. Michael Marullus, *Carmina*, ed. Alessandro Perosa (Turico: Thesaurus Mundi, 1951). For Marullus I have also consulted *Poetae tres Elegantissimi* (Paris, 1582), the edition of Marullus Jonson owned.

20. Laudatory epigrams of this kind are common throughout fifteenth and sixteenth-century Neo-Latin poetry, particularly when one man of letters is writing of or to another. The summary of praises Jonson includes in epigram 7 to Donne ("thy language, letters, arts, best life") much resembles the catalogue of Politian's distich, "In Marsilium"—"Mores, ingenium, musas, sophiamque supremam" ("Manners, wit, muses, and supreme wisdom")—with which Politian would sum up Marsilius's praises (Leodegarius a Quercu, *Flores Epigrammatum* [Paris, 1555], 1.49v). Jonson's autograph volume that contains Giovanni Battista Pigna, Celio Calcagnini, and Ludovico Ariosto also yields many complimentary epigrams to literary figures. Pigna compliments Bartholomew Cavalcanti on his Platonic studies; Calcagnini praises Lilio Gregorio Giraldi on his learning and the purity of his style (Ioannes Baptista Pigna, *Carmina*, Caelius Calcagninus, *Carmina* [Venice, 1554], p. 7, pp. 184–85). Jan Gruterus (*Epigrammatum Libellus* [Heidelberg, 1587] in another collection that Jonson owned includes among his epigrams addressed to friends a complimentary epigram to Jan Dousa on his completion of his edition of Plautus (p. 161). Those very figures who address epigrams to literary friends are in turn the subject of complimentary epigrams written by other poets. See, for example, the epigrams to Calcagnini and Politian in Quercu's collection (1.79v, 80r).

21. Epigrams to learned and noble ladies, in which they are compared to goddesses, are common throughout the Renaissance. See, for example, the following included in Quercu's anthology: an epigram by Ercole Strozzi to Lucretia Borgia, "Sis Venus ore, opibus Iuno, Minerua manu" (Be Venus in face, Juno in riches, Minerva in skill), (76v), or an epigram by Pietro Bembo to Diana Ariosta, in which he remarks that the lady is just like Diana in appearance, in dress, in hair, in name, and in wit (55r).

Printing and "The Multitudinous Presse": The Contentious Texts of Jonson's Masques

Joseph Loewenstein

Jonson was a quarrelsome man. As a young soldier he was fascinated with the flashy gravity of military display; as a slightly older actor he was imprisoned for duelling.[1] As a playwright he sustained and perhaps instigated what came to be known as the War of the Theaters, and he gloried in the fact that when John Marston threatened him with a pistol he had beaten his assailant and taken the weapon. Age—by which one might mean fatherhood, or mourning over lost offspring, or imprisonment for various offences, or popular success, or persistent aristocratic attention and patronage, or religious conversion, or any number of things—slightly distilled his general belligerence, boiled and cooled it, into a passion for polemic.

Under James, the making of masques became both a focus and a vantage for Jonson's polemical engagement with England's aesthetic culture. If all of Jonson's works are marked—and in some instances a better word would be scarred—with furious intensities, the masques are in no way exceptions. Responsible criticism will preface its account of those furies with some acknowledgment of the genuinely remarkable composure conjured in these creations, a ravishing composure, a luminous poise. Since Stephen Orgel turned his attention to Jonson's masques, critics have been alert to their successes, but it will again bear noting how much was accomplished in the form.[2] English indoor spectacle had never been so complex. To be sure, there were some splendid botches—machines that didn't work, audiences too unsophisticated or too willfully obtuse to make sense of the event, performances cancelled because of insoluble diplomatic problems in the seating of spectators, audiences and performers so drunk that entertainment and revelry degenerate into fuddled chaos.[3] But when the event did come off, it involved astonishing achievements in logistics and etiquette: dancing master, composer, architect and poet working in concord; noble participants blandished into cooperation, their actions insulated from and coordinated with the labor of mechanicals; a huge scale of communal aestheticization, charged with the energies of Saturnalia, but checked from dissipation. The form itself was an accomplishment: Inigo Jones and Jonson imbued the loose conventions that had accumulated in Tudor royal entertainments with form, with recognizable generic coherence. And there is even more to the achievement. Even as Jonson participated in making the form of masques, even as he negotiated the ethical problematics of flattery (and so secured for a time the most sustained hearing that an English poet had ever received from a monarch, with the possible exception of the hearing Elizabeth accorded Lyly), even as he was composing some of his most musical, and "settable" verse, he was sternly, carefully grutching.

D. J. Gordon has mapped the large ideological range of Jonson's quarrel with Inigo Jones, and others—Orgel and Jonas Barish most notably, myself as well—have continued to examine the terms and implications of the quarrel.[4] But recently Jonathan Goldberg has remarked on another of Jonson's adversaries:

> The entrance of the witches in Queens is self-consciously reminiscent of another masque of twelve ladies, Daniel's Vision of the Twelve Goddesses (1604), and when the queen of the witches arrives, Jonson launches into a lecture that seems aimed at Daniel: "For to have made themselves their own decipherers, and each one to have told upon their entrance what they were and whether they would, had been a most piteous hearing, and utterly unworthy any quality of a poem, wherein a writer should always trust somewhat to the capacity of the spectator, especially at these spectacles, where men, beside inquiring eyes, are understood to bring quick ears" (lines 92–97). Although Jonson seems here to be minimizing the importance of the words spoken, that is not his point. Daniel's masque, in which the characters announce their identities, lacks the proper encouragement to decipherment that Jonson favors.[5]

Small matter that I think Goldberg not quite correct in suggesting that Jonson is "minimizing the importance of the words spoken," even in so polemical a circumstance, for Jonson is arguing against Daniel's vulgarization of the verbal component of masquing. He is quite right about Jonson's emphasis on decipherment, on what Eco calls "the role of the reader."[6] For the masque to realize fully its ideological function, the mutual heightening of the prestige of maker—poet, architect, dancing master—and monarch, production of meaning must involve reciprocal exchanges along that axis which is itself symbolized by the line of royal vision around which Jones's perspective was organized. Goldberg deserves credit for noticing an episode in what turns out to have been a sustained competition between Jonson and Daniel for a favored position as court entertainer. The competition is primarily articulated as a debate—a debate somewhat more sober than that carried out between Jonson and Jones—on the place of explicitness with respect to courtly making. To track Jonson's relation with Daniel is to trace a crucial development in that theory of the masque and of its textuality which ultimately led to their publication in the 1616 Folio.[7]

Jonson's pointed remark on the unworthiness of explicitness is, of course, not only a statement of aesthetic conviction: it is also an attempt to score off Daniel. There is evidence that differences between Jonson and Daniel antedate Jonson's comment on the unworthiness of Daniel's courtly aesthetic in the Queenes manuscript by several years, although the very first signs of Jonson's awareness of Daniel are innocuous enough. Neither Matheo's plagiarism of the opening of Delia in the quarto text of Every Man In His Humour (1601, but performed two years earlier) nor Fastidious Brisk's near-quotation of Daniel's Complaynt of Rosamond in Every Man Out does a particular disservice to the original author.[8] But by the time Jonson rewrote Every Man In (probably in 1612) he has Matheo distort the lines from Delia and so provoke the unambiguous response, "A Parodie! A parodie! with a kind of miraculous gift, to make it absurder then it was" (5.5. 26–27), and when he once again imitated the passage from the Complaynt of Rosamond, this time in The Staple of News (1626), awareness had blossomed as firm derision.[9]

As far as one can judge, Jonson consolidated his hostility to Daniel in the first years of the century and, as is often the case with Jonson, it is difficult to establish precedence for pique or principle.[10] In 1619 he reported that he and his friend, Sir John Roe, "were ushered by my Lord Suffolk from a Mask" and that Roe wrote "a moral epistle" on the event. Though Roe's epistle is dated 6 January 1603 (O.S.), it strongly suggests that the masque from which they were ejected was in fact Daniel's Vision of the Twelve Goddesses, performed later during the

Twelfth Night festivities for that year, on the eighth of January 1603/4.[11] "Let them increase / In riot and excesse" writes the smarting Roe of the revelrous courtiers,

> as their meanes cease;
> Let them scorne him that made them, and still shun
> His Grace, but love the whore who hath undone
> Them and their soules. But; that they that allow
> But one God, should have religions enow
> For the Queens Masque, and their husbands, far more
> Then all the Gentiles knew, or *Atlas* bore!
>
> (ll. 23–30)

This is the second time in the poem that Roe specifies the queen's masque—Daniel's *Vision* was commissioned by Anne, who took the role of Pallas—whereas the masque of 6 January was a "mask of Scots" which seems to have been a simple disguising and dance, probably without text.[12] Surely it was a performance of Daniel's masque from which Roe and Jonson were expelled. Roe's emphasis on the polytheism of the queen's masque seems to specify the ethos of Daniel's text, which concludes with Iris adumbrating a gallant theology:

> These deities by the motion of the all-directing, Pallas, the glorious patroness of this mighty monarchy, descending in the majesty of their invisible essence upon yonder mountain found there the best (and most worthily the best) of ladies, disporting with her choicest attendants, whose forms they presently undertook as delighting to be in the best-built temples of beauty and honour.[13]
>
> (ll. 406–12)

Casting as hierophany: a jealous dramatic poet could easily make of this an occasion for pious disdain, might even be so imprudent as to cause some slight disruption, however imposing the social circumstance. So, early in 1604, Jonson incarnated himself as Rabbi Busy, though he failed to stop the performance.

Perhaps he felt licensed to such self-assertion by his noble companion. Jonson relied heavily on the influence of aristocratic friends, and often overestimated or misconstrued the nature of their patronage. Perhaps Jonson expected the protection of Suffolk, whose appointment as Lord Chamberlain in May of the preceding year he had celebrated in verse (*Epigrammes*, 67). Jonson had already been the beneficiary of Suffolk's kindness during the trouble over *Sejanus* and indeed Suffolk would assist him again in a few months, helping to secure his release from prison, where he had been confined for various libelous aspects of *Eastward Ho*.[14] Jonson's plays, like those of many of his contemporaries, frequently brood or sneer over the vagaries of personal allegiance; loyalty was as important to Jonson as it was mysterious. Interested as he was in clientage, he was stunningly obtuse about gauging the precise configurations of Suffolk's allegiance; he misjudged Suffolk, as he would often misjudge his patrons, thinking that the Lord Chamberlain would be as indulgent toward social gaffe as he was toward political indiscretion. He would attempt to mitigate a poet's punishment for imprudent flirtings with topicality, but he would not tolerate a mere citizen's disturbance of courtly ceremony.

The event must have consolidated Jonson's nearly perpetual sense of having been slighted. The expulsion was simply the crowning blow; bad enough that Jonson had not himself been asked to script the queen's masque, the most elaborate entertainment in this the first holiday season of the new reign. He had, after all, provided the text for an entertainment during the preceding June on the occasion of Sir Robert Spencer's reception of Queen Anne and Prince Henry at Althorp.[15] Worst of all, Daniel's commission to provide the queen's masque had come to him through the Countess of Bedford, whose patronage Jonson had himself been cultivating since at least 1601.[16] Daniel had received pointed signs of Lady Bedford's favor since the previous spring, when she commissioned his *Panegyrike Congratulatorie* in celebration of the new king's progress south. This patronage either confirmed or qualified (depending on how the epistle is dated) the terms of Jonson's references to Lucy and to Daniel in his verse epistle to the Countess of Rutland; Lady Bedford is

>   that purest light
> Of all Lucina's traine; Lucy the bright.
> Then which, a nobler heaven it selfe knowes not.
> Who, though shee have a better verser got,
> (Or Poet, in the court account) then I,
> And who doth me (though I not him) envy,
> Yet for the timely favours shee hath done,
> To my lesse sanguine Muse, wherein she'hath wonne,
> My grateful soule, the subject of her powers,
> I have already us'd some happy houres,
> To her remembrance.[17]
>
>   (*The Forrest*, 12, ll. 65–75)

Jonson's remark to Drummond, years later, that "Daniel was at Jealousies with him" (*Conversations*, 152), repeats the ascription, although the slightly curious phrase, "to be at jealousies with" suggests a reciprocity that seems more credible than does the explicit denial of reciprocity in the verse epistle. Though Jonson is obviously projecting his own envy onto Daniel, it could still be maintained that before the decade was out, there would be something more than mere projection in Jonson's ascription of envy to Daniel. If one can fairly assume that Jonson was jealous of Daniel, and that his jealousy got the best of him during the holiday season of 1603–1604, there is reason to believe that the feeling was mutual.

The Vision of the Twelve Goddesses was published surreptitiously soon after its performance: as early as 2 February Lord Worcester annotated a copy of the edition and sent it to Lord Shrewsbury, who had asked for details of the season's festivities.[18] On the nineteenth of March, Edward Blount entered for publication a volume of Jonson's specifically "Jacobean" devisings to date—the texts of the Althorp entertainment, of the speeches Jonson had composed for James's coronation progress through the city of London, and of Jonson's "Panegyre" on the occasion of James's first attendance in Parliament, taking place that very day. Thus, Jonson's text matches two crucial texts by Daniel from the preceding year, Daniel's *Panegyrike Congratulatorie*, published in the early summer of 1603, and the *Vision*. But it is not only Daniel with whom Jonson competes here. The title page reduces James himself to a kind of pretext, an occasion to the Poet:

B. JON:
HIS PART OF
King James his Royall and Magnifi-
cent Entertainement through his
Honorable Cittie of London,
Thurseday the 15. of
March. 1603.

The characteristic Jonsonian self-promotion is palpable.[19] Before the end of the title page, the self-promotion will be elegantly restated. More than flattery and knee-jerk neoclassicism motivate the Latin epigraph to the volume:

Quando magis dignos licuit spectare triumphos!

When could one have seen such noble triumphs!

(l.3)

The epigram from which the line is taken, Martial 5.19, gets beyond brassy encomium

est tamen hoc vitium sed non leve, sit licet unum,
    quod colit ingratas pauper amicitias

Yet there is a defect—only one, but not a small one:
    that a poor man must seek from ungrateful friendships.[20]

(ll. 7–8)

The complaint is so tired that one might not bother to track Jonson in Martial's lines: Jonson, of course, was appealing to James's patronage. Still, Jonson must have found a good deal of his own predicament in Martial's lines—must have animated those lines, as it were—for as Martial goes on to detail and measure the meanness of contemporary patrons he consolidates a fine shrewdness that Jonson often sought and imitated from Martial. Moreover, Jonson shares Martial's professional position:

quatenus hi non sunt, esto tu, Caesar, amicus:
    nulla ducis virtus dulcior esse potest.
iam dudum tacito rides, Germanice, naso;
    utile quod nobis do tibi consilium.

Since these are not, Caesar, be you my friend;
    Nothing can be sweeter in a leader.
Yet all this while, Caesar, you've been laughing in your sleeve
    Because I council you, but on my own behalf.

(ll. 15–18)

Though Caesar's *tacito naso* asserts superior social knowledge, Martial checks the imperial sneer, which must adjust itself to join the poet in chuckling over the poet's predicament. The last line shows poet and patron to be possessed of matched social knowledge. This joining and matching is the fundamental tactic of the epigram; only by favoring the poet can Caesar hope to distinguish his *amicitia* from the *ingratae amicitiae* of others. And Jonson here matches Martial, for his title page proposes quite the same relationship between himself and his king, a relationship that will be reasserted at the end of the "Panegyre," where Jonson quotes Florus: "Solus Rex, & Poeta non quotannis nascitur." The title page nevertheless proposes to distinguish the scholarly monarch from such fickle patrons as the Countess of Bedford.

Working thus, by slant allusion, Jonson's volume lodges only the slightest, the most barely particularized protest against the Countess of Bedford. The epigraph—a sly and fragmentary "Epistle to Lucy, Countess of Bedford"—is distinguished by its very subtlety of implication, its inexplicitness ("a writer should always trust somewhat to the capacity of the spectator," Jonson asserted). This, too, is part of the complex self-promotion marshalled on Jonson's title page.

The self-promotion in this volume works subtly and firmly to Daniel's disadvantage. Hardly surprising, thus, that it is here in the Entertainments volume, and not in the text of *Queenes*, that Jonson made his first published swipe at Daniel's overexplicitness; hardly surprising, too, that it is something more than a mere swipe:

> The *Symboles* used, are not, neither ought to be, simply *Hierogly-phickes*, *Emblemes*, or *Impreses*, but a mixed character, partaking somewhat of all, and peculiarly apted to these more magnificent Inventions: wherein, the garments and ensignes deliver the nature of the person, and the word the present office. Neither was it becomming, or could it stand with the dignitie of these shewes (after the most miserable and desperate shift of the Puppits) to require a Truchman, or (with the ignorant Painter) one to write, *This is a Dog*; or, *This is a Hare*: but so presented, as upon the view, they might, without cloud, or obscuritie, declare themselves to the sharpe and learned: And for the multitude, no doubt but their grounded judgments did gaze, said it was fine, and were satisfied. (ll. 253–67)

A remarkable stratagem: once more, principle—the Jonsonian position—emerges from a positioning. Jonson here grounds his characteristic assertion that the finest poetry discriminates its audience on the implication that base overexplicitness actually condescends to a noble audience. Some of the richest effects of Daniel's masque are thus devalued. It is an elegant compliment to the ladies in Daniel's masque to assert how easily goddess and noble mortal can interpersonate each other, yet as Jonson would have it, when Lucy presents herself, it is a rather tawdry business:

Next holy Vesta in bright majesty
Appears with mild aspect in dove-like hue:
With th'all-combining scarf of amity
T'engird strange nations with affections true.

(ll. 299-302)

According to Jonson, Daniel has contrived that the Countess drag herself into a wholesale degradation of court culture simply by reciting her lines. It is as if Daniel had required that she and her fellow-masquers each prance forward and each insist, "Don't we look *divine?*"

Because the Entertainments volume slights Daniel in this and other ways, one suspects that the second printing of *The Vision of the Twelve Goddesses,* also in 1604, is partly a response to Jonson's volume (if not to Jonson's attempted disruption of the performance of *The Vision*) and to what Jonson was beginning to stand for. One cannot be certain: the precise date of the authorized edition of Daniel's masque cannot be fixed, and it could have preceded Jonson's (in which case one may simply wish to reverse one's sense of who is responding to whom). Certainly Daniel's printed preface, in the form of a proper epistle to the Countess of Bedford, claims the unauthorized edition as sole pretext. He begins,

Madam,
In respect of the unmannerly presumption of an indiscreet printer, who without warrant hath divulged the late show at Court, presented the eighth of January, by the Queen's Majesty and her Ladies, and the same very disorderly set forth: I thought it not amiss, seeing it would otherwise pass abroad to the prejudice both of the masque and the invention, to describe the whole form thereof in all points as it was then performed. (ll. 4–16)

This is plausible enough: the first edition does show signs of hasty preparation. Yet it also establishes a fundamental difference from Jonson's attitude to print. Daniel preserves the traditional English poet's prejudice against the vulgarity of the press. The ostensible privacy of his epistle to the Countess of Bedford claims the ethos of manuscript culture and laments the indiscreet, commercial presumption of the printer. If Jonson had not yet gone nearly as far as later he would toward embracing the technology of print, there is, nonetheless, none of Daniel's grudging relation to the press in the Entertainments volume.

This is hardly the limit of the differences articulated in the two publications. Others are so pointed that they seem to reveal two poets settling into adversarial roles. Consider the rather obscure but important principles of signification that each invokes. Jonson asserts of his coronation entertainment that "the *Symboles* used, are not, neither ought to be, simply *Hieroglyphickes, Emblemes,* or *Impreses,* but a mixed character, partaking somewhat of all." The scholarship of Dieckmann, Allen, Gordon, and others has failed to gloss adequately these distinctions—and there may be a certain amount of chic (and scholar-thwarting) theoretical mumbo-jumbo in Jonson's assertion—but his defense of semiotic complexity may be contrasted with Daniel's commentary on the figurative status of the impersonated goddesses:

> Though these images have oftentimes divers significations, yet it being not our purpose to represent them with all those curious and superfluous observations, we took them only to serve as hieroglyphics for our present intention, according to some one property that fitted our occasion, without observing other their mystical interpretations, wherein the authors are so irregular and confused as the best mythologers, who will make anything to seem anything.[21] (ll. 31–37)

"Hieroglyphics for our present intention." Thus Daniel insists on a semiotic straitened by authorial will, an event of determined meanings. This is not to suggest by contrast that Jonson's entertainment was conceived as somehow indeterminate. "The garments deliver the nature of the person, and the word the present office": such determinations are possible. But such determinations as are possible are conditioned by the audience, and depend upon a variety of semantic registers, "*symboles* . . . [of] a mixed character." We must note, then, the generosity of signification that Jonson proposes.

This is a fairly important point, since it bears upon the insufficiently modulated critical issue of Jonson's pedantry. Jonson was a quarrelsome man, but not exactly a fussy one. However learned an early Jonsonian masque may have been, its semiotic plenitude is intended as part of a fully occasional, fully theatrical dazzle. When Jonson wrote out the text of *Queenes* for Queen Anne, five years after his first polemical engagement with Daniel, he prefaced it with a letter that carefully inflects that gross distinction between the scholarly (which today is vulgarized as "the pedantic") and the theatrical (a term that requires no special labor of vulgarization); in the letter to Anne he speaks of Prince Henry's "command, to have mee adde this second labor of annotation to my first of Invention." He knows the difference, and indicates a clear priority: it bears remarking that masque performance is not nostalgic for the archive. This is not to deny the undeniable, that Jonson was proud of his learning. In the dedicatory letter to Prince Henry, that pride, joined by self-promotion, speaks—"though it hath prov'd a worke of some difficulty to mee to retrive the particular *authorities* (according to your gracious command, and a desire borne out of judgment) to those things, which I writt out of fullnesse, and memory of my former readings" (ll. 32–36). The "*symboles* . . . [of] a mixed character" are "writt out of fullnesse": invention for the masque-performance is cornucopian, text-preparation is ancillary.

Jonson must have thought of *Queenes* as a particularly fine achievement, a perfect means of securing his place as chief court poet. The antimasque, Jonson's most obvious contribution to what would become the canonical form of the Stuart masque, was first employed as a fully articulated feature in *Queenes*. It was a brilliantly responsive innovation, perfectly attuned to the resources of Inigo Jones's stagecraft. Jonson had been working with Jones since 1605, working with alert and jealous appreciation; the fashionable *serio ludere* of antimasque's mock dissipations provide a fine scenic occasion in and of themselves, an occasion, too, for a scenic foil to the ensuing Palladian symmetries of the main masque; more important, the turn from antimasque to main masque exploits Jones's astonishing skills in engineering abrupt transformations. With its fiction of historical teleology, in which civil magnificence dazzlingly replaces grubby superstitiousness, *Queenes* invigorates courtly masquing by importing the dynamism of rudimentary plot. Daniel's *Vision of Twelve Goddesses* is linked by structural affiliation with medieval dream-vision (Night rouses Sleep, who invokes Iris, who speaks to a sibyl, who acts as presenter to a pageant of twelve goddesses) and the new Jonsonian sequence of antimasque and masque repudiates such a static structure. With its allusion to the formal model of the neoclassical triumph, *Queenes* thematizes Culmination. Such allusions would grow firmer in the next decades of Jonson's career as a masque-maker. Indeed, Jonson must have thought that his new masque had so outdistanced Daniel's finicky and overexplicit construction that it had achieved Culmination.

*   *   *   *   *   *

The competition with Daniel is quite a small episode in Jonson's career, but it edged him toward certain positions and precipitated some discriminations that criticism will do well to appropriate. First, it helped him to articulate a preference for what Barthes would have called "readerly" reception of masque performances, a courtly deference that entailed an emphasis on esoteric representation. When, in the quarto text of *Hymenaei*, Jonson contrasts "the things subjected to *understanding*" to "those which are objected to *sense*" (ll. 1–3), the former is not a fully antitheatrical category. One may recall the gallantry of his remark on one of the dances in *The Masque of Beautie*: "*Here, they danc'd a third most-elegant, and curious dance, and not to be describ'd againe, by any art, but that of their owne footing*" (ll. 374–76). At this stage in his career, Jonson is certainly not promoting reading at the expense of spectatorship. He is simply promoting the sort of reception that might best be characterized as "curious." The term might just as well have been taken from the much-quoted passage that comes shortly after the opposition of understanding and sense in the text of *Hymenaei*, a passage that deserves an unsettled scrutiny; it begins in deference to "the most noble royall *Princes*, and greatest *persons* (who are commonly *personaters* of these actions)" and who are

> not onely studious of riches, and magnificence in the outward celebration, or shew; (which rightly becomes them) but curious after the most high, and hearties *inventions*, to furnish the inward parts: (and those grounded upon *antiquitie*, and solide *learnings*) which, though their *voyce* be taught to sound to present occasions, their *sense*, or doth, or should alwayes lay hold on more remov'd *mysteries*. (ll. 10–19)

Those mysteries, "subjected to understanding," are not fully at odds with the occasion—Jonson has used the same word, *sense*, to describe both the fugitive experience of the spectator and the purport of the masque's "inward part." Mysteries are accessible within Jonsonian masque-performance, not transfixed, flattened, or exposed as they are in Daniel's *Vision*; mysteries defer to the spectators' curious constructions.

Many commentators have taken Jonson's endorsement of "more remov'd *mysteries*" primarily as an antioccasional assertion, a scornful withdrawal from Whitehall, perhaps to the library. Certainly Jonson had had his antioccasional, antitheatrical moments—as early as *Cynthia's Revels*—and more would come, but the text of *Hymenaei* does not quite constitute one of them, for here Jonson is formulating a courtly aesthetic, not an anti-courtly ethic. But it is also the case that the masque text itself makes possible a set of experiences obviously unavailable to performer or spectator. This observation occasions a return to the matter of Jonson's so-called pedantry, ostensibly evidenced by the obtrusive annotations to the masques.

In many ways the annotations destabilize the format of Jonson's page, announcing, gravely insisting, that these are not scripts. The strange appearance of these texts is often over-looked. A certain amount of typographic chatter is common to many Renaissance texts, although it is not quite so common in works of vernacular literature. The dense play of roman and italic type (sometimes further unsettled by Greek), the visual interruptions worked by stage directions (both tabular registers and prose descriptions, the latter of sometimes Shavian length), and, above all, the printed marginalia, with their pointed clog of abbreviation and textual reference—the combined effect of all this is to produce a textual coruscation that disrupts the easy symmetries of verse array.[22] Elucidation seldom makes such difficulties for contemplation. In a sense, of course, the typography of these texts achieves something analogous to the semiotic dazzle of masque performance, so that, once again, Jonson is more complex than Daniel.

The comparison is not a random one. The conspicuously complicated Jonsonian page makes its first appearance in the Entertainments volume of 1604. I have already suggested that this volume, which includes Jonson's "Panegyre" for James may specifically engage Daniel, who had published his own *Panegyrike Congratulatorie* in 1603. Daniel's volume had been, in its own way, a fine piece of self-promotion; it included both the coronation panegyric—no serious match for Jonson's quasi-official coronation entertainments—and the *Defence of Ryme*. The *Defence* is a learned response to Campion's attack on rhyme, the *Observations in the Art of English Poesie* of 1602. Jonson's thoughts on the arguments on both sides of this dispute are known—his opinion is recorded in the very first paragraph of Drummond's *Conversations:*

> He had ane intention to perfect ane Epick Poeme intitled Heroologia of the Worthies of his Country, rowsed by fame, and was to dedicate

it to his Country, it is all in Couplets, for he detesteth all other
Rimes, said he had written a discourse of Poesie both against Campion & Daniel especially this Last, wher he proves couplets to be
the bravest sort of Verses, especially when they are broken, like
Hexameters and that crosse Rimes and Stanzaes (becaus the purpose
would lead him beyond 8 lines to conclude) were all forced. (ll.
1–11)

Of course, Jonson had written his coronation entertainment and
his "Panegyre" in the obtrusively caesural heroic couplets at-
tacked by both Daniel and Campion. Even the lyric Althorp
entertainment, also included in the 1603 Entertainments volume, is largely given over to strange quatrains rhymed *aaaa*,
a prosodic choice that suggests itself as an overt flouting of
both Campion's and Daniel's standards. But the passage from
the *Conversations* betrays more than a difference of opinion,
for Drummond shows Jonson responding specifically to his fellow artists' claims as scholarly theorists. And the Entertainments
volume may be equally specific, its marginalia a way of insisting
on Jonson's own claims to scholarly authority. The format was
not unprecedented: Jonson and his printers had experimented
with a marginal format for stage directions as early as 1601
with the publication of *Cynthia's Revels*, a format that gives
the page a scholarly look and hints at the affiliations of the
play with traditions of classical mythography. With the publication of *Poetaster* early in the next year, stage directions give
place to terse references to classical source-texts in the margins.
But the pages of *Poetaster* are only lightly spattered with annotations, and so can hardly be said to anticipate the thickly en-
crusted page of *Sejanus* (1604). Clearly the Entertainments
volume is the first to take on the obtrusive and distinctive Jonsonian format, which offers itself as the complex product of the
compounded poet and scholar. The tangled scholarly hedge
works as an immanent Defence of Poesie. Here again, perhaps,
a skirmish with Daniel.

But by far the most significant difference articulated during
the engagement with Daniel was the attitude toward print. Daniel affects a dislike for publication; Jonson relies on it, even
relishes it. The Entertainments volume not only exploits the
range of typographic possibility, it is the first Jonsonian text
to insist on the differences between the fugitive event and the
disseminable exfoliation:

Thus hath both Court- Towne- and Countrey-Reader, our portion
of devise for the Cittie; neither are we ashamed to professe it, being
assured well of the difference betweene it and Pageantry. If the
Mecanick part yet standing, give it any distaste in the wrye mouthes
of the Time, we pardon them; for their ambitious ignorance doth
punish them inough. (Q, recorded by Herford and Simpson as a
note to 1.674)

The profession of publication enables an assertion of the dignity
of the device and frees that device from the tyranny of the
momentary and the local. Scribal, post-Gutenberg, and post-
McLuhan, we may find this latter sensitivity to the resources
of print unremarkable; for Jonson they are strategic. They enable
him to distinguish his text from Daniel's, to distinguish the
device from its nonverbal vestiges. On the one hand, the performance of the Jonsonian masque is readerly in the extreme;
on the other hand, once that performance has passed, Jonson
seeks to extricate his device from occasional constraints which
he regarded as epiphenomenal. Print redeems the device from
Place and Time.

I have argued that the publication of the masques, which
involved Jonson directly with printers in text preparation, was
an important turning point in his intellectual career—perhaps
an important moment in the history of Western literary culture—
for it provoked a reorientation of Jonson's attitude to the phe-
nomenology of the literary work.[23] Engaged as editor and as
his own publicist, Jonson experienced a propriety in the printed
masque text that he had never felt in the printed dramatic text;
that propriety eventually became the model for his relation to
the dramatic and lyric texts of the 1616 Folio. As early as 1605,
Jonson was exploiting his control over the printed text of *Sejanus*
as an attempted revaluation of the play: it had bombed in the
playhouse and Jonson was trying to make it a success on the
page. This constitutes a quiet revolution in dramatic publishing.
The play was printed with a polemical letter to its readers,
and with its pages crowded with marginal notes indicating classical sources and allusions: the masque-format was becoming
generalized as Jonson's dramatic format. Because in this instance
the printed text entails a full-fledged renunciation—perhaps a
denunciation—of the performance, we also find here the beginnings of an important feature of much of Jonson's late textuality,
including the textuality of the Folio: text as transhistorical and,
frequently, as antioccasional, text as antitheater.

It will perhaps bear repeating that this form of textuality is
by no means established as a fixed institution at the publication
of *Sejanus*. The quarto texts of the masques, for example, do
not attempt to remove mystery beyond the reach of performance.
"A *Writer*," says Jonson in the text of *Queenes*, "should alwayes
trust somewhat to the capacity of the *Spectator*, especially at
these Spectacles" (105–7), and though trust did not come easily
to Jonson, the masque quartos repeatedly embed the record of
the spoken text in deferential reconstructions of performance.
But reverence for the event is by no means unqualified. The
quarto texts for the wedding masques of both 1606 and 1608,
Hymenaei and *The Haddington Masque*, improve upon the event
or, rather, claim an authority for Jonson's conception that *rivals*
the authority of courtly enactment (what the gallant language
of *Pleasure Reconcil'd to Virtue* describes as "the wisdom of
your feet" [l. 268]). Thus in the quarto *Hymenaei*, the rival
claims are balanced:

> After them, the *musicians* with this song, of which, then, onely
> one *staffe* was sung; but because I made it both in *forme*, and *matter*
> to emulate that kind of *poeme*, which was call'd . . . *Epithalamium*,
> and (by the ancients) us'd to be sung, when the *Bride* was led
> into her chamber, I have here set it downe whole: and do heartily
> forgive their ignorance whom it chanceth not to please. (435–41)

And in *Haddington*, the performance is shown to have been an
obstacle to comprehension:

> Here, the *musicians* . . . sung the first staffe of the following *Epitha-*
> *lamion:* which, because it was sung in pieces, betweene the *daunces*,
> shew'd to be so many severall *songs;* but was made to be read
> an intire *Poeme*. (338–42)

Moreover, it becomes clear in these texts that the assertion of
the authority of the text, its counterauthority with respect to
performance, entails Jonson's contentious jealousy of his own
cultural authority. Jonson describes the intermittent music and
dances that disrupt the integrity of the epithalamion in Haddington, and then makes attributions:

> The two latter [dances] were made by M. THO. GILES, the two
> first by M. HIE. HERNE: who, in the persons of the two *Cyclopes*,
> beat a time to them, with their hammers. The tunes were M. AL-
> PHONSO FERRABOSCO'S. The Device and act of the *scene*, M.

YNIGO JONES his, with addition of the *Trophaees*. For the invention
of the whole and the verses,
Assertor qui dicat esse meos, Imponet plagiario pudorem. (348–55)

A crucial passage. From the "made by" of manufacture to a
more interested "his," a word common to the language of production and of property: Jonson is adjudicating claims, asserting
his own. He is now, of course, staking claims to the disadvantage
of Jones and not Daniel, but what we have here is not so much
a transformation as a transfer of animus. Nevertheless, the force
of self-assertion may be read from the concluding Latin phrase,
a philological nicety adapted from Martial 1.52. A *plagiarius*
is a kidnapper; the modern meaning of *plagiarist* derives from
metaphoric extension, but that extension was first enacted in
Martial's own poem and first introduced into English by Jonson
himself—not here, but in that most contentious, most defensive
early text, *Poetaster* (1601). It is by means of Jonsonian self-
assertion that England gains the word *plagiarism* as we now
use it, and here that self-assertion is supported by the permanent
registration of the printed text. Here is an event in personal
and lexical history significant enough to stand as a key moment
in cultural history as well.

This event does not, of course, make for a revolution, for
others would write and publish considerably less jealously. Daniel, to take a conspicuous example, preserves a deferential attitude to collaborators and to performance:

> But in these things wherein the onely life consists in shew: the
> arte and invention of the Architect gives the greatest grace, and
> is of most importance: ours, the least part and of least note in
> the time of the performance thereof; and therefore have I inserted
> the discription of the artificiall part which only speakes M. *Inago
> Jones*. (*Tethys' Festivall*, E2)

This passage from *Tethys' Festivall*, performed and published
in 1610 after the Jonsonian idiom in, and attitude toward,
masques had steadied, suggests that Daniel wished to distinguish his own masque-making from Jonson's as much as Jonson
wished to distinguish his from Daniel's. If by now Jonson was
showing his dislike for working with Inigo Jones, Daniel will
celebrate their collaboration. Indeed, Daniel will go so far toward
commemorating the joint effort that he does what Jonson
would never have done: he surrenders his own singularity of

voice and allows his text to subside into a literal polyvocality.

> Tethys with her Nymphes appeares, with another Scene, which I
> will likewise describe in the language of their Architector who con-
> trived it, and speakes in his owne mestier to such as are understand-
> ers & lovers of that design.

The celebration of the transient sparkle of Jones's displays is
not an afterthought, not a contrivance for the printed commemo-
ration. The very songs of *Tethys' Festivall* do homage to Jones's
art:

> Pleasures are not, if they last,
> In their passing, is their best.
> Glory is most bright and gay
> In a flash, and so away.
>
> (ll. 344–52)

This homage to Jones's whirling mutabilities modulates into
a gallantry that Jonson was carefully purging from his own
masques. As Mercury enters to restore the masquers to their
proper shapes, to make a queen of Tethys, and noble ladies
of her nymphs, Triton announces the preeminence of this last
change, calling this return to the normalcy of the Jacobean court
"a transformation of farre more delight" than even Jones could
work.

The Daniel of *Tethys' Festivall* is thus pure anti-Jonson. He
prides himself in the fictive purity and consequent social exclu-
siveness of his masque: "in al these shewes, this is to be noted,
that there were none of the inferiour sort"—no antimasque and
thus no professionals performing—"mixed amongst these great
Personages of State and Honour" (323). He refuses to make ex-
cuses "for these figures of mine, if they come not drawn in
all proportions to the life of antiquity (from whose tyrannie,
I see no reason why we may not emancipate our inventions
. . .)" and he sneers at annotation and commentary—"neither
do I seeke in the divulging hereof, to give it [that is, his account
of the masque] other colours then those it wore, or to make
an Apologie of what I have done" (306). Above all Daniel continues to base his self-assertion on his resistance to print. "It is
expected (according to the custom)"—the Jonsonian custom—
"that I beeing imployed in the busines, should publish a description and forme of the late Mask."

Which I doe not out of a desire to be seene in pamphlets, or of
forwardnes to shew my invention therin: for I thank God, I labour
not with that disease of ostentation, nor affect to be known to be
the man *digitoque monstrarier hic est,* having my name already
wider in this kind then I desire, and more in the winde then I
would.

Daniel has worked his way into favor; Jonson was still working
his way toward the Folio.

In the Folio, devaluation of the impermanent event is more
definitive (and more anti-Danielian) than in any of the preceding
quartos. Again, the text of *Queenes* is exemplary. In 1616, the
dedicatory letter to Prince Henry was removed. It is easy enough
to explain the deletion, but it is worth considering that, by
thus transforming the quarto text, Jonson willingly sacrifices
the distinction between the primary fullness that generates a
device conceived for performance and the secondary reconnais-
sance that annotates a literary text, which means that a crucial
argument on behalf of the priority of performance has been
attenuated. The Folio texts are far less commemorative than
the quartos. Though the alteration is by no means systematic,
in several instances lists of noble participants included in the
quartos were simply dropped in the Folio. Judicious references
to the contributions of Giles, Ferrabosco, and Jones in the quarto
of *Hymenaei* were also dropped, leaving the text as Jonson's
own and permanent artifact. The masques first printed in the
Folio, *Prince Henries Barriers, Oberon, Love Freed from Ignorance, Love Restored, A Challenge at Tilt, The Irish Masque
at Court, Mercurie Vindicated,* and *The Golden Age Restored,*
contain no cast lists, few stage directions, virtually no descriptions of scenery, no mention of Jonson's collaborators. Text as
antitheater.

Hence the notorious conclusion to the Folio: *The Golden Age
Restored,* printed last though performed one year prior to *Mercurie Vindicated,* and printed with a text that manifestly scram-
bles the conclusion as it was performed in 1615. Much has
been made of the politic conclusion of the printed text, wherein
Astraea seems to admire some ideal Jacobean "place":

> What change is here! I had not more
> Desire to leave the earth before,
>   Then I have now to stay
>
> . . . .
>   This, this, and onely such as this,

> The bright *Astraea's* region is,
>   Where she would pray to live,
>   And in the midd'st of so much gold,
>   Unbought with grace or feare unsold,
>   The laws to mortals give.
>
>   (222–24,234–39)

When the masque was performed, this speech was inconclusive, for at Whitehall an ascending Pallas had called out a final corrective to this Jacobean puff, "'Tis now inough, behold you *here,* / What JOVE hath built to be your sphere" (200–201; the emphasis is mine), to which a choir, firmly and conclusively, responded, "To *Jove,* to *Jove,* be all the honour given, / That thankefull hearts can raise from earth to heaven" (219–20). The performance had been contrived to praise James and then to check and chasten that praise; the text is more free and more lavish. It is also sneaky. In performance Astraea points to that bright region beyond the proscenium where sits the king and she does not have the last word; on the page, the deictic insistence—"This, this, and onely such as this"—claims a textual authority without semantic closure, for no gesture and no delighted gaze directs our own attention to an elsewhere of ideal political stability. In performance, Pallas ends by pointing heavenward; on the page, Astraea ends by pointing, but in a direction that it lies within the power of the printed page to withhold. This may be Jonson's purest contention.

                    *   *   *   *   *   *

The title of this essay alludes to a note in the published text of the Althorp entertainment, a note that introduces a final address to Queen Anne:

> There was also another parting Speech; which was to have been presented in the person of a youth, and accompanied with divers gentlemens younger sonnes of the countrey: but by reason of the multitudinous presse, was also hindred. And which we have here adjoyned. (ll. 292–96)

Such adjunction, a recurrence in the history of Jonson's masque texts, is Jonson's printed signature, the characteristic inscription in moveable type of his particular authorship. Against the multitudinous "presse"—against, that is, the pressures of historical instance that erode verbal construction—Jonson counterposes the bulwark, the polemical stability of the Press.

Notes

1. I take these details from the biographical account in vol. 1 of the eleven-volume edition of his works edited by C. H. Herford, P. Simpson, and E. Simpson (Oxford: Clarendon, 1925–52). I wish here to acknowledge the generosity of the American Council of Learned Societies, which assisted work on this essay with a research grant.

2. Stephen Orgel, *The Jonsonian Masque* (Cambridge: Harvard University Press, 1965).

3. I have given a short list, leaving out such instances of mere failure to please as that of *Pleasure Reconcil'd to Virtue*, of which Sir Edward Harwood remarked, "the conceite good the poetry not so" (*State Papers, Domestic, James I,* vol. 95, no. 10; cited in Enid Welsford, *The Court Masque: A Study in the Relationship Between Poetry and the Revels* [Cambridge: Cambridge University Press, 1927; repr., New York: Russell & Russell, 1962], p. 205). Welsford is a connoisseur of such lapses, recording Harwood's censure as well as Sir Dudley Carleton's, this time of Jones's seascape for *The Masque of Blacknesse*—"all fish and no water" (cited from R. Winwood, *Memorials of Affairs of State in the Reigns of Q. Elizabeth and King James I* [London, 1725], 11.44.178). Campion speaks with gentler dismay of the machines for his *Lord Hay's Masque* (1607): "Either by the simplicity, negligence, or conspiracy of the painter, the passing away of the trees was somewhat hazarded" (*The Works of Thomas Campion,* ed. Walter R. Davis [New York: Doubleday, 1967; repr., New York: Norton, 1972], p. 222). But Jonson himself is the great, and greatly exultant memorialist of scenic disaster; see his joyously splenetic description of the "shows" for *Chloridia* in "An Expostulation with Inigo Jones," ll. 33–39.

The performances of masques always caused problems of diplomacy, particularly with respect to the tense protocol of seating the audience. Perhaps the worst difficulties arose at the performance of *The Golden Age Restored* (1615); on the similar difficulties involved in the protocol for other masque performances, see Mary A. Sullivan, *Court Masques of James I* (New York: G. P. Putnam, 1913).

4. Gordon's seminal essay, "Poet and Architect: The Intellectual Setting for the Quarrel between Ben Jonson and Inigo Jones" is most easily accessible in *The Renaissance Imagination,* ed. Stephen Orgel (Berkeley: University of California Press, 1981), pp. 77–101. Jonas Barish first remarked the antitheatricality of Jonson's position in the quarrel in "Jonson and the Loathed Stage," *A Celebration of Ben Jonson,* ed. William Blissett, Julian Patrick, and R. W. Van Fossen (Toronto: University of Toronto Press, 1973), pp. 27–53. My own contribution to this line of critical inquiry may be found in chapters three and four of my *Responsive Readings: Versions of Echo in Pastoral, Epic, and the Jonsonian Masque* (New Haven: Yale University Press, 1984).

5. *James I and the Politics of Literature* (Baltimore: Johns Hopkins University Press, 1983), p. 58.

6. I take the phrase from the title of Umberto Eco's collection of early studies in semiotics, *The Role of the Reader: Explorations in the Semiotics of Texts* (Bloomington: Indiana University Press, 1979), from which the introduction is perhaps most germane to this essay. But see also the short exploration of "The Poetics of the Open Work," pp. 47–67, which sustains a discussion of the performance and reception of scores of serial music that is particularly

suggestive for the criticism of such heavily mediated cultural productivities as play and masque.

7. Goldberg is not the first to draw attention to the competition. F. G. Fleay made an overstated case for Daniel as the object of some very early attacks by Jonson (*A Biographical Chronicle of the English Drama, 1559–1642*, vol. 1 (London: Reeves and Turner, 1891), pp. 92–98, particularly pp. 96–98. More measured are the suggestions made by Joan Rees in her *Samuel Daniel* (Liverpool: Liverpool University Press, 1964), to which I am much indebted.

8. Again, see Fleay, *Biographical Chronicle*, pp. 92–98; E. K. Chambers judiciously remarks on these borrowings as touches of satiric characterization: "What other poetry, then, would affected young men at the end of the century be likely to imitate?," *The Elizabethan Stage*, vol. 3 (1923; repr. Oxford: Oxford University Press, 1961), p. 273.

9. See *The Staple of News*, 3.2.267–73. By this time Jonson had seen fit to make other accusations against Daniel's verse, accusations not germane to my inquiry. In *Volpone* (1605), Lady Would-Bee reviews the contemporary literary scene:

> Here's PASTOR FIDO—. . .
> . . . All our *English* writers,
> I meane such, as are happy in th'*Italian*,
> Will deigne to steale out of this author, mainely;
> Almost as much, as from MONTAIGNIE:
> He has so moderne, and facile a veine,
> Fitting the time, and catching the court-eare.
>
> (3.4.86–92)

Daniel is undoubtedly the thief glanced at. His translation of *Il Pastor Fido* was entered in the Stationers' Register on 16 September 1601, although never published; more pertinently, Daniel's *The Queen's Arcadia*, performed in Oxford on 30 August 1605, is heavily indebted to Guarini's tragicomedy. Jonson was not the first to cast such aspersions on Daniel, for the last of the three university satires, the so-called Parnassus plays, finds Iudicio passing judgment:

> Sweete hony dropping *Daniell* may wage
> Warre with the proudest big Italian
> That melts his heart in sugred sonetting:
> Onely let him more sparingly make use
> Of others wit, and use his owne the more,
> That well may scorne base imitation.
>
> (*The Second Returne from Parnassus*, 1.2.235–40; *The Three Parnassus Plays*, ed. J.
> B. Leishman [London: Nicholson and Watson, 1949])

The anonymous author is probably not making reference to Daniel's indebtedness to Guarini; presumably the indebtedness of *Delia* to Italian sonneteering, and to that of Tasso in particular, is primarily at stake here.

10. If the date of the Epistle to Elizabeth, Lady Rutland, can be fixed as early as 1 January 1600, this would provide the earliest evidence of Jonson's hostility to Daniel. (For the problems of dating this poem, see note 17.)

11. I cite Roe's poem from *The Poems of John Donne*, ed. Herbert J. C. Grierson, vol. 1 (Oxford: Oxford University Press, 1912), pp. 414–15.

12. Chambers, *The Elizabethan Stage*, p. 279.

13. I cite Daniel throughout from *The Complete Works in Verse and Prose of Samuel Daniel*, 5 vol. ed. A. B. Grosart (1885, repr. New York: Russell and Russell, 1963).

14. Herford and Simpson collect Jonson's correspondence from prison to various prospective intercessors; see vol. 1, Appendix 2, pp. 190–200. Daniel must have approved the play, having been made licenser to the Blackfriar's Company at James's accession; since this was the season of his censure for *Philotas*, his quick recovery of royal favor is evidence of his extraordinary diplomatic skills.

15. Moreover, Jonson had clearly been thinking of himself as a court entertainer—as Lyly's proper heir—since 1600, when he wrote *Cynthia's Revels*. For a discussion of that play as an act of self-promotion, see my *Responsive Readings*, pp. 78–84.

16. In 1601, Jonson sent a printed copy of *Cynthia's Revels* to Lady Bedford, inscribed with a very charming envoy (Herford & Simpson, *Inscriptions*, 2); the poem implies an identification of Lucy with the character, Arete, in *Cynthia's Revels*, she who protects and patronizes the poet-moralist, Crites. Around this time Jonson also seems to have sent her a manuscript of four poems on the subject of the phoenix and the turtle, *Forrest*, 10 and 11 and *Ungathered Verse*, 4 and 5.

17. It has become a commonplace of Jonson scholarship that the poem was sent to Lady Rutland on New Year's Day 1600, wishing her the blessing of a son. Elizabeth Sidney married Roger Manners, fifth Earl of Rutland early in 1599; the poem mentions the Earl's absence from England and Rutland was probably in Holland during the winter of 1599–1600. Yet there is no surviving evidence for Lady Bedford's interest in either Daniel or Jonson from before 1600. (Daniel may have come into Lady Bedford's notice through either Herbert or Clifford influence.) In 1939, the weakness of the Daniel connection with Lucy at mid-century was urged by R. W. Short in "Jonson's Sanguine Rival," *Review of English Studies* 15 (1939): 315–17 as part of an argument for taking the "better verser" as Drayton, and not Daniel; though Percy Simpson resisted this argument when it first appeared (*Review of English Studies* 15: 464–65), by the time of the publication of the Herford and Simpson annotation to the poems (1952), Short's thesis had prevailed. It has since been discredited, for in 1965, J. R. Barker noted in "A Pendant to Drummond of Hawthornden's *Conversations*," *Review of English Studies*, 16:284–88 that Drummond of Hawthornden had obligingly annotated the lines in the Epistle to Lady Rutland in his copy of the 1616 Folio with the single word "Daniel." (One might ingeniously suppose that Jonson meant Drayton in 1600, but by the time of the publication of the Folio, Daniel had supplanted Drayton in Jonson's disfavor).

Short's argument had taken much of its force from the assumption that the epistle's date must be fixed at 1600; the date is generally accepted, but unsubstantiated. Rutland was known to have been a great traveler and may well have been conveniently out of the country on New Year's days subsequent to 1600. My own preference is for fixing the date of this poem at the beginning of 1603, before the death of Jonson's own son in that year which would have rendered the last lines of the epistle too plangent for the serious gallantry of the poem, before the Earl of Rutland's impotence had been widely noised about, and while Elizabeth was still alive to bolster the reference to "Lucina's traine," but late enough for the Countess of Bedford to have manifestly favored Daniel over Jonson.

18. Chambers, *The Elizabethan Stage*, 3, p. 281.

19. Still, the essential strategy of the title page is, as always in Jonson's fantasies of the relation of monarch to poet, mutuality. Jonson explains why he included the Althorp entertainment in the Entertainments volume—the title page of which really announces itself as Jonson's Coronation volume: he claims to be honoring Lord Spencer, going on to assert that the text is "not here unnecessarily adjoyned, being performed to the same *Queene & Prince;* who were no little part of these more labord and Triumphall shewes." James's royalty, significantly mediated and decentered through his family, is a principle of unity counterpoising the unifying fact of Jonson's authorship.

20. I cite Martial from the edition in the Loeb Classical Library, ed. Walter C. A. Ker (Cambridge: Harvard University Press, 1947).

21. For a general introduction to the place of hieroglyphics in European culture, see Liselotte Dieckmann, *Hieroglyphics: The History of a Literary Symbol* (St. Louis: Washington University Press, 1970). Studies more specific to Jonsonian hieroglyphics are D. J. Gordon, "The Imagery of Ben Jonson's *Masques of Blacknesse and Beautie," The Renaissance Imagination*, pp. 134–56 and D. C. Allen, "Ben Jonson and the Hieroglyphics," *Philological Quarterly* 18 (1939): 290–300.

22. For related remarks tending to rather different conclusions, see Timothy Murray, "Ben Jonson's Folio as Textual Performance," *Proceedings of the 10th Congress of the International Comparative Literature Association*, vol. 1, ed. Anna Balakian, James J. Wilhelm, Douwe W. Foukkema, Claudio Guillén, and M. J. Valdés (New York: Garland, 1985), p. 325–30.

23. "The Script in the Marketplace," *Representations* 12 (Fall 1985): pp. 101–14, and see also Timothy Murray, "From Foul Sheets to Legitimate Model: Antitheater, Text, Ben Jonson," *New Literary History* 14 (1983): 641–64.

"Noe fault, but Life": Jonson's Folio as Monument and Barrier

Jennifer Brady

By 1629, Jonson's uneasy heirs were beginning to admonish him publicly for what they persuaded themselves had been the blunder of his career: the Rhodian colossus had found himself surprised by longevity. "No book was ever spared out of tenderness to the author,"[1] Samuel Johnson wrote in his Preface to the *Dictionary*. Ben Jonson found the obverse true. The solicitude of his contemporaries was entirely for his *Workes* while his immodestly prolonged life spawned apprehension even in well-wishers, who advised Jonson to justify his claim to laureate status by, in effect, wrapping himself in his writings as his "winding-sheet."[2] Nicholas Oldisworth bluntly counsels the aging writer:

> Die: seemes it not enough, thy Writing's date
> Is endlesse, but thine owne prolonged Fate
> Must equall it? For shame, engrosse not Age,
> But now, thy fifth Act's ended, leave the stage,
> And lett us clappe.
>
> (11.397)

For Oldisworth, Jonson had "noe fault, but Life." From the vantage point of this Caroline aspirant to the disputed legacy, the *Workes*, Jonson's willful "length of dayes" was an unconscionable engrossing of his patrimony. The "Bodie" of the father, his warm breath, stands between Oldisworth and his inheritance. "Cold authors please best," he observes candidly. It is a point on which the epistles addressed to Jonson during the last decade of his life reach a remarkable consensus. These verse letters invert the *soteria* tradition, anticipating instead the sudden parricidal closure of Dryden's "Mac Flecknoe," with Jonson cast as the "yet declaiming Bard"[3] who must be hustled summarily

192

off the stage. The fifth act of Jonson's career could be described as an abject lesson in the hazards of constructing a monument to oneself in mid-life—and then, through bad judgment or miscalculation, surviving long enough to see one's *Workes* proclaimed one's cenotaph.

The canonicity of the 1616 Folio is not disputed in the Caroline censures of Jonson's protracted life and his later works. The Folio is rather invoked to a strategic end: to hold Jonson hostage to a remembered perfection. Parricidal impulses are, as it were, authorized by the Folio itself. "Thy workes make us mistake / Thy person" (11.396), Oldisworth claims. He wishes to adore a pure, stellified Folio, removed from its author's intrusive, embarrassing presence. Not surprisingly, the *Workes* become a convenient locus for charges that Jonson's talent is in eclipse. "Wee pittye now, whom once, wee did Admire," the anonymous critic of *The New Inne* writes, noting that wits "have their date" (11.344). Or Goodwin, advising Jonson not to respond to the venomous attacks directed at his age, physical disabilities, and waning prestige, cites as consolation "The other workes, rais'd by thy skillfull hand, / . . . [that] shall stand / As Monuments of thee" (11.343). Examples of this kind could be multiplied. What interests me in this body of poetry is the use to which the *Workes* are being put. To a son, these Caroline poets believe themselves justified in judging Jonson's later career by the standards set by his 1616 Folio. Jonson is held endlessly accountable to his authoritarian classic. The spectacle of the undignified, bedridden writer "Stain[ing his] . . . Well-gaind Honour" (11.341) with impassioned defences of his last works, and resisting the proferred roles of Good Gray Poet or Old Possum, requires the sons' intervention. The Jonson who refuses to "Die, for [his] . . . own sake" (11.397) is, to their minds, engaging in a high-risk behavior; alive, he threatens to become a spoiler, his own heir.[4] In contradistinction to Jonson himself, Oldisworth, Felltham, Carew, Goodwin and the other Cavalier offspring emerge as conservers—conservers, that is, of the definitive, canonized *Workes*. The stellification of those *Workes* is a necessary prelude to deposing their author. As Lawrence Lipking has remarked, "Stellification is a very safe method of disposal,"[5] especially if the heirs to a legacy can find themselves sinecures, as in this case, by claiming to be the custodians of the true, unchanging text.

A curious parenthetical aside in one of the elegies published in *Jonsonus Virbius* in 1637 speaks to the appropriation of the

Folio *Workes* by the Caroline sons. Mourning Jonson's passing, Jasper Mayne suddenly interjects a different note, an admission that ruptures the elegy's conventional *topoi* of loss: "wee all conspir'd to make *thy Herse* / Our *Workes*" (11.451).[6] The compression of this aside is itself telling. Mayne identifies the heirs as conspirators involved, out of envy, in a hostile takeover. For Mayne, the *Workes* are disputed property; once Jonson's, they are now "ours." Proprietary claims have nonetheless one considerable drawback: Mayne posits bleakly that "no *Posteritie* / Can adde" (11.452) to or better the Folio's achievement. Could it be that the *Workes* can have only custodians? Is their self-sufficiency such (Mayne remarks that "th'had their whole growth then / When first borne, and came aged from thy *Pen*") that the *Workes* preclude progeny?

Mayne is responding to a particular quality of the 1616 Folio *Workes* that Richard Newton has called their "closed coherence."[7] Newton has argued that Jonson became a textual poet by discovering the potential of print to "endow [a] . . . text with autonomy."[8] He suggests that the very impression of completeness and self-containment achieved by the Folio legitimized Jonson's essentially "coercive authority."[9] The poems I have been citing support a historical revision of Newton's thesis. By the last decade of Jonson's life, the Folio had gained a canonical life independent of its author and maker. The *Workes* supplanted Jonson as the authority that coerced. The poet's monument to himself had become an albatross, or at least a barrier to new work. Newton is utterly persuasive when he depicts Jonson's symbiotic identification with his Folio in 1616.

> Jonson, as our first textual poet, as the (re-)inventor of the book is, in a way new to English literature, possessed of his text. That is to say, he possesses his texts, and he is possessed by them. He lives in his texts in a way unprecedented because the texts themselves have an unprecedented existence.[10]

That Jonson possessed his texts, as opposed to being possessed by them, was no longer clear by the late 1620s. The evidence of the Caroline poems and of Jonson's own *Under-wood* suggests that his decision to publish as *Workes* texts so apparently impervious to change or to development exacted a psychological cost. Unprecedented closure of the kind Jonson engaged in by exploiting the fixity of print had unforeseen consequences. To put it differently, tomes have an uncanny way of mortifying their makers.

The very success of the Folio was double-edged. Jonson survived the publication of his collected *Workes* by some twenty years. For many of his heirs, the Folio represented the fruition of his talents, the apex of his career, and its logical terminus. The reception of his last plays, the vicious invectives circulated by the literary sons Henry Coventry would style the "prophaner *Parricides* in verse" (11.442) begin to suggest the price Jonson paid for having realized laureate status in mid-life. William Cartwright's elegy for Jonson captures what it can mean to be "read as Classick in [one's] . . . *life*" (11.457). The acuity of this elegy impresses. Like Coventry, Cartwright was skeptical of the motives underlying the Caroline censures of Jonson. While both poets identify the attacks on his late work as originating in a Bloomian-inflected anxiety of influence, Cartwright focusses on the psychic costs for Jonson of his having become a purely textual poet. He evokes those last years:

> th'exacting *age*, when deeper yeeres
> Had interwoven *snow* among *thy haires*
> Would not permit *thou* shouldst grow *old*, cause they
> Nere by *thy* writings knew thee *young*.
>
> (11.458)

Cartwright, who was Jonson's intimate during his years of eclipse, states that for Jonson "to have *writ* so well" earlier has proven to be not simply a burden but a curse. While the elegist believes that Jonson's controversial late plays "will come up *Porcelaine-wit* some hundreds [of years] hence," he acknowledges in a suggestive line the imposing barrier to such a reappraisal. "*Thine Art*," he says simply, "was *thine Arts* blurre." Cartwright's partisan prediction that Jonson's last plays would achieve canonical status may still be premature. About the Folio, his judgment could stand unamended.

1

In the poems eventually published posthumously in 1640 as *The Under-wood*, Jonson made his marginalization from the Caroline court and his bodily infirmity subjects of his work. Both conditions entailed crises of self-confidence. *Under-wood* maps the topography of the body's decay, Jonson's own and others'. These poems treat the body that is subject to "the accidents and dispersions of historical reality,"[11] the body no text can redeem. Susan Stewart has remarked in *On Longing* that

> the printed word lends the book its material aura; as an object it has a life of its own, a life outside human time, the time of the body and its voice.[12]

She argues that the "transcendent authority" of the classic inheres in the capacity of print to escape "the constraints of an immediate context of origin."[13] Jonson's 1616 Folio can be said, in Stewart's phrase, to have achieved a place and status outside "the time of the body and its voice." *Under-wood*, however, explores another terrain, the untranscended body. In these poems, the poet's body becomes shapeless. The boundaries of that body alter; projected into a world ("human time") that no longer has space for it, and which spurns its gross materiality, the body is reconstituted. Its topography, metaphorically, is the grotesque.

Jonson's body becomes a deformed text in "My Answer. The Poet to the Painter." Addressed to his friend Sir William Burlase, this poem conveys the poet's response to what seems to him to be the idealizing fictions of Burlase's art. Jonson will apply a self-lacerating corrective to his friend's partisan perspective. His own portrait, a tissue of punning revisions of the painter's flattering *trompe l'oeil*, draws a different likeness.

> WHy? though I seeme of a prodigious wast,
> I am not so voluminous, and vast,
> But there are lines, wherewith I might b[e]'embrac'd.
>
> 'Tis true, as my wombe swells, so my backe stoupes,
> And the whole lumpe growes round, deform'd, and droupes,
> But yet the Tun at *Heidelberg* had houpes.
>
> You were not tied, by any Painters Law,
> To square my Circle, I confesse; but draw
> My Superficies: that was all you saw.
>
> Which if in compasse of no Art it came
> To be describ'd [but] by a *Monogram*,
> With one great blot, yo'had form'd me as I am.

But whilst you curious were to have it be
An *Archetype*, for all the world to see,
You made it a brave piece, but not like me.

(52)

When Dryden wants to exclude the poetasters who would arro-
gate Jonson's name from claiming kinship to the lineage that
is his alone, he quotes "The Poet to the Painter." "A *Tun of
Man* in thy Large bulk is writ," Flecknoe charges his dull offspring, Mac Flecknoe, "But sure thou'rt but a Kilderkin of wit"
(ll.195–96; the emphasis is mine). Dryden's mockery is restora-
tive; he salvages laughter from Jonson's self-portrait. The tone
of the original is far less comic. Jonson's poem images his body
as distended by having given birth to prodigious works. His
back stoops as a result of his labors, of going into labor as
his literalized metaphor for creativity painfully insists. Thomas
Carew invokes what had become a truism about Jonson's art
when he wrote in 1629 that "Thy labour'd workes shall live,
when Time devoures / Th'abortive ofspring of [thy sons'] . . .
hasty howers" (11.336). Jonson makes the generative metaphor
more concrete, dilates it into the grotesque. His fecund, femi-
nized body droops with fatigue. The poet's womb produces
prodigies, volumes, Folios, but at considerable cost to Jonson:
he has been deformed by the struggle. Michael Seidel reminds
us in *Satiric Inheritance* that satire (whose locus is the body)
is "conditioned to be out of shape."[14] Jonson images this as
a loss of distinct boundaries. The self is, as it were, projected
into space until it covers the whole canvas in "one great blot."
  The epithet "blot" has, of course, a peculiar power for Jonson.
"The Poet to the Painter" ought to be required reading for those
who have never forgiven Jonson's snub of Shakespeare. Jonson's
answer in *Discoveries* to contemporaries who claimed Shakespeare "never blotted out line" is famous: "Would he had blotted
a thousand" (8.583). And in *Under-wood* he commends John
Selden's rigor, exclaiming "What blots and errours, have you
. . . purg'd / Records, and Authors of!" (14). To blot out for
Jonson means to purge one's writing of excrescences; the revised
work is bounded by the compass of the poet's critical judgment.
In the poem to Burlase, however, Jonson's body expands to
"one great blot." Here the stigma redounds on Jonson. His body
swells, grows lumps, metastacizes. "With one great blot, yo'had

form'd me as I am": at this moment of self-reckoning, Jonson
is not Selden's ally in editorial scrupulosity, not Shakespeare's
scold. He looks in anguish at what he is and winces at the
sight.

Jonson's epistle to Selden forms an apt contrast to his self-
portrait in "The Poet to the Painter" in another respect. Praising
Selden's *Titles of Honour* in 1614, Jonson finds himself "lost,
/ To see the workmanship so' [e]xceed the cost" (14). It is precisely this cost, the psychic depletion exacted by artistic labor,
that Jonson fixates on in the poem to Burlase. When he writes
"I seeme of a prodigious wast," the punning line communicates
not simply (as Robert Adams would have it) his body's bulk
but a thought resonating with considerably more pathos.[15] The
poet seems aware suddenly of the prodigious waste of body
and self that a lifetime in the service of art can demand. The
poet continually in labor may come to see himself less as a
"Tun of Man" than as a drab. It may be for this reason that
Jonson rejects Burlase's portrait, which would represent him
as "An *Archetype,* for all the world to see." Burlase draws
Jonson's "Superficies," his achievement as a master poet. From
a different vantage point, Jonson gazes at the same canvas and
speaks his own exhaustion.

In *Under-wood* the body engrosses age, space, the matter that
is the unregenerate stuff of satire. Jonson begins by making his
body the subject of compulsive jokes. These jokes seem freighted
with a mortifying awareness that his is the body his culture
no longer embraces. In the "Epistle to my Lady Covell," Jonson
recommends his "nimble" and chaste muse to a prospective
patron. Even here, in an occasion that calls for tact, Jonson
obtrudes his body.

> So have you gain'd a Servant, and a Muse:
>   The first of which, I feare, you will refuse;
> And you may justly, being a tardie, cold,
>   Unprofitable Chattell, fat and old,
> Laden with Bellie, and doth hardly approach
>   His friends, but to breake Chaires, or cracke a Coach.
>
>   (56)

Jonson's muse is inoffensive, arousing the jealousy of neither
husband nor suitor. On inspection, however, that very security
turns out to be the body's subversive doing. Lady Covell "fan-
cie[s] not the man." Her acceptance of his muse is itself provi-

sional; the poet is relegated to making the bored aristocrat "merry" at her "Dressing stoole," and later to amusing her maid. The downward spiral of Jonson's career narrated in these poems of the body suggests how the aging poet experienced his altered state. An "Unprofitable Chattell" in the eyes of the Caroline elite, Jonson now takes up unwarranted space. No longer the authoritarian presence of the Folio, he is reduced to pleading. About the closing years of Jonson's life, one might say as Lily Bart does at a comparable juncture of her career, "I have lived too long on my friends."[16] Like Wharton's heroine in *The House of Mirth*, Jonson found himself designated excessive baggage, the servant a frivolous culture can do without.

In *Under-wood* the body of the poet is a mortifying spectacle.[17] It is proffered up repeatedly to friends, to prospective or former patrons, to the indifferent bureaucrats withholding Jonson's pensions. Jonson's fear that his necessities will be refused saturates the begging poems that close the volume. Jokes about financial need, deft and controlled in his "Epistle to M[r] Arthur Squib," are recycled in contexts that sour their original grace. Ultimately the joking tone disappears altogether. When Jonson tells Lady Covell that "His weight is twenty Stone within two pound; / And that's made up as doth the purse abound," he is, of course, reminding her of the tavern wager that occasioned his earlier epistle to Squib. He is also nudging her to duplicate Squib's gesture; but Squib's friendly loan of sufficient silver to make good Jonson's weight of "Full twentie stone" (54) for the weigh-in at the tavern is of a different order. The tone of the original petition is intimate and assured. Jonson can admit without subterfuge his "corporall feare" that he will lose his bet, together with the precarious state of his finances.

> One piece [of silver] I have in store,
> Lend me, dear *Arthur*, for a weeke five more,
> And you shall make me good, in weight.
>
> (54)

He offers Squib "this letter / For your securitie," confessing with blunt charm, "I can no better." The approach to Lady Covell conveys more desperation. Her generosity, which in a patron takes the form of anticipating need, may not be assumed. Nothing in this epistle suggests that Lady Covell will appreciate what it might mean to have to resort to making wagers on one's fat. The aristocrat at her dressing stool is far removed from the world Jonson inhabits, where "A Merchants Wife is Regent of the Scale" and where to lose such a bet will "stink" the poet's already shaky credit. In repeating the story of his wager, Jonson gambles that his verses will pry open an aristocrat's purse. What he hazards out of need is his self-respect. "I can lose none in tendring these [verses] to you," he writes Lady Covell. It is not a claim he has to make in petitioning Arthur Squib.

The epistle to Squib has its own undercurrent of the rueful. Jonson requires a loan from the teller of the Exchequer to "make me good, in weight." He is obese enough to wager his heft but not, it seems, weighty enough to be certain of winning the contest. Squib's intercession reifies the poet's substance. Without the ballast (and backing) of the Exchequer's silver, Dame Justice will determine against Jonson in adjudicating the bet. She is, he tells Squib, already predisposed to do so, suspecting rightly that Ben Jonson is an "ill commoditie." Even in play, Jonson is utterly cognisant of how his culture perceives him. One might say alternatively that only in play could he bear to know what this epistle knows. The verses to Squib communicate the poet's recognition of his marginalized, dependent position: this awareness begins to enter the poetry of Jonson's last years as a felt shame. The poet's aging body is a commodity that engrosses too much space. Variously imaged as a blot on the canvas of his age; as a lump "deform'd and droup[ing]" from its unprofitable labors; or as an unwanted chattel that breaks chairs and cracks coaches, Jonson's body inflicts itself on his culture. He is in turn afflicted by his contemporaries' rejection of that body, which is to say their repudiation of who he now essentially is. It is not the magisterial Jonson of the 1616 Folio *Workes* the Caroline sons vilify in their invectives of the 1630s. It is the Jonson who falters, who in eclipse turns inward to salvage what he can of a self fragmenting before their collective gaze, whose vulnerability licenses parricide.

2

"For, what is life, if measur'd by the space, / Not by the act?" (70). The question Jonson poses in his ode to Sir Lucius Cary and Sir Henry Morison resonates throughout *Under-wood*. Empty bulk, the slow accumulation of "dayes summ'd up with feares": both are included in the poet's invocation of negative

space. The mortifying wager narrated in his epistle to Squib
explores this terrain. The bet makes disconcertingly literal that
a man's life can come to be weighed and appraised not by
his accomplishments but by the space his body takes up. When
Jonson writes of Morison's premature death that "in short measures, life may perfect bee," the consolation he finds is distinctly
unrhetorical. By 1629, Jonson was experiencing the indignities
that came with age, penury, obesity, and disabling strokes. In
the Cary-Morison ode he writes himself into the past tense and
speaks as though from beyond the grave:

> And there he [Morison] lives with memorie; and *Ben*
>
> *The Stand.*
>
> *Jonson,* who sung this of him, e're he went
> Himselfe to rest.
>
> (70)

Living in pain, the poet continues to write: he is Ben Jonson
still. Self-affirmation nonetheless wrestles with a counterlong-
ing, a desire to take a sabbatical (as George Fortescue would
say) from the labor of "dispensing Life immortally" (11.446).
Jonson inscribes himself into the poem but the self no longer
has complete integrity: it is split between stanzas, poised between memory and death. These twin impulses to affirm in
and through poetry and to relinquish its onerous labors ("he
went / Himselfe to rest") inform the poems of Jonson's Caroline
period. It derives, I believe, in part from the poet's experience
of degradation when his life began to be measured by space
alone.

Jonson had reason to fear that he might live long enough
to vex time. The censures circulated by his increasingly vocal
detractors provide substantive evidence confirming these anxieties. The Caroline poems, which were widely read, are performance pieces. Their vitriol gets out of hand. The sons hurl Molotov
cocktails of abuse, spatter insults calculated to enrage and maim.
Invariably, the locus for hostility is the poet's body. The parricides chart its decay in fulsome detail, in language appropriated
from Jonson's own work but directed to quite other ends. Seidel
observes in *Satiric Inheritance* that when "degeneration and
disinheritance predominate, satire takes over the body."[18] His
perception could be extended as follows: Master poets, once

the season of their hegemony is passed, are subject to satire's
revision. They will be treated as though space, not achievement,
defines the negative essence of their worth. Jonson's Caroline
heirs fear a dwindling inheritance. For them, it seems grotesque
that the father should still inhabit (or "engrosse") his own body.
For the sons standing in the wings, eager to displace Jonson
from the stage, his bulky frame becomes an arena for competitive
exercises in laureate-bashing. They imagine they too will grow
"fatt" with "Laughing" (11.347) at the poet who in his last poems
hazards his sacrosanct, authoritarian status by taking instead
the measure of his own infirmity.

Jonson's "Epistle Mendicant," sent to the Lord High Treasurer
in 1631 to plead his desperate straits, became for his contemporaries a rich source of denigrating jokes. Jonson represents his
needs with consummate dignity. His poem to Lord Weston narrates the body's decay, its betrayal of the poet in him. The
muse that promised to "tread the Aire" (56) for a Lady Covell
is now entrapped by disease and want, bedridden with the poet
himself, who speaks candidly of his debilitating strokes:

> MY LORD;
> POore wretched states, prest by extremities,
> Are faine to seeke for succours, and supplies
> Of *Princes* aides, or *good mens* Charities.
>
> *Disease*, the Enemie, and his Ingineeres,
> *Want*, with the rest of his conceal'd compeeres,
> Have cast a trench about mee, now, five yeares;
>
> . . . .
> The *Muse* not peepes out, one of hundred
>   dayes;
>
> But lyes block'd up, and straightned, narrow'd in,
> Fix'd to the bed, and boords, unlike to win
> Health, or scarce breath, . . .
>
> Unlesse some saving-*Honour* of the *Crowne*,
> Dare thinke it, to relieve, no lesse renowne,
> A *Bed-rid* Wit, then a *beseiged* Towne.

(71)

During the last decade of Jonson's life, the charity of good
men seems to have been a scarce commodity. When *The Mag-*

sion in the Workes—birthday poems, poems on the queen's "lying in," poems acknowledging gifts of ink or the one hundred pounds the king sent Jonson "in my sicknesse"—are preserved in Under-wood. Epigrammes dates only one poem. Under-wood's titles insist on the occasion (and, to some degree, the occasionality) of a poem's writing. Fully eleven poems are given explicit dates and others, such as the epigram to Lord Ellesmere "the last Terme he sate Chancellor" (31) or a comparable one to Sir Edward Coke "when he was Lord chiefe Justice of England" (46) are equivalently precise in their historicism. There is a new emphasis in Under-wood on the precariousness of what can be salvaged, in solitude, in and from time. That precariousness is underscored when Jonson restores a "lost" ode written in the Elizabethan era to Under-wood and places it after his meditation on Ralegh's History of the World. It is further underlined when he (or Digby)[26] chooses to publish fragments of poems in his last collection in clear violation of the first Folio's insistence on textual integrity. More pressing concerns than aesthetic coherence dictate the publication of these incomplete works; their presence as truncated texts complements Under-wood's focus on loss, its muted affirmation of the imperfect. Poems are, like their maker, fragile constructs in Under-wood. The poems of the late 1620s and the 1630s make uncharacteristically minimal claims for transcendence. The book is suffused with what it is a poet comes to know when he faces death and his own "darke oblivion" (24). The magisterial confidence we associate with the Folio Jonson could not have caught this— the accent of vulnerability that permitted Jonson, subsequent to the Folio, a "later growth."

Annabel Patterson has drawn attention to Jonson's ode to Desmond and its significant placement in the volume. The Pindaric ode "writ in Queene ELIZABETHS time, since lost, and recovered" (25) follows Jonson's poem vindicating Ralegh and his history. The juxtaposition in Under-wood of an ode for the man known in eclipse as the 'Tower Earl' and Jonson's meditation on The History of the World, written by Ralegh in the same Tower where Desmond had been imprisoned, is telling. As Patterson argues, Jonson in Under-wood both appropriates and "privatize[s] the historian's role," defending Ralegh and Desmond "in whispers"[27] from accusations of treason. The poet like the historian is "Times witnesse" (24); in his work, the good who are elsewhere "defrauded" of a defence will be vindicated. Patterson claims rightly that the emotional intensity of these poems is effectively "recharged by history" after Ralegh's execution in 1618 and the suppression of his book. Her insight can be extended. Jonson's unwieldy title to the Desmond ode begs certain questions: How did the poem come to be lost? Lost, or tactfully omitted from the 1616 Folio? How recovered, and why restored now? The title, in other words, withholds as much as it communicates; its withholding constitutes a communication. In *Under-wood*, historical retrieval is always only partial, always a mere fragment of what could be recovered. If this ode manages to survive "the wash of time,"[28] its fate is exceptional; not all can be redeemed by the "life of Memorie." In this instance, the poet's verses act

> like strong Charmes, [to]
> Breake the knit Circle of her [prison's] Stonie Armes,
>   That hold[s] your spirit:
>   And keepes your merit
> Lock't in her cold embraces, from the view
>   Of eyes more true.

                                                                    (25)

Disgrace, the "jealous errors / Of politique pretext," censorship: these are the stony arms of historical contingency from which the poet would liberate the Desmonds and the Raleghs. Men's lives are vulnerable to these forces. When other voices are mute, poetry is the life of memory that seeks to preserve. The ode to Desmond, in following the warm tribute to Ralegh's *History*, substantiates Jonson's belief that the poet must emulate the historian in breaking silence. Its title also implies that art can be the frailest of bulwarks against time and oblivion: historical recuperation is itself contingent, a salvage operation whose victories are to be weighed in the balance against the loss of other works that will never be recovered.

The Desmond ode has the power it does not only by virtue of its strategic placement in *Under-wood* but because the volume publishes portions of poems, parts of Jonson as it were, that have been salvaged from imperfect manuscripts. The sole precedent for this is *Forrest* 12 where the epistle to the Countess of Rutland breaks off in mid-line with the cryptic note "The rest is lost." The circumstances were unusual. The epistle exists complete in its manuscript form. Jonson struck from the Folio the last section, which wished the Countess a son, to save her family from further embarrassment when her husband's impotence became widely known. One excision in Under-wood, the deletion of a single obscene word from "Epigram, to my Bookseller," serves a comparable function of tact. The others are significant departures from the editorial practices of the 1616 Folio. What they suggest, I think, is the new susceptibility of the Jonsonian text to dispersion and loss. The 1640 Folio restores a "lost" work to a place of honor; it simultaneously records the permanent loss of all or parts of four others, Under-wood 20, 84.2, 84.8, and 84.10. The loss is documented with unusual elaboration in the editorial notes to "Eupheme." The hand here is doubtless Digby's, whose pain at the irreparable loss is palpable when he describes the missing quaternion containing "Eupheme 8." The loss is for him and for Jonson especially distressing; the manuscript belonged to the sequence of ten poems Jonson had written to commemorate Lady Venetia Digby, the editor's wife, in 1633.

> A whole quaternion in the middest of this Poem is lost, containing entirely the three next pieces of it, and all of the fourth . . . excepting the very end: which at the top of the next quaternion goeth on thus. (84.8)

Digby writes. He then publishes in Under-wood a fragment of a letter addressed by Jonson to Lady Digby's surviving sons; the source of this is clearly the family's autograph manuscript of "Eupheme." In the surviving remnant, the poet advises Lady Digby's heirs not to trust to the mere "reedes" of title but to pursue deeds worthy of their noble lineage. It is signed "with his latest breath expiring it, B. J." Jonson's carefully wrought sequence of elegies for Lady Digby is incomplete, published in a truncated form. The second Song terminates abruptly in mid-line, "the rest . . . lost." The tenth, which was to have been the "CROWNE" of the sequence, is missing altogether. The felt absence of these works, coupled with Digby's retrieval of a fragment of Jonson's poignant exhortation to Lady Digby's children, reiterates in whispers what the ode to Desmond had suggested earlier in the volume: Art is as pervious to destruction as paper itself, as susceptible to extinction as human memory. Knowing this, as both Digby and Jonson did, one preserves what one can.

4

The imperfect is distinctly not our paradise in Jonson's later work any more than it was in his classical period. He affirmed it in himself provisionally and with difficulty when his diminished circumstances and his utter dependency on others—the Digby family, the king and the bureaucrats dispensing his charity at increasingly irregular intervals, the unnamed woman Jonson lived with—made adaptation a necessity. It was that painful accommodation that also made possible the "later growth" of *Under-wood*. "Eupheme" crowns that autumnal book: it is the work in which Jonson "summe[d] up mine owne breaking" in his "Elegie on my Muse." The final poems of *Under-wood*, "Eupheme" and the poet's Jacobean translations of Horace, Petronius Arbiter, and Martial are all fragments. Chronologically, they span some twenty years of the poet's career, but the effect of their placement in the volume suggests that the earlier works, restored decades later to the canon, carry with them the recharged intensity of the backward glance. The "Elegie on my Muse" and Jonson's translation of Martial's epigram on "the happier life" (90) warrant particular attention.

The ninth poem of the sequence on Lady Digby is a sustained probing of private loss. In *Under-wood* 12, the epitaph on Vincent Corbett, Jonson had written "I feele, I'm rather dead than he!" By 1633, fourteen years after Corbett's death, that thought has sharpened into a new urgency. The poet's puns emphasize the fragility of his own hold on life; each exhalation is a "latest breath expiring." In Jonson's elegy, an epitaph for the poet in him, he revises his earlier study of loss. The poem reverberates with an aging poet's oblique self-quotation.

> 'TWere time that I dy'd too, now shee is dead,
>   Who was my *Muse*, and life of all I sey'd,
> The Spirit that I wrote with, and conceiv'd;
>   All that was good, or great in me . . .
> Thou hast no more blowes, *Fate*, to drive at one:
>   What's left a *Poêt* when his *Muse* is gone?
> Sure, I am dead, and know it not! I feele
>   Nothing I doe; but, like a heavie wheele,
> Am turned with an others powers.

> (84.9)

When Corbett died, Jonson berated himself retrospectively for his scant understanding of a man he had thought exemplary. His epitaph for Corbett centers on missed opportunities; theirs had been a relation of respect that might have deepened over time into intimacy. By 1633, the season of new relations and new beginnings is over: "'TWere time that I dy'd too." For the poet, the world emptied of Lady Digby's presence is a "dungeon of calamitie," the years ahead a limbo of numbness. His grief cannot be circumscribed or measured; it is so weighty that the capacity to feel is anaesthetized. "I feele" is immediately cancelled by the next line, "Nothing I doe." Nothing that can be done or made out of this bereavement will restore Jonson's muse: it is dead, gone, undone by "*Vulture death*, and those relentlesse cleies."

In memorializing Corbett, Jonson takes refuge in the thought of the man's courage. Corbett's struggle with disease exemplified the strength of the human will, its capacity to endure and surmount pain, terror, and the affliction of remorse. Vincent Corbett, he wrote

> long
> Had wrestled with Diseases strong,
> [And] . . . though they did possesse each limbe,
> Yet he *broke* them, e're they could him,
>   With the just Canon of his life,
>   A life that knew nor noise, nor strife:
> But was by sweetning so his will,
> All order, and Disposure, still.
>
> (12; the emphasis is mine)

Jonson in his "Elegie on my Muse" depicts his own bodily affliction in language that interrogates his celebration of Corbett, not only when he sums up his own breaking but when he declares Lady Digby's death and the corresponding extinction of his muse to have been the intolerable "stroke" of misfortune that his "wounded mind cannot sustaine." Jonson cannot and, in his candor, does not emulate Corbett's composure. Partially paralysed by a succession of strokes, he is now a "heavie wheele, / . . . turned with an others powers." There are reasons for us to read that 'metaphor' of fortune's inexorably revolving wheel with a certain stubborn literalism. It needs to be understood as a statement of fact. Jonson was bedridden by 1633 and according to Lord Winton, who visited him "in his long retyrement, and sicknes," the poet was "govern'd"[29] by the woman "with whome he livd and dyed" (1.181–82) near Westminster Abbey. This is hearsay but I am inclined to credit it. The very obscurity of the accounts of Jonson's final years is itself suggestive of his ignominious state. Utterly absent from his formal tribute to Corbett is Jonson's stress in "Eupheme" on his dependency: he is dependent as a poet on his muse; dependent on patrons and their charitable memories of better days; dependent, finally, on an obscure, anonymous mistress for the nursing his condition required. Given these realities, it is perhaps not surprising that the body in Jonson's later poetry becomes a locus of misfortune that no Stoic example can prepare one for. To be immobilized by recurrent strokes is, one might say, to be condemned to "perish, piece, by piece," to be kept "dying a whole age" (43). In this line, taken from "An Execration upon Vulcan," Jonson's fantasy centers on the cruel, agonizingly slow death of an author's works when they are rejected by the public.[30] The poet's fantasy is subsumed (and privatized) in "Eupheme" by the humbling reality of disease, a reality that, as Susan Sontag has passionately argued, resists the consoling transformations of metaphor.[31]

In life, the body is the muse's precarious habitation. "Eupheme" anticipates the "fleshes restitution" after death, at the "last Trumpe." For Lady Digby and her family, the last judgment can be joyfully anticipated as the occasion of their reunion and elevation into the ranks of the elect. God's judgment is nevertheless a "finall retribution." Penetrating "the hearts of all," Jonson writes, God "can dissect / The smallest Fibre of our flesh; he can / Find all our Atomes from a point t[o]'a span." Broken by disease in life, dispersed after death into fibres and atoms, the body is resurrected and reconstituted. Corbett will be rewarded for the just canon of his life; the Digbys' bodies will be transfigured into a new nobility. For others, however, God's dissecting judgment awaits: for them, the flesh's restitution will indeed prove to be a grimly final retribution.

Under-wood concludes appropriately with a recovered fragment, Jonson's translation of Martial's portrait of "the happier life." Significantly, neither Jonson nor Martial subscribes to Gulliver's delusion that longevity contributes to human happiness. For both, happiness is contingent and circumscribed; under certain favorable conditions we can be happier, but that ideal state of being is qualified by the knowledge that happiness is precarious and that "thy latest day" inevitably awaits. Restored decades later to a prominent place in Under-wood, the epigram is darkened by the circumstances of Jonson's later life. As wish, however, the poem is utterly without irony.

> THE Things that make the happier life, are these,
> Most pleasant Martial; Substance got with ease,
> A Soyle, not barren . . .
> A quiet mind; free powers; and body sound;
> A wise simplicity; freindes . . .
> Thy table without art, and easy-rated:
> Thy night not dronken, but from cares layd wast;[32]
> Sleepe, that will make the darkest howres swift-pac't;
> Will to bee, what thou art, and nothing more:
> Nor feare thy latest day, nor wish therfore.

(90)

Over a life, these unexceptionable wishes accrue a certain poignance; they often remain unrealized. *Under-wood* closes with what could be described as a prayer. Fortune, fate, life will determine whether one will enjoy the blessings of a "body sound" or "free powers." What the poet can choose is to "bee, what thou art," to affirm his own limitations and imperfections and, through that affirmation, to bring in his late harvest. "Some grounds are made the richer, for the Rest; / And I will bring a Crop, if not the best" (57). That, for Jonson, is what it meant to have a "Soyle, not barren" in his old age. And that is also the achievement of his *Under-wood*, not substance got with ease—the 1616 Folio must have seemed that in retrospect—but a poet's provisional self-acceptance.

Jonson closes the volume with quiet tributes to enabling fathers, Horace and Martial. The values he endorses in his translations reiterate his affinity for the classical tradition, and something more. Through them Jonson reclaims his literary sires. He finds comfort in what they have left him. The figures of Martial and Horace provide a continuity back to Jonson's own earlier work, the continuity the Caroline sons would deny him. To close with translations of these writers is to go home again, not in the attitude of nostalgia but as self-recuperation. Translating Horace and Martial, Jonson rereads himself; he recovers who he has been and wishes for his last years the will to be who he now is, and no more. The poems that close *Under-wood* stretch back through time, Jonson's and his sires, to speak of desires that are both personal and communal. Old poets who have no fault but life have, it seems, a common prayer.

Notes

1. Samuel Johnson, *Preface to A Dictionary of the English Language*, in *Samuel Johnson*, ed. Donald Greene (Oxford: Oxford University Press, 1984), pp. 327–28.

2. Dudley Diggs, "AN ELEGIE ON BEN. JOHNSON," in *Ben Jonson*, ed. C. H. Herford and Percy and Evelyn Simpson, vol. 11 (Oxford: Clarendon Press, 1925–52), p. 444. References to works about Jonson will be cited by volume and page number. The allusion to Jonson as a kind of Rhodian colossus is taken from Nicholas Oldisworth, "A letter to Ben. Johnson. 1629" (11.398). I have also consulted throughout Ian Donaldson's edition of Jonson's *Poems* (Oxford: Oxford University Press, 1975).

3. John Dryden, "Mac Flecknoe," in *The Poems of John Dryden*, ed. James Kinsley, vol. 1 (Oxford: Clarendon Press, 1958), p. 270.

4. The most eloquent expression of this sentiment is Dryden's. His Neander reflects of Jonson, Fletcher, and Shakespeare: "Yet give me leave to say thus much, without injury to their Ashes, that not onely we shall never equal them, but they could never equal themselves, were they to rise and write again. We acknowledge them our Fathers in wit, but they have ruin'd their Estates themselves before they came to their childrens hands. . . . All comes sullied or wasted to us: and were they to entertain this Age, they could not now make so plenteous treatments out of such decay'd Fortunes." Neander is, however, quick to couch his critique of the Renaissance fathers in language that conveys Dryden's veneration of their memories: "They are honour'd, and almost ador'd by us, as they deserve; neither do I know any so presumptuous of themselves as to contend with them." See John Dryden, "An Essay of Dramatick Poesie," in *The Works of John Dryden*, ed. Edward Niles Hooker and H. T. Swedenberg Jr., vol. 17 (Berkeley: University of California Press, 1956–1984), p. 72–73.

5. Lawrence Lipking, *The Life of the Poet: Beginning and Ending Poetic Careers* (1981; rpt. Chicago: University of Chicago Press, 1984), p. 177. See further Jonathan Arac, "Afterword: Lyric Poetry and the Bounds of New Criticism," in *Lyric Poetry: Beyond New Criticism*, ed. Chaviva Hošek and Patricia Parker (Ithaca: Cornell University Press, 1985), p. 346.

6. Jasper Mayne, "To the Memory of Ben. Johnson" (11.451–54). That the sons' conspiracy centers on the 1616 Folio *Workes* is, I think, clearly established by the rest of Mayne's elegy. See especially in this context lines 37–42.

7. Richard C. Newton, "Jonson and the (Re-)Invention of the Book," in *Classic and Cavalier: Essays on Jonson and the Sons of Ben*, ed. Claude J. Summers and Ted-Larry Pebworth (Pittsburgh: University of Pittsburgh Press, 1982), p. 36. Newton's study of Jonson's achievement in the 1616 Folio is justly renowned. Also central to an understanding of the monumentality of the Folio is Timothy Murray's *Theatrical Legitimation: Allegories of Genius in Seventeenth-Century England and France* (New York and Oxford: Oxford University Press, 1987). Murray argues convincingly that "Whereas the domain of the public theatre might be understood to nurture significational free play and intertextuality, the printed text offers the playwright the opportunity to transcend authorial anonymity and linguistic ruin through various operations of textual self-representation. The textual materialization of authorship thus enacts the regeneration of the figure of the Self through its objectification in the printed text" (p. 16).

8. Newton, "Jonson and the (Re-)Invention," p. 42.

9. Ibid., p. 35.

10. Ibid., p. 44.

11. Susan Stewart, *On Longing: Narratives of the Miniature, the Gigantic, the Souvenir, the Collection* (Baltimore: Johns Hopkins University Press, 1984), p. 158.

12. Ibid., p. 22.

13. Ibid.

14. Michael Seidel, *Satiric Inheritance, Rabelais to Sterne* (Princeton: Princeton University Press, 1979), p. 9.

15. See Robert M. Adams, "On the Bulk of Ben," in *Ben Jonson's Plays and Masques*, ed. Robert M. Adams (New York: W. W. Norton, 1979), pp. 482–92.

16. Edith Wharton, *The House of Mirth* (New York: Scribners, 1905), p. 474. I have in speaking of a frivolous culture adapted Wharton on the subject of her novel. Wharton claimed that "a frivolous society can acquire dramatic significance only through what its frivolity destroys." See R. W. B. Lewis, *Edith Wharton: A Biography* (New York: Harper & Row, 1975), p. 150.

17. "Spectacle risks misapprehension and invites the lowest response in an audience; the playwright longs for hearers and understanders, not spectators. Yet in these late poems, paradoxically, Jonson tends to make a spectacle of himself," notes John Lemly in his "Masks and Self-Portraits in Jonson's Late Poetry," *ELH* 44 (1977): 250. Jonson offers himself up as a "dubious prize package" (p. 249) in the epistle to Lady Covell, Lemly suggests. His argument complements my own at several points. See further on this subject, Susan Stewart's discussion of "the freak of culture" in *On Longing*. Stewart argues that in freak shows the viewer is 'normalized,' safely distanced from the aberrant object of his speculative curiosity. The freak, transformed into spectacle, is further degraded by 'speculation' (pp. 108–110). Jonson's grotesque visual self-portraits do distance; they lend his audience a spurious, illusory normalcy. As in *Frankenstein*, however, or for that matter *The House of Mirth*, speech breaches that hierarchized separation of viewer from spectacle: Jonson engages in dialogue with the addressees of his epistles, and thus affronts the presumption of distance that preserves the illusion of all spectacle.

18. Seidel, *Satiric Inheritance*, p. 56.

19. Annabel Patterson, "Lyric and Society in Jonson's *Under-wood*," in *Lyric Poetry: Beyond New Criticism*, pp. 148–63; and on the Pindaric traits of the Cary-Morison ode, see Stella P. Revard, "Pindar and Jonson's Cary-Morison Ode," in *Classic and Cavalier: Essays on Jonson and the Sons of Ben*, pp. 17–29. Revard terms the splitting of "Ben" and "Jonson" an "extreme case" that is nevertheless consistent with the Pindaric practice of "carry[ing]-over [the] . . . sense from one stanza to another" (p. 17).

20. Lipking, *Life of the Poet*, p. xi, 70.

21. Newton, "Jonson and the (Re-)Invention," p. 38.

22. Joseph Spence, *Observations, Anecdotes, and Characters of Books and Men*, ed. J. M. Osborn, vol. 1 (Oxford: Clarendon Press, 1966), p. 258, quoted by Lawrence Lipking in *Life of the Poet*, p. 68. The phrase "poetical prudence" is, of course, Samuel Johnson's in his *Life of Pope*.

23. See further Jennifer Brady, "'Beware the Poet': Authority and Judgment in Jonson's *Epigrammes*," *Studies in English Literature* 23 (1983): 95–112; and Timothy Murray, *Theatrical Legitimation: Allegories of Genius in Seventeenth-Century England and France*, pp. 39–93.

24. The classic study is W. David Kay, "The Shaping of Ben Jonson's Career:

A Reexamination of Facts and Problems," *Modern Philology* 67 (1970): 224–37. Kay's important essay is supplemented and to some degree superseded by Newton's "Jonson and the (Re-)Invention of the Book."

25. Lipking, *Life of the Poet*, p. 131.

26. My argument does not seek to adjudicate between the editorial decisions made by Jonson and Sir Kenelm Digby, who acted as Jonson's executor in preparing *Under-wood* for the posthumous 1640 Folio.

27. Patterson, "Lyric and Society," p. 154.

28. Newton, "Jonson and the (Re-)Invention," p. 32.

29. The source of this account is Isaac Walton, who communicated Lord Winton's memories of Jonson in his years of eclipse to John Aubrey, who preserved Walton's notes. The explicit passage reads: "in that time of his long retyrement his pentions (so much as Came In) was given to a woman that govern'd him. with whome he livd and dyed" (1.182). Jonson's dependent state is here recalled as especially abject because his nameless mistress apparently took charge of his royal pensions.

30. See further the excellent reading of "An Execration upon Vulcan" in Sara van den Berg, *The Action of Ben Jonson's Poetry* (Newark: University of Delaware Press, 1987), pp. 143–59; and, for an alternative perspective on *Under-wood* that emphasizes "acts of grace" and the "Christian and classical values" (p. 172) that frame the collection, pp. 170–81.

31. Susan Sontag, *Illness as Metaphor* (New York: Farrar, Strauss and Giroux, 1978).

32. Walton elaborates with delight on the subject of Jonson's inebriation in his later years. His source is again Lord Winton, but the gusto with which he reconstructs the laureate's last days is all his own: "nether he nor she [Jonson's mistress] tooke much Care for next weike: and wood be sure not to want Wine; of which he usually tooke too much before he went to bed, if not oftner and soner. . . . so much for brave Ben" (1.182).

Contributors

WILLIAM BLISSETT is Emeritus Professor of English at the University of Toronto. He was the editor of *University of Toronto Quarterly* from 1965 to 1976 and coedited *Ben Jonson: A Celebration* (1973). He has published extensively on Renaissance literature, particularly on Shakespeare, Jonson, and Spenser, and he is the author of *David Jones: The Long Conversation* (1983). He is currently a coeditor of *The Spenser Encyclopedia*.

JENNIFER BRADY teaches Renaissance and Restoration literature at Rhodes College. She has published several articles on Jonson's poetry, as well as essays on Marlowe, Samuel Richardson and Joan Didion. Her current project is a study of poetic affiliation in the seventeenth century, centering on Jonson and Dryden.

KEVIN DONOVAN is Assistant Professor of English at the University of New Hampshire. He recently completed his doctoral degree at the University of Wisconsin and has published on bibliographic problems in the 1616 Folio in *Studies in Bibliography*.

WYMAN H. HERENDEEN is Professor of English at the University of Windsor. He is the author of *From Landscape to Literature: The River and the Myth of Geography* (1986) and has published articles on Renaissance literature in *Studies in Philology, Medievalia et Humanistica, The Journal of Medieval and Renaissance Studies*. He served as editor (1981–88) of the *Directory of Renaissance Scholars in Canada* for the Canadian Society for Renaissance Studies.

JOSEPH LOEWENSTEIN writes on Renaissance literary history. His articles on Guarini, Sidney, Spenser, and Jonson have appeared in such journals as *MLQ, ELH, Representations*, and *ELR*. His first book, *Responsive Readings: Versions of Echo in Pastoral, Epic, and the Jonsonian Masque*, was published in 1984. He is currently writing a book on Renaissance intellectual property, an institutional history of early modern creativity. He is an Associate Professor of English at Washington University in St. Louis.

KATHARINE EISAMAN MAUS teaches English literature at the University of Virginia. She is the author of *Ben Jonson and the Roman Frame of Mind* (1984) and a number of articles on political and gender issues in Renaissance and Restoration drama and poetry.

STELLA P. REVARD is Professor of English at Southern Illinois University, where she also teaches Greek. Her book *The War in Heaven: Paradise Lost and the Tradition of Satan's Rebellion* (1980) was awarded the Holly Hanford Award for the "most distinguished book published on Milton in 1980." In 1984 she was President of the Milton Society of America. Her publications include articles on classical, Neo-Latin, Renaissance, eighteenth- and nineteenth-century English and Continental literature.

SARA VAN DEN BERG is Associate Professor of English at the University of Washington. She is the author of *The Action of Ben Jonson's Poetry* (1987), and she has published essays on Jonson, Milton, and Freud in *ELH, Shakespeare Studies, Studies in Philology, Modern Language Quarterly,* and *Psychoanalysis and Contemporary Thought.*

Index

PR
2643
.B46
1991

PR
2643
.B46/1991

AUTHOR

TITLE
Ben Jonson's 1616 Folio

DATE DUE	BORROWER'S NAME

Gramley Library
Salem College
Winston-Salem, NC 27108

Gramley Library
Salem College
Winston-Salem, NC 27108